Butter Cream

Butter Cream

A Year in a Montreal Pastry School

Denise Roig

Signature Editions

Cover design by Doowah Design.
Cover photos by Ariel Tarr.
Photo of butter cream by Ardis Root.
Photo of Denise Roig by André Forget.

Printed and bound in Canada.

We acknowledge the support of the Canada Council for the Arts and the Manitoba Arts Council for our publishing program.

Library and Archives Canada Cataloguing in Publication

Roig, Denise
Butter cream : a year in a Montreal pastry school / Denise Roig.

ISBN 978-1-897109-30-4

1. Roig, Denise. 2. Authors, Canadian (English)--20th century--Biography. I. Title.

PS8585.O3955Z462 2008 C813'.54 C2008-905750-3

Signature Editions
P.O. Box 206, RPO Corydon, Winnipeg, Manitoba, R3M 3S7
www.signature-editions.com

for my mother, Jacky Roig,
who started it all

1

A Checkered Future

I am the only one wearing the bloody uniform. Not only am I the oldest one here—judging from a quick scan of younger and way younger faces—but I look like a dork. A keener. And I know, since I'm usually teaching kids this age at this time of year, that there's nothing less cool than a first-day keener. I take the last available stool, shove my massive toolbox and bulging backpack under the chrome counter, fumble for pen and paper. Everyone is dressed in late-summer casual, while I glow extra-white in my high-necked chef's jacket. Just last night Beauch, my husband, asked if I was going to tell my classmates at the start that I'm writing a book about this. No, I said. I want to blend in, be a student among students in the beginning. Sure.

"Welcome to Pastry!" Ardis Root, the director of the program, is at the front of the classroom and looking so genuinely glad we're all here that I feel almost okay. In a long pastel skirt and fitted T, she's dressed in exactly the summer clothes I would be wearing if I hadn't come dressed as a true beginner. Slender, with long red hair and green eyes—I'd put her in her early forties—she sends out warmth and reassurance.

We'd met several times during the winter as I was contemplating enrolling in the program. I had so many questions: What was studied? How was it taught? Who was this program for? Underneath everything I asked was the question: Can you see *me* doing this? "I would love to have you in class," Ardis had told me back in March. "We'd have so much fun!" Implying, I'd guessed, that it would be nice to have a fellow teacher, a grown-up, a university grad, among the young ones.

Altogether we are twenty-three women and one man. Six of the women are Chinese. The man is also Chinese. "We'll be nice to you," Ardis promises him. She says that if we call her "Chef" she probably won't answer, will assume we're talking to someone else. "Call me Ardis. In pastry we're more informal than in cooking."

If your career destination is to become a pastry chef, we'll help you get there, she promises. If you just want to have fun, make knock-out desserts for the family, that's fine, too. "You can do what you want with this." Other things she promises: we'll make *crème pâtissière*—pastry cream—so many times we'll be able to do it in our sleep. We will learn a tradition that is centuries old: classic French pastry. We'll gain ten to fifteen pounds over the course of the year. Instinctively, I tug down my extra-small chef's jacket. I've had my size six houndstooth-check pants (uniform of culinary students the world over) taken in at the waist. Will I have to let them out? Move up to the next size?

We go around the room, introducing ourselves by a dessert we like that begins with the first letter of our first name. I'm Denise and I like Danishes. (I once ate half a barrel of my Jewish grandmother's Danishes, but it's probably too soon to admit this to my classmates, if I ever tell them at all.) There are young names in here, names like Madison—who likes mousse—and Avedon, apple pie.

I'm glad to not have to reveal more than this the first day. What would I add? That I'm fifty-six, a writer for close to thirty years, a teacher of writing, too, and that it was after reading a so-called academic evaluation from one of my university journalism students the previous winter—"The room smells like ass"—that made me think it was time to do something else. I'd never intended to be a teacher, had fallen into it as I'd fallen into so many other things that I thought could earn me a living while I did what I really wanted to do: write. I loved my Concordia University kids, but I found myself less and less enthusiastic about reading and marking their poorly punctuated, lazily researched, hazily conceived stories. This semester when I talked about "the *craft* of writing," I'd noticed there were more blank looks than ever. Me and teaching? Maybe it wasn't such a great fit.

Driving home from teaching that winter day, I'd stopped at one of my favourite neighbourhood spots: the Pearson School of Culinary Arts, a vocational school that runs a restaurant and store as part of its professional cooking, pastry and butchery programs. In line for whatever students had cooked up that day, I'd chatted with a woman whose husband had taken both the cooking and pastry courses after he retired. So this wasn't just for the young and ambitious, for career chefs. This could be for someone a little older, a little in between things. Someone who needed a respite from smelly classrooms. Someone like me.

"I'm going to pastry school," I announced to Beauch when I got home five minutes later. Okay, it was a little out of the blue, but we both knew I'd long dreamed of moving into food writing, admiring writers like Anthony Bourdain, Calvin Trillin, Amanda Hesser, Michael Ruhlman, not to mention the great M.F.K. Fisher herself. And if I ever had a heroine, it was the late Laurie Colwin. A writer of funny, wise, warm short stories, she also wrote funny, wise, warm food columns for *Gourmet*. I've been a serious baker ever since I was seventeen and attempted crêpes suzettes and *croquembouche* in the same week, a serious writer since I was twenty-one. With some formal training, could I not combine my enduring passions for a late-life career swerve?

Truth is, I'm not entirely sure why I'm here. I realized this when trying to explain my year's plan to friends over the summer. Pastry school? But you're a writer. Isn't this an awfully long detour? No one was actually saying this, but I could see it in faces and hear it in voices. I'd assumed that my mother, a baker without equal who, in her eighties, still makes the best cheesecake on the planet, would be happy, proud even, at the news that I was going to professional pastry school. No, she thought I was nuts. What did I still have to prove to myself? she seemed to imply in our long-distance phone conversations. She'd said to my sister recently, "Deni's eyes are bigger than her life."

Luckily, Beauch—himself a novelist and newspaper editor—seems to get it, telling people I'm writing a Tracy Kidder-type book, like *Among Schoolchildren*. Kidder attended Grade Five in an inner-city school for a year, absorbing every bit of that school's life, sponging up its characters so he could write about it. The comparison makes me slightly uncomfortable—I'm no Kidder—but this explains it more neatly than I seem able to and raises my efforts to a literary level I like.

But now that I'm actually here, I'm scared, doubtful, overwhelmed. This morning I prayed in bed before I swung my already aching right leg up and over. I prayed the way Georgia, my eight-year-old, does when she serves mass, hands flat and together:

Please keep my body in one piece—no flare-ups with my herniated disks, no dizzy spells, no fibromyalgia crises, none of the half-dozen chronic conditions that kick in under stress.

Please help me juggle school, special-needs child, house, husband and the unfinished book of short stories promised to my publisher last year.

Please keep my eating sane. No bingeing on cream puffs. I cannot, *cannot* come out of this twenty pounds heavier.

Please help me remember that I'm not out to become the next Pierre Hermé, Alice Medrich, Jacques Torres or anybody fancy like that.

Please help me to do this in the right spirit.

And please...make it fun?

Ardis reminds us there are waiting lists to get in here. The Pearson School of Culinary Arts offers the only government-supported pastry-making program in English in Montreal, and, according to Ardis, the only program like it in Canada—a $10,000 education free to Quebec residents that's on a par with Montreal's snootier, male-dominated French counterpart: the ITHQ, l'Institut de tourism et l'hôtelerie du Québec. Pearson is even on equal educational footing with $30,000-a-year programs, like those at George Brown University in Toronto, she says.

About the uniform, which she cheerfully makes me get up and model for everyone: We are to wear our whites and checks every day and to get dressed in the school locker room. We even have to keep our shoes here. This changes my idea of my mornings slightly. I'll have to leave the house on foot fifteen minutes earlier, meaning that once Georgia's on her school bus, it will be a push for the front door. No more freelance writer's leisurely reading of the paper, no more easing into days.

No backpacks allowed in "the Lab" either, Ardis says. (I want to ask why it's called "the Lab" instead of "the Kitchen," as if we'll be conducting science experiments in there, but there isn't time to interrupt.) We are allowed to take in a fanny pack with keys, and a bit of money, but not much, because already there have been thefts since the school became an adult and vocational education centre this summer. Drug dealing, too. Living in the neighbourhood, I've passed this building almost daily. It looks tough, one of those massive brick 1970s fortresses that seem more low-security prison than school. It's hard to imagine something as refined as French pastry coming out of this place.

Other no's: rings, earrings, necklaces. No jewellery at all. The young girl next to me touches her lip stud protectively, as Ardis tells us that she took her wedding ring off this morning when her husband dropped her off for work. "'Well, honey, that's it till July!' I told him." Watches are to be worn on our apron straps. Nails are to be kept short, no polish. A piece of nail polish could chip off and land in our crème anglaise. Most important: hairnets at all times in the Lab. "It's not elegant," says Ardis, who also suggests wearing one of those little hats that resemble cotton pillboxes, kind of a Jackie Kennedy look. And absolutely no cell phones.

She hands out a sheet of paper with our curriculum: twenty-two modules over nearly eleven months covering everything from creams and fillings to food safety to ingredients to bread, chocolate and decoration. No wonder this is full time—eight hours a day, five days a week from now through next July. ("How can it be full time?" my friends keep asking me. "How much can there be to learn?") We'll write a paper for our first module, Pastry as a Trade. "Spelling doesn't count, grammar doesn't count. All I care about is your ideas," says Ardis, not exactly what I tell my third-year journalism students. We'll take a written exam for safety/hygiene, Module Two; do a written and fifteen-minute practical for the equipment module; write an exam for ingredients. All the rest of the modules—five through twenty-two—will require practical exams. We'll be given recipes, ingredients and a certain amount of time to make something. We will be marked each step along the way.

Ardis checks our faces, must sense the worry around her. "Evaluation!" she says. "I know. It's really scary. But a teacher's job is to get you through. If you don't do well on an exam, we'll stay after and work with you. Ninety percent of the time it's fine." Still, we won't get a diploma without passing every single module. I feel my stomach drop. What if my pies burn or my meringues go splat? How can a whole year hinge on a moment of what might just be bad luck? Is this what my J-school students feel like when I read the course outline at the beginning of a semester? I've taken all kinds of courses in recent years, but not for grades. Is anyone else in here breathing?

What's brilliant about the design of the course, though, and I can see this already, is that the baking modules are spread out over weeks, even months. "Creams, pies, batters goes into the brain better than cream, cream, cream for a hundred and twenty straight hours," she explains.

But back to the uniform. Ardis makes me stand up again. "Why do you think it's important to wear it every day?" she asks. Hygiene, uniformity, we offer. Yes, but more than anything, Ardis says, "those pants and jackets say who you are." We may not be chefs yet, not by a long shot, but we're chefs-in-training and that warrants looking like one. I sit down again, grateful.

Suzy, one of the older students, an attractive, cool blonde with a tired face, asks, "How do you become a chef? I mean, who decides when you become a chef?"

"The English-Canadian interpretation would be someone who really, really knows his or her stuff, someone with expertise," Ardis says, smiling as if she knows we're getting into something chewy here.

"So when you walk out of here would you be considered a chef?" Suzy presses.

"Absolutely not," says Ardis, and tells us about Fabrice Frelat, one of our instructors, who started working in a patisserie in his native France when he was in his teens. He was not considered a "chef" until ten years later. "In France there's a very set system," she says. "A chef is the chief. We have one graduate from eight years ago who's at the Ritz-Carlton. She's the only graduate of this program I would call 'Chef' at this point."

There's silence as this sinks in. "You'll see as you go," says Ardis. "Watch me and watch Claudette and you'll see the difference."

First, there's their training. Claudette Groulx is a graduate of the ITHQ who went on to spend thirty years as a pastry chef in the city's top hotels. Ardis, who's been teaching for twenty years, studied home economics with the idea of becoming a sewing teacher. "But it was awful!" she says. "Students would bring up these dreadfully messed-up seams and we'd have to rip the whole thing out. With food you can fix things!" And then she repeats what she told me last winter in one of our little chats. "I love this, but I'm not a chef. I went to chefs in the city and asked them to teach me. I can do a cake in ten minutes. Claudette can do it in two and it will look better than mine. I like food fine, but what I love is to teach. And I really like it when you come in knowing nothing."

"Think of it this way," she says, trying to get the point to sink in. "Think of sports or music. In education we now put a number on the hours it takes to become an expert in something. It's *ten thousand*." And then, so we're not too staggered by that number, seeing as we're only one hour into it, she says, "If you're good, if you're dedicated and work hard, you'll go far."

We must look doubtful still because she hastens to reassure us. Have you heard of The Zone? she asks. It's that place where you love what you're doing so much that you're completely engrossed. "My gut feeling is that most of you are in The Zone when you're baking."

It's true. Things fall away when I'm melting butter and chocolate, when I'm peeling fruit for jam or folding in nuts. Worry about my daughters, about the waiting pile of student marking, about a misunderstanding with a friend—gone in a puff of flour. Baking connects me to myself. Baking makes things hum.

Ardis runs through the lineup of teachers, starting with Claudette, whom she calls "a great role model. She's got strength in her mind and in her body." I'd attended a class of Claudette's the winter before as a student-for-a-day, showing up in a tie-dyed apron and low heels. I'd been stunned at Claudette's speed of movement, the volume of her voice and the number of small, complex pastries produced by twenty student chefs. It was jitterbug baking.

Another of our teachers will be Alfred de Luca. "He's a bread guy, owned his own bakery for years. He knows everybody and is a very nice man." Fabrice, another nice guy. We won't have him as a teacher for another month because he's on his way to Paris for a pastry tour with the graduating night class. Did someone say Paris?

And, finally, Edward Kraczyk. "He's the real world, the real European thing. He might yell at you, he might call you a name, he might tell you your cake is ugly. He's the pastry chef at the Queen Elizabeth Hotel and I call him '*Chef*.' He has a ton to teach you. But be forewarned."

It's now ten and this is school, so we take a fifteen-minute recess. I intend to call Beauch and tell him I'm surviving, but instead I get into a conversation with Trina, a dark-haired, round-faced young woman who's *garde-manger,* prep chef, at La Transition, a Westmount restaurant I passed every day this summer. "I said I'd never do desserts when I was across the hall studying professional cooking two years ago," she tells me. "But then I made a friend's wedding cake this past summer and found I totally loved doing it." Her dream is to open a bed and breakfast.

Trina is friendly and bright and a reader (Anthony Bourdain, Michael Ruhlman), so we talk chefs and books and cooking magazines and it's lovely. I tell her how jerky I feel being the only one in uniform. "Don't worry about it," she says. And the way she says it, as if it really doesn't matter, as if she only now noticed it, makes me feel finally at ease.

Back in the classroom, Ardis stands at a table pulling things out of a toolbox. "You travel with your tools. You'll have these hopefully the whole of your career." How big should the box be? I ask, having bought the longest box I could find at Canadian Tire, but now finding it hugely heavy to haul around. My back won't love it for long. "I bought it big so the rolling pin would fit in," I explain.

"Your rolling pin won't fit in no matter how big a box you get," she says. "Get a box you can carry." Someone asks just how big the rolling pin has to be. "Huge. I don't know exactly. Eighteen inches?" She goes through the long list of equipment, telling us which things we can get at the dollar store (like oven mitts) and which must be of professional quality (zester, paring knife, cake knife, spatulas…many more items, really.) The lot might cost up to $500. She warns us about the French star tips with their jagged little edges. "Don't stick your finger in. You can't pull it out." The only way out is to pry open (and wreck) the star tip. Yet every year, apparently, a student will do this. I look around at the serious, listening faces. *Please don't let that be me.* We're all praying the same thing.

When she gets to pastry bags (we're to buy polyurethane ones, better than canvas, and in a range from small to large, smaller being easier to use since we'll hold the bag with one hand and fill it with the other), Ardis tells us a little story. A couple of years ago she went to do an internship, or *stage* as it's called in Quebec, with a Montreal chocolatier. "All they had were *big*—twenty-four-inch—pastry bags. I was sure I would make a fool of myself and I did. Ganache squished out the top of my bag, it smeared on my jacket, it dripped on my shoe. But none of the chefs laughed and I survived." She's telling us, I think, that we will, too.

"Hey, here's another chef and tools story for you," she says. "A pastry teacher, who will remain unnamed, tells a student, 'You must use an offset spatula to ice this cake!' In his first job, the student works with a chef who says, '*Never* use an offset spatula for that cake!' So practise this every night before you go to sleep: '*Oui, Chef! Oui, Chef!*' You'll be saying that a lot."

Since this is school, there's a textbook. We're each given a turquoise, plastic-bound, three-inch-thick tome with one word on the cover: Pastry. It's overwhelming just to peruse: photos of scroll work, intricate diagrams of how to assemble a petit four, recipes that go on for pages. Every year, apparently, the pastry teachers look for a published text they might use, since there are many fine pastry books on the market. Ardis cites Charlie Trotter and Jacques Torres, whose books, she promises, "will be a snap" after the course. But still, every year the four teachers end up putting together their own book, one beyond the skills and knowledge of even the most ambitious home baker, one made for will-be professionals.

She urges us to get organized now, over the Labour Day weekend, suggesting the purchase of several binders, twenty-two dividers, and a lot of loose-leaf paper. Plus a three-hole punch because there will be many handouts. And, interestingly, a recipe box. "As you get a recipe in class you'll write it down on a card and put it in the box. The card will just have the ingredients." Quizzical looks go around the room. "The method will be in your head," she explains.

And through the rest of this long first day, as we tentatively learn how to operate the rotating oven, the blast freezer, the giant Hobart mixers, I keep coming back to this astonishing possibility. I have been a serious baker for forty years. Yet I still read and reread recipes, squint at them, recheck them: Do I add the sugar now or later? Do I have to flour the pan for this? I've been making the same beloved brownie recipe forever and yet I don't always remember what comes next. *The method will be in my head.*

Up front with her overhead projector, Claudette Groulx stands tiny and mighty in a bare-all ecru lace camisole and tight jeans. It doesn't jive with my memories of the stern, perfectly coiffed (even with a hairnet) blonde woman storming through the Lab last winter as the class sculpted mice from marzipan and tempered chocolate for Easter eggs. ("Yeah, she's tough," several students told me then.) I'm still in the minority in my whites and checks (and secretly wondering why Claudette herself is so obviously not *en forme*), but this morning at least I'm one of seven. By the end of this week we're to have it together: uniforms and equipment.

"I try to memorize your names," Claudette says, surprisingly remembering me from my student-for-a-day. Again, we go around the room, this time explaining why we're here.

"I didn't want to go into anything boring," says Andrea, the twenty-year-old sitting next to me at the counter. We were in these same places the first day, already creatures of habit.

"I like to eat dessert!" giggles another girl.

"I'm bad with knives," says Anna, a gorgeous honey-blonde who's come from working restaurants in Vancouver. She holds up a bandaged finger and we wince. "Besides, everyone's crazy in Vancouver. People here are more sane." Lane, further down the table, lives on the Mohawk reserve of Kahnawake, making and selling fruitcakes and cheesecakes to friends and neighbours. She wants more training.

"My daughter, she loves the cakes," says Yujie, one of the adorable, smiling Chinese women. "I want to make for her."

"I love the desserts," says "Shirley," who's apparently given up on anyone getting her Chinese name right. She looks so happy when she says she loves desserts, all lit up.

When my turns comes, I explain that I'm a teacher and freelance writer who wants to move into food writing. I don't say anything about a book.

Although Ardis has already made a big point about Claudette's being the real thing, a Chef, Claudette asks to be called by her first name. "When you call me 'Chef,' already there's starting to be a wall between me and you." She's been in the pastry business since 1975, working at the Bonaventure, the Ritz and the Château Champlain, big hotels with serious pastry departments. "But then, I'm a serious lady," she tells us. "I'm a strict lady, but open-minded. You promise me that as soon as you have a problem you come to me. You don't keep it for too long."

For the next month, Claudette will teach safety and hygiene—a serious topic. She hands out a huge packet of stapled papers, our text for this module, on top of the regular text. Already we're swimming in paper. By way of introduction to hygiene, she tells us about the time she got "hill from heggnogs" and I'm thankful for fourteen years of living with Québécois English.

She's right: She's serious and straight. I think we'll do okay.

We're in the Lab. We're in hairnets. We've got ingredients. We're making bread. We cluster around Ardis at the front work station, which has a demonstration mirror and stainless counters. She's a different person in her white jacket, her long red hair neatly tucked under a checked pillbox. Still warm, but more official.

Already Ardis has she's told us that in professional baking everything is weighed in grams and measured in millilitres. Forget the measuring cups. "You put your empty container on the scale"—every table has two large, stainless scales—"and weigh it first. You have to if you're going to get accurate measurement." She taps out some all-purpose flour into a clear, plastic container, pyramids of which stand on shelves above each work table. "Oh, I'm making a mess," she says, laughing, as she spatulas flour back into the container.

We're making bread, but this isn't the bread module. This is Ingredients, where we'll learn the science of pastry components. "If you know how ingredients work, you can figure things out," Ardis promises. "There are a lot of chefs who don't know the science, which is unfortunate when things go wrong."

Earlier, we'd copied phallic shapes in our notebooks, marking off endosperm, bran and germ, looking up every few seconds at the enlarged wheat kernel on the overhead. Whole wheat, Ardis told us, is what you get when you grind all three parts together, but in French pastry we'll be working almost exclusively with white flour, which comes only from the endosperm. She talked about winter wheat versus summer wheat and the gluten differences between all-purpose, bread, pastry and cake flours, passing around samples of each to rub between our fingers. I've always used cake and pastry flour interchangeably, but now I know cake flour has been bleached a little more and milled a little finer. On the Ingredients exam we'll be given five different ingredients to identify by sight and touch, she warns. For now, they all look and feel pretty much the same to me.

For today's bread, we'll use instant yeast, a good place for beginners to start. "Fresh yeast looks like an ugly chunk of good, smelly French cheese. You'll work with it when you get to the Bread module," Ardis explains as she mixes powdered yeast, flour and water. "It can take a while to get the right consistency, but use your hands all the way." She turns her doughy little mound onto the wood table. "Kneading is pushing with the left hand, turning one-quarter to the left, then folding with the right, the reverse if you're left-handed." The ball of dough swivels obediently, rhythmically. Already it is becoming something different. Under her small, deft hands it turns smooth and springy. She dashes a bit of flour on the table, nestles the dough under the stainless dome of her bowl. It will grow there until it's time to form into baguettes.

And then it is our turn. Twenty-four people fly off in every direction. What to do first? My mind goes totally blank, like a loaf of Wonder Bread. Only the ingredients are written on the large, moveable blackboard. I've got no rudder. I've been baking most of my life, but now I seem to remember nothing. Luckily, Jen, who sits on the other side of me in class, has asked if I would work next to her. "Because I don't know anyone in here," she said. She is small and pretty with a long brown ponytail and a high little voice. She's maybe eighteen. The oldest with the youngest. I've got no method, but I've got Jen.

Somehow the ingredients get assembled, weighed and combined, though my dough looks stickier than everyone else's. At 10:50 I limp out of the Lab, one of the last to leave for break. I'm worrying about my little lump of dough. Will it rise? Will it hold together? Will it become a real loaf of bread? And then I have to laugh because it's so damn obvious: Those little domed lumps, they're us.

Claudette goes around the room, naming names. "Don't tell me, don't tell me," she says, reaching deep into what seems a formidable memory. "I wait for you later," she tells the Chinese contingency. I, too, am having trouble remembering their names: Min, Feng, Jing, Xiu Li, Yujie, Shirley (but that's easy). And Xue Qiang, pronounced Chang, who became X-Man.

Claudette scares us right off with a video of food-poisoning case studies: a food handler with a boil on his finger, a boy who almost dies from eating a tainted can of smoked oysters for an afternoon snack, a family stricken with E-coli from drippy hamburger meat. The little girl, my daughter Georgia's age, now has permanent kidney damage.

The bad news, says Claudette, is that food-borne illness is on the rise in Canada: More than two million cases are documented in this country each year. And that's just what's reported. Half the time when you think you have a touch of the flu, it could very well be contaminated food. Claudette waves a finger at us. Most of us make ourselves sick from our own fridges because we don't keep them cold enough or empty them out often enough. She passes out stick-on fridge thermometers so we'll have no more excuses. Most of us also leave food on the counter or stovetop for too long. One hour, two hours tops. Never, for example, leave butter out for days at a time, as I do. And then there are leftovers. Even rice and pasta should be tossed after two or three days.

"I'm afraid to eat now," says Michèle. She's a tall nineteen-year-old who sits across from me. "This is how you *lose* ten to fifteen pounds in pastry school."

"But don't become paranoid about bacteria," says Claudette.

We feel better for exactly one second before she tells us how she got food poisoning at the Ritz-Carlton where she once worked. Already we've been told: The world out there—patisseries, hotels, restaurants—will be dramatically, even disgustingly, different from our clean little bubble here. "Hey," adds Claudette, "I once saw a chef washing his underwear in the same sink as he was washing dishes."

She goes on to tell us about the salesman who tried to convince her to buy a year's supply of frozen meat. "I gave him shit. He never called me again." She must hear that she's just said "hagain," because she starts laughing. "When I first started teaching, my English was worse than it is now. Can you imagine? I can remember..." she continues, looking out over our heads. "Oh, I have a lot of things to remember, I've been in this trade so long. But in the old days the regulations for food safety weren't so tight. We used to suck out the butter cream from a blocked pastry tip."

Now Claudette herself has joined the bacteria brigade as an inspector for MAPAC (Quebec's Ministry of Agriculture, Fisheries and Food). Ministry regulations are tough, she tells us. If an inspector comes into a kitchen and catches a chef wearing a ring he can get slapped with a $250 fine. "Across the hall in professional cooking they wear plain wedding bands. Hey, if they want to get caught, that's their business," she says.

We won't be getting away with any of that. After provincial inspectors made Alfred de Luca, one of our teachers, cut off his wedding band last year—he couldn't get it off—the Pastry department has cracked down on everyone.

This goes for nails, too. A student a couple of years back lost a fake nail in a vat of batter. "She called me over," Claudette recalls. "'Claudette,' she said, 'You don't want to know.' She couldn't find the nail. I made her make the batter all over again."

At break I drift into a discussion with Michèle and Trina about air-brushing equipment for cake decorating, and I find again that I'm interested in *all* of it—bacteria, the structural properties of wheat grain, chef stories, egg washes, cake triangles. I've not always wanted to admit how...what's the least damning word? domestic? non-intellectual? inconsequential? at least some of my interests are, especially to my writer friends, especially my male writer friends. But now I have people to talk cake with. Now tiny details fill my days.

In these first days of Baking U, it strikes me again that I'm studying a profession so many feel proficient in, even if this means opening a box of Duncan Hines topped off with a can (a can!) of Pillsbury frosting. ("Whipped cow fat," my brother calls it.)

Why is it that most of us think we can bake? Dry snickerdoodles, grainy fudge, raw apple pie. I've scanned bake-sale tables hopefully for fifty years, dipped into Granny's prizewinning something and almost always come up disappointed.

Am I a snob? Is that what this year is about? Am I trying to put distance between myself and home bakers with their unearned pride? I'm guilty of the sin of pride, too. I adore bringing something divinely baked to the table, relish showing up for a party with a cake, a pie, a torte that I know will be the subject of conversation. I love dazzling with dessert.

It's kind of like writing. When I tell people I'm a writer, at least half say, "I always wanted to be a writer! I have a story that would make a great book!" They just haven't gotten to it yet.

When I told one of my aunts that I was going to full-time professional pastry school this year, her response was, "Oh, your cousin Janice makes the most wonderful chocolate cake. Have you had it?"

No, I said.

My cousin—someone I've always been able to talk cake with—is a marvellous, dedicated baker, who tackles the most ambitious recipes on *Epicurious*. But this isn't about having a fun home baker time in the kitchen. This is another world altogether.

He's printed his name clearly on the board: Alfred de Luca. "That's me!" Alfred is a short, bald, teddy-bear chef who's had a few spoons of mousse in his time. "I'll be your teacher for the biggest module of the year, Module Eight—Creams, Fillings and Glazes. You're stuck with me for 120 hours." He quickly fills us in: graduated from the ITHQ in 1970, worked as first chef in the bakery at the Manoir Richelieu in Charlevoix, then moved on to small bakeries around Montreal, "putting in sixty to seventy hours a week for ninety cents an hour. Today? It hasn't changed much." He later worked as a lab tech for Robin Hood, testing flours, before opening his own "very successful" West Island bakery.

The name? He won't tell us. Is it still operating? He won't tell us that either. "I can't tell you everything at once, can I?"

Alfred, though, has lots to tell us about *crème pâtissière*, the basic custard filling in many French pastries. We'll put ours into strawberry tarts today, but the point of this module, he says, isn't to come out of here and say, "Wow! I made a beautiful whatever today." Here we'll be focusing on making the components, like crème caramel, mousseline, lemon curd, chocolate mousse, *crème bavaroise*. And butter cream, butter cream and still more butter cream. "I'll leave the finishing of the cake to other teachers," he tells us and winks.

He writes a recipe for *crème pâtissière* on the board, everything in grams and millilitres, of course, and we copy it furiously. He watches us, then says, "I ask you not to memorize a recipe. It's useless. Just memorize the procedure."

Each time someone says *procedure*, I get nervous. How am I ever going to remember how to do a million recipes? Already I'm worried about what he's going to ask of us today. Alfred looks back at the board, gets up from his stool and changes the amount of cornstarch. As he turns back to us, I notice he has flour on his cheeks. "A little modification," he says, and repeats: "A recipe is not important. Is there a better recipe for *crème pâtissière* than this? Yes, you and your mother probably have a better recipe."

But seeing Alfred in the Lab in his tall, white chef's toque one would think he was making the show-stopper of *crèmes pâtissières*. He demos the blending of sugar and eggs, telling us to never, ever let sugar sit unmixed in a bowl with eggs—"the sugar 'burns' the raw egg"—then warms milk to a simmer on a gas range. He shows us how to temper the egg and sugar mixture with some of the steaming milk, then how to whisk this back into the milk and how to cook, but not burn, the flour taste out of the crème.

In France, where he did a short *stage*, "they do pastry cream every, every morning. You have to. Hey, if a chef wants to keep pastry cream longer than five days, let him poison his customers. Let him get his bakery closed down." Okay, think about Christmas, he tells us: You pick up your cake on the morning of the $24^{th,}$ but most likely the chef made it on the 23rd, so by the time you eat it on the evening of the 25th, that pastry cream is three days old. Alfred makes a face and repeats what he's already said two or three times this morning: "Make it as fresh as possible."

Alfred made fresh pastry cream every single day as a pastry chef, but as he whisks and talks, darts from stove to counter, so intent, so present, it's as if he, too, is doing this for the very first time. Still, this is Alfred making pastry cream. As I watch, I find my heart thumping, my palms sweating. How am I going to remember all these steps? That same blankness hits as Jen—it's now assumed we're together—and I run to gather up the milk and eggs, sugar and cornstarch. Watching everyone scatter and dash, Alfred yells out, "Today is not a speeding contest, guys!"

It takes a long time to measure everything, but then I find myself at the stove stirring the milk and half the sugar. At our table Jen whisks the egg and egg yolks with the other half of the sugar, then adds the cornstarch. The tempering isn't so hard, though the pot is heavier than I'd expected, as I tip it into Jen's stainless bowl. The cream thickens fast, Jen whisking like mad for the requisite two minutes. Back at our table, she pours it quickly into a shallow plastic tray lined with plastic wrap, sprinkles the top with sugar so the plastic won't stick. I write "Jen & Den" in marker on the plastic and place it in the fridge. I feel as if I have been teaching all day, or recovering from the flu: completely done in.

Alfred stays to have lunch with us in the classroom, though he doesn't seem to be eating anything. "There's a big problem in France," he says. "The old father-son lineage has been broken and now they're having to change their attitude. You know: 'Ah, women…they cannot lift a bag of flour!' Listen, I had two girls working for me and they were the same height as…" Alfred points to Jen, even though he is not that much taller…"and they were amazing. There's no difference between men and women in this trade. If it's heavy for you, it's heavy for me. I'm not Superman."

"Alfred, did you sell your business?" asks Trina.

Alfred pauses. "In a way," he says. "Listen, it's good to have a woman in the kitchen. In North America, acceptance of women chefs has come more quickly. And that's a good thing. If you look at what women do at home, I'd rather go to work every day. I see what my wife does."

Alfred has said he'll leave the finishing touches to other teachers, but today, our first real day, he wants us to bring home something more impressive than plastic containers of pastry cream. He's come in early and baked up batches and batches of mini tart shells and ordered baskets of fresh strawberries.

"Demo!" he yells and we cluster at one of the stoves. "Hey, Stinky!" calls Michèle, and makes a space for Andrea, her partner. Andrea (a perfectly groomed young woman) grins and squeezes in. It's only day five, but already there are nicknames, already we're some kind of group.

Alfred pries open a Day-Glo yellow vat, rolls up one sleeve and sticks his short, wide, hairy hand in, drawing out a slab of what looks like stiff orange marmalade. It adheres to his palm. "Spoons? In the trade? Forget it!" he says, adding, "Ardis would have a fit if she saw me doing this. Am I going to change? Nah, I've been doing this forever." He shows us how much water to add to the gelatinous substance so that it will spread like the sheerest shellac, then holds up one tart, daubs it lightly with a glaze-dipped pastry brush, turning it for all to see.

Et voilà! We have patisserie-worthy strawberry tarts, sweet little crusts filled with our very first, our very own, pastry cream, studded with whole strawberries and apricot glaze. Most of us pop at least one into our mouths. The crust is flaky, the strawberries are luscious under their glaze, and the custard is creamy. As she lines up her tarts in a bakery box at the end of the afternoon, Jen says at least three times, "This is so neat!"

Crème Pâtissière (Pastry Cream)

2 cups (500 mL) whole (3.25%) milk
1/2 cup (125 mL) sugar
1 egg
2 egg yolks
1/3 cup (75 mL) cornstarch
2 teaspoons (10 mL) vanilla

In a heavy, medium saucepan heat milk with 1/4 cup (50 mL) of the sugar over medium-high heat. In a small bowl, whisk other 1/4 cup (50 mL) of sugar with cornstarch to eliminate lumps. In another small bowl, vigorously whisk egg, egg yolks and sugar/cornstarch mixture until pale yellow. Whisk in vanilla. When milk is simmering, stir 1/2 cup (125 mL) hot milk into egg mixture; whisk smooth. Off the heat, slowly pour egg mixture into nearly boiling milk, whisking constantly. Return to stove and quickly bring pastry cream to boil, whisking vigorously to prevent lumping and scorching. Cook for 1 minute more, until pastry cream is pudding-thick. Quickly pour into small plastic tray, or bowl, sprinkle lightly with sugar and spread plastic wrap directly onto hot cream. Refrigerate until using.

2

Oui, Chef!

I grew up with a Hungarian-Romanian Jewish mother, a woman born to bake. As was her mother and her mother's mother. I just had to tie on an apron and trot along behind. I don't remember my mother actually standing next to me at the kitchen counter saying, "Here, sweetie, this is how you separate an egg, this is how you test for doneness." I watched. I smelled. I tasted. My mother baked nearly every day of my growing up. None of it came from a box.

She baked *pogácsas,* Hungarian butter cookies—not sweet, with a fork's cross-hatching on top and a lovely yolk glaze. The recipe came from Rosa Green's *The Art of Hungarian Cooking: Culinary Gems from World-Famous Hungarian Recipes, Especially Adapted to American Tastes,* a 1938 cookbook that drove my mother crazy with its vague measurements and directions. My mother and my aunt Tobi referred to the book simply as "Mrs. Green." I didn't know who this maddening Mrs. Green was, but I pictured her like my grandmother, Regina: ample bosom, light hair, and a stand-back attitude. I imagined her intoning the words from the introduction with a Zsa Zsa accent: "Cooking, dahling, is an art in which the Hungarian excels. It is her heritage…"

My mother also baked sugar cookies from the red-and-white-checked *Better Homes and Gardens Cookbook.* She made chocolate mousse from Escoffier. And when Julia Child's *Mastering the Art of*

French Cooking came out in 1961, my mother was among the first to have it in her arsenal. She had cookbooks on cookbooks, and she *used* those books, not to mention bulging files of clips from the food sections of *The New York Times* (some dating to the forties) and the *Los Angeles Times*.

At eighty-something, my mother can still bake me under the counter. Only recently did she confess, "You know, I really enjoy baking much more than cooking. I think I always did." But no, she doesn't get this year of mine. Not yet.

I love days with Ardis. She's friendly, upbeat, teacherly. Funny, too: in the last class, she cautioned us about the disinfectant we'll use when washing dishes. It's a clear liquid called Quatromyacide and (in the wrong dosage) will kill you sooner than it will protect you. "Let's say we're having a piña colada party in the Lab," Ardis posed by way of example. But somehow we get mixed up and take a swig of Quatromyacide instead. On the way to the hospital, we're to grab a fact sheet—a pad of them hangs on the Lab wall—detailing the cleaning product we've accidentally imbibed. I can see it: one of us, green, retching, already maybe in a coma, remembering, oh, yes, the fact sheet.

Today Ardis has another sheet for us, a maze in the shape of a chef wearing a toque. "This year of pastry will be like this puzzle," she says, as we each try to snake our way to the end. "There will be days when it's all fine. And there will be days when you'll think 'Oh, this is just awful.'"

And so we don't take only her word on the high and low of it, she's brought in a guest speaker, Dora Floros, for this morning of Module One, The Trade and the Training Process. I interviewed Dora the previous year, after being a student-for-a-day with Claudette, still trying to see how this might fit. Dora (short for Theodora) is a woman on a large scale, and not just physically. She's Greek, which my friend Bea—who's Italian, but whose husband, Louie, is Greek—would say explains a lot. "With us Italians life is like opera; with them it's all Greek tragedy," says Bea. Even Dora's long, brown curls are dramatic, weighty, screeching for attention. I like her, but know she'd run over me in a minute.

Dora tells us she started her cooking career like us—right here in the pastry program five years before. "This kicked everything off." After pastry school she went on to complete Pearson's professional cooking course and its advanced cooking course, Cuisine Actualisé. Last spring I attended her Big Fat Greek Dinner in our school's restaurant, Le Saucier. For dessert she turned her grandmother's traditional baklava literally on end, standing the batons upright on the plate, sprinkling them with crushed pistachios, making them into something *haute*.

Out in the real world, she plated desserts at Château Lake Louise for a summer, then moved on to the Plateau's trendy meatery, Au Pied de Couchon. She's now pastry *garde-manger* at Passe Partout, the restaurant owned by James Maguire, Montreal's emperor of bread. Dora tells us she's also just earned her Red Seal, Quebec's highest rating for a chef. (I'll have to ask Ardis later if she calls Dora "Chef.")

"You can do anything you want with pastry. You can make wedding cakes. You can cater to your ethnic community. Your imagination will be what determines how far you go," Dora promises us.

Wendy, who plans to open her own bakery as soon as she graduates, asks about money. "Money?" says Dora. "Okay…" She inhales. "The stress, the cut fingers, the grey hair, the shattered nerves. That's what comes first." She's now making between $11 and $14 an hour in her various kitchen jobs, caters on the side and still works a couple of days a month in her old hospital administration job.

"The best chefs don't always pay you the best," Ardis throws in. "It's assumed they can pay less because you're learning from them."

Dora nods. She has a deep reverence for Maguire. "His puff pastry looks like a pillow. His butter budget is higher than some kitchens' entire budget."

The stress is correspondingly high. "You work, work, work, fast, fast, fast. You're into the fridge, you're out of the fridge. You've got twenty things on that list before service begins," she tells us.

I see my panic reflected on the faces around me. "Don't be scared!" says Dora. "Everyone here is multi-tasking. Just cooking dinner at home is multi-tasking."

But the pressure is different, we insist. Wendy says she doesn't think she'll be able to bear being yelled at. "I take things personally."

"Okay," says Dora and breathes in again. "I've cried often and I'm a strong person. Chefs yell at you when they're under pressure. Of course, you don't yell back."

She tells us a story she heard about a chef who turned a vat of over-whipped cream onto a student's head. "But that's France," she says, laughing. "Those guys tend to be a little rough."

Chef Maguire? "He doesn't have to yell," Dora says. "He just looks at you and you're already upset. It's never right. It's undercooked, it's overcooked. But I've learned so much from this man."

We've gotten quiet, so Dora moves in with some softness. "I was very insecure when I began. But I worked days and I worked nights and I worked days and nights. I was on my feet twenty-four hours sometimes. It didn't matter. I was doing what I love. And eventually doing this made me more confident."

It's also made her crazier, she admits. But then "you have to be a bit cuckoo to be in this business. It's made for artistic personalities. So lose your mind now. Just let it go!" As for this next year, she urges us: "Enjoy your time here, forget who washed what, learn, don't be scared, and don't give up."

Ardis tells us, with a teasing smile, that Dora has just gotten engaged.

"And guess what?" Dora says, "He thinks I can't cook."

"My husband thinks the same about me," says Ardis, looking equally incredulous.

We're a roomful of women—Qiang, our only man, is smiling, though I'm not sure he knows what we're on about—so we laugh about this for a while.

"Where do you see yourself in five years?" I ask.

"At the top! At the top!" says Dora, who, after slipping out a few minutes later, pokes her head back in and orders us again: "Don't give up!"

Giving up is actually my biggest fear. When I was in my twenties and thirties, even my forties, I had a pattern of not finishing things. Of promising lots and delivering less—be it freelance stories or college credits or volunteer gigs. My eyes *were* bigger than my life, certainly bigger than my time, energy and focus. But since meeting Beauch, a follow-through guy in all aspects of his life, finishing has become really important to me. With his support, I finally graduated from university, thirty-eight years after I'd begun.

But this isn't English 101; this promises to be Graduate Pastry, demanding all of me and more. Do I really want to devote myself so completely to something I'm doing as a bend in the path? I'm not Dora aiming for the top. Still, it would be mortifying to quit partway through, especially after all my pronouncements: Hey, everybody, listen up: guess who's going to pastry school!

Georgia throws a fit getting dressed for school, an arch-her-back, fall-on-the-bed tantrum, one of those times when her appositional behaviour makes her cerebral palsy and hearing impairment look like (what she herself considers) no big deal. Georgia's got a will of hard metal, thank God. This is what enables her to do so much. But sometimes she turns that will against us. This morning I'm frantic with the hopelessness of it. Georgia will miss the bus. I will be late. But somehow she gets on the bus, I drive the van halfway to school (all of four blocks), then park it in the students' parking lot, still a good five-minute walk to the back entrance. I arrive exhausted, still tired from the weekend, still tired from the week before.

Claudette never looks tired, even on a Monday morning. We're beginning a new module with her this week, Design and Esthetics. "The point isn't to be the best artist," she tells us after we take out coloured pencils and blank paper. "What's important is being able to draw on a cake, to work with a team." It takes me an uncomfortable hour of wondering why no one makes a move to work together to figure out she means theme.

We begin with flowers and fruits. "Get a kids' colouring book for ideas," Claudette suggests. We draw first with dots, like would-be Seurats, then with lines. Everyone is intent, bent over paper. There are a few protests at the beginning—"I can't draw!"—but then, as in every art class I've taken, we get lost in the line. Will those years of drawing and painting classes at the Saidye Bronfman School for the Arts help me here? Already Claudette has told us that drawing with royal icing or gel or butter cream is not the same as drawing with pencil.

But the stress of my early morning is disappearing. I'm here with my classmates and we're drawing. I look around, realizing I now know most everyone's name and that slowly I'm getting a sense of who's who:

Jen and Trina, of course—already my anchors.

Michèle—nearly six feet tall, nineteen and from a long line of bakers. We registered together last May, and her older sister, who'd driven her in, told me with much pride and some envy, "Now *she'll* be the pastry queen in the family."

Andrea (Michèle's partner, "Stinky")—looks tough, but is a sweetheart. She's my counter partner still and we compare answers after our quizzes.

Rena—early thirties, from Saskatchewan. She's just graduated from professional cooking, seems grounded and serious. She told me that this group seems wonderful compared with last year's cooking class. "I had to take a week off, it got so bad in there." The teachers? I ask. The students? All of it, she says.

Wendy—same age as Rena, big personality, but seems down-to-earth. A suburban mom with two little kids, she's hell-bent on starting her own business, with her friend...

Diane—Momsville, too. Pleasant, seemingly small ego. Diane often winks at me when we rush past each other in the Lab. This helps more than I can ever tell her.

Tara—young, *zaftig*, single mamma, talkative, funny, sharp.

Suzy—mid-to late forties. In fine, but edgy, shape. Tara's partner. Like me, has a Hungarian/Jewish background.

Madison—just out of high school. She has a long, blonde ponytail, a pink complexion and wears her checks like hip-huggers.

Nadia—Madison's partner. Italian, round, fun.

Avedon—tiny, dark, beautiful, of Indian ancestry, but born and raised in Trinidad.

Tamara—a black-haired beauty, half-Armenian, half-German. She really wanted to study art history at university but didn't have the grades.

Cindy—half Mohawk, half black. Early forties with two sons.

Lane—also Mohawk, the maker of fruitcakes.

Anna—the beauty from Vancouver.

Qiang—our guy, already nicknamed X-man. He often runs in late, working most nights as a line cook in an upscale restaurant. He smiles whenever he sees me and exclaims, "Deni!"—my childhood nickname, though he couldn't know this.

Xui-li, Feng, Jing, Shirley, Min, Yujie—I don't like lumping them together, but I'm only now beginning to be able to spell the Chinese women's names, and to connect those names with faces. I wonder often how they are managing with all this English. They team up with each other in the Lab and stay separate at breaks, sitting together in the school dining room, speaking Mandarin and sharing noodles and dumplings. I want to know them.

Alfred wears a hairnet even when he's lecturing in the classroom, the band slipping down his forehead, a man with no vanity.

"First," he asks, "how did the strawberry tarts hold up?"

"They made it to Sunday, but then the apricot glaze started dripping off," Wendy tells him. He nods, seeming to have expected this. After all, his guiding principle is make it fresh, eat it fresh, nothing lasts forever. Those tarts didn't survive two days in my household, were devoured the afternoon I brought them home.

Today we're making crème caramel, basic cream number two.

Crème caramel and I go way back. I acquired a taste for flan, the Spanish version, when I was eighteen and living in New York. My Puerto Rican bachelor uncle, George, was being wooed that year by an older Cuban lady. Lola would make us dinner, always finishing with her flan, a satiny custard in a pool of deep caramel sauce—knowing how I loved it, knowing how my uncle loved me. Dinners at Lola's included gold cutlery and multiple courses. For my birthday that year she made a pineapple upside-down cake that refused to bake after three and a half hours in the oven. She spent the evening apologizing, comforted only by my insisting on taking the cake home where I toasted sodden slices of it for the rest of the week.

Sadly, George loved Lola's cooking, but he didn't love her. My days of flan were numbered.

I expect everyone to know about crème caramel. But only a few people—Trina among them—have even tasted it before.

"What we call caramel in French pastry is only water and sugar," says Alfred. "It's not soft cream like we find in the centre of a candy bar. I'm not Parisian, but give me a crème caramel where the sugar is dark..." He closes his eyes, lifts his shoulders. "Oh, the flavour!"

Suzy asks if crème caramel can be made with cream instead of the milk called for in today's recipe. Sure, says Alfred, "though it's more like a crème brûlée then." Suzy looks happy, and she doesn't often look happy.

"But are you checking your cholesterol levels?" he asks. "Are you trying to kill your boyfriend? This would be a very good solution."

The tricky part of crème caramel is getting the just-right amount of caramelizing from our water and sugar. Cook it for half a minute too long and the stuff gets bitter and hard as a lollipop. Half a minute too short and the colour will be pale and the taste too sweet. On the blackboard, Alfred draws a picture of a bowl filled with water, then pantomimes taking a pot from the stove and placing it inside. "Psssssshhh! Cold water stops the cooking just in time."

We're also making pastry cream with a different recipe today, using milk powder instead of regular milk. Powder takes a long time to go bad, he tells us, a plus for some pastry chefs.

What else would we use milk powder in? Trina asks.

"You name it," says Alfred. "A lot of bakeries don't even keep fresh milk."

I'm beginning to get a sense of this industry of ours. Lots of shortcuts, lots of "cheats," as Alfred and Claudette call them. And lots of products not even available to home bakers, such as Covo Sm, the commercial shortening we'll use this morning in our first go at Swiss meringue butter cream. It's not lost on me that we are making three things today, not one as we did a few days ago. Things are speeding up.

Someone asks why we're making butter cream with part butter and part shortening. "Personally I don't like something that tastes of shortening," says Alfred with a sigh. "But it's very difficult to handle butter cream that's 100-percent butter. You have to make your life easy. It's easier to pipe, to spread, to make flowers when you've got twenty-five percent shortening in there."

Plus, it keeps longer. How long do you think? he asks. It's like an auction as we yell out the possibilities: Three days? Six months? Ten years? He tells us finally: butter cream lasts in the fridge one month; on the counter up to a week in winter, three to four days in summer. In the freezer, six months. But why freeze it for six months? he asks. In less than a week we already know Alfred's credo: Make it fresh.

He tells us that by now, mid-September, most patisseries are finishing up their *bûches de Noël* for Christmas and stacking them by the dozens and hundreds of dozens, in their walk-in freezers. "By mid-October, production is completely over."

We must be making faces, because he says, "Hey, we kept our wedding fruitcake in the freezer for seven years until our first kid was born. You think it was dangerous to eat? It's more dangerous to get married and have kids."

He's promised us that today won't be "pressured or sweaty," but right away I feel both. Our pastry cream nearly burns on the bottom. When the cream begins to boil you have to whisk fast and furiously, he tells us too late. "And don't say, 'I'm not strong. I'm very delicate.' I don't believe that."

In Alfred's former shop he made twenty litres of pastry cream at a time. "And I did it by hand with a whisk so big it came up to my shoulder. I was losing ten pounds each time I made it."

Twenty litres at a time? We're incredulous. "Try to forget that you're going to do a home-based bakery, making things in small batches," he says. "This is commercial baking in the typical French pastry tradition."

Back in the cool classroom four hours later, I gulp down a bottle of iced tea and try to make sense of the day's notes. Does the mind ever get beautifully clear and precise in the face of baking on command? Today I was bushed by the second recipe. Still, there is the beginning of routine in this new life of ten-minute lunches and apricot glazes, of dirty dishes by the dozens and rotating ovens. I'm struck again by the difference between all those slow, cozy years of baking in my own kitchen and this.

Crème Caramel (Caramel Custard)

makes 6 ramekins (3.5 oz, 4 inches wide, 1 1/2 inches high)

1 cup (250 mL) sugar
1/2 cup (125 mL) water

2 cups (500 mL) 3.25% milk (or 2%)
1/3 cup (75 mL) sugar
2 eggs
2 egg yolks
1 teaspoon(5 mL) vanilla

Have 6 ramekins or small custard cups and a bowl of ice water ready. In a small, heavy saucepan cook the sugar and water over medium heat. To avoid crystallization, do *not* stir, brushing down the sides of the saucepan with a clean pastry brush dipped in water. Swirl the pan slightly when sugar begins to take on colour. When sugar syrup turns a deep amber colour, and the syrup just begins to smoke, quickly take the saucepan off the heat and place bottom of pot into bowl of ice water to stop the cooking (do this double quick before the caramel thickens). Then quickly pour the syrup into the ramekins, just coating the bottoms. (Rewarm the syrup if it becomes too difficult to pour.)

While heating the milk over medium-low heat, whisk the sugar, whole eggs and egg yolks together in a small bowl. When milk is steaming, whisk a ladle of it into the egg mixture. Remove pot from heat, pour the milk over the sugar/egg mixture and whisk vigorously. Strain the mixture. (This is very important in case there are any bits of egg.) Pour milk/egg mixture into caramel-coated ramekins. Then place ramekins in a shallow baking dish and fill with warm water until midway up the sides of ramekins. Bake in 325°F (165°C) oven for 45 minutes or until knife inserted in custard comes out nearly clean. Let cool before refrigerating (it's best to refrigerate for at least one day so the caramel liquifies). Just before serving, run a thin knife all the way around the ramekins, then turn the ramekins upside down on serving plates.

Every now and then, as I grease cake pans or turn up the speed on the KitchenAid, I wonder what my long-time sponsor in Overeaters Anonymous would say about my current project.

My name is Denise and I am a compulsive overeater. I have to use the present tense, though I haven't binged in years, nor been anorexic. I am an...alcoholic, addict, gambler, compulsive overeater. I am. That's what we say in a 12-step program. Amazing to think that for six and a half years—those skinny mid-eighties when I was in my mid-thirties—no refined sugar passed my lips. I was a confirmed candy-holic, a sugar junkie. I would still rather eat a slice of cake than a slice of cheese.

The difference, and it's a big one, is that I can now eat a slice of cake, not the whole cake. And that I can enjoy that slice, not feel guilty, not crave more. There's no cure for any of this compulsive shit. But there is relief, and I am grateful to be in what I guess my sponsor would call "recovery." She'd also say Easy Does It, One Day at a Time, and Keep it Simple, Stupid (KISS), all those over-used, beloved program slogans that helped me get here.

Still, it's a slippery slope. I watch some of my classmates wolfing down bowls of pastry cream, notice their jackets getting tighter, and know that could be me. Pastry school could just be an excuse.

I didn't start really bingeing until I was eighteen and living in New York. I was there to study dance at the Juilliard School of Music. It was a place where bodies mattered. When I'd auditioned six months earlier, in February 1965, I'd weighed 105 pounds. "A sylph," one of my Juilliard teachers called me. Six months before that, I'd weighed in at an anorexic 96 pounds.

But by the time I arrived in New York that September for the start of school, I was up twenty pounds, having anxiously packed away whole boxes of ice cream sandwiches in what I thought would be my last summer at home. By December I was 140 and letting out the seams in all my new winter clothes. By the time I got off the plane in LA in June, I was 170. "I didn't recognize you at first," my mother admitted a few years later.

What happened that year? I'm not sure I know even now, forty-plus years later. I was terribly homesick. By December I was lovesick. The composer who'd loved me in October was already going out with one of my classmates two months later. I was facing a kind of competition as a young dancer I'd never known before. Getting into Juilliard was tough, but staying in was tougher. "Half of you will not be coming to Lincoln Center with us when we move there in two years," was the greeting we first-year Juilliard students got from the school's director. Having already disappointed myself so spectacularly over the summer—eating too much, crying too much, not dancing nearly enough—I seriously wondered which half I'd land with.

I began buying candy bars by the handful, halvah by the pound, eating bowls of hot cereal late at night, rice, noodles, anything cheap, starchy and filling. I ate to calm my fears, to bolster my fragile ego, to subdue the ache of being far from home. I ate, as I was later to learn in Overeaters Anonymous, because of what was eating me.

It took four years to lose that weight. By then I was back in LA, having gotten kicked out of Juilliard at the end of the school year for gaining weight and skipping classes. General sloth. But at twenty-three, newly married to my first husband, the other half of my eating disorder kicked in: not eating. I lost thirty pounds in the first thirty days of being married.

I had more than a problem with food.

"Rena's not going to be back for a while," Anna tells Alfred. "She's figuring some things out." Tall, dark-haired Rena of the high-wattage smile has been out most of this week. I'm disappointed. She's smart and focused and a little older than most of the class and I've been hoping to get to know her better.

Alfred nods solemnly as if he understands this. Every class has its casualties. We'll be lucky if we still number in the twenties by year's end. But before we can get started on another day of creams, fillings and glazes, Ardis comes in to tell us we've all passed Module 1. It's not a huge feat. Module One has consisted of showing up for two classes and writing a paper on our impressions of the profession so far and how we saw ourselves fitting in or not. "One credit down, eighty-nine credits to go!" she chirps.

In the Lab it's one demo after another as Alfred shows us how to finesse pie crust. We're making flan today as our basic cream. But again he doesn't want us going home with only a plastic container of custard, so he came in early to whip up a giant mixerful of pie dough.

"In professional cooking we went home with a litre container of pastry cream," says Trina.

"It sat there and went bad, right?" asks Alfred.

"Something like that," says Trina.

He dashes flour across Tara and Suzy's wood counter. The flour flies diagonally out of his hand like the finest ski powder. "Don't trust your rolling pin. Trust your hands," he says and rolls a small ball out into a perfect circle, gives the circle a half turn, rolls again. He folds the circle in half, slips it into the waiting pie pan and taps it, the dough filling in every little crevice. Then he picks up his rolling pin and rolls it right over the top of the pan, the excess falling at his fingers. All of this takes, I don't know, a minute?

When I try this a half-hour later, it takes ten times longer, and my pie crust has the patched-together look of dough that's been rolled and re-rolled. Jen tells me she's never made a pie in her life, but she rolls her little mound of dough out into a perfect circle the first time and gets it into the pan without mishap.

"How did you do that?" I ask. I've tried making pie dough many times. Though I hate store-bought anything and pride myself on being a from-scratch baker, I've come to rely on ready-made crusts.

"I just watched Alfred's hands," Jen says. "I just did it the way he did it."

I'm so tired these mornings, Beauch is having to nudge me off the bed as if he were a baker peeling bread, sliding a long-handled wood paddle under a heavy, resistant loaf at the back of the deck oven. Oooph.

We're all in a bit of a scramble with Claudette this morning, meaning some of us are late, and she threatens to lock the classroom door at 8:15. There's a new student in the front row: Lorrie, Trina's friend from professional cooking. Lorrie is tall with long blonde hair and ice-blue eyes. She's so pretty and Trina and she are such good friends, I find myself a little jealous. Will Trina want to talk to me as much now?

Our first cake designs are due this morning—a cake for someone taking a trip. I see boats and palm trees handed up to Claudette. I did an RV on the open road with a lake full of sailboats in the background, *Happy Sails, Happy Trails* in a round, casual font. It looks breezy, but I had stayed up till all hours searching for photos of Winnebagos on the Internet. A bit busy, Claudette will tell me later, but "nice."

Looking around the classroom, it's hard to believe this was the same group of fighting women at the rotating oven Friday afternoon. We'd just made our first clafoutis, pudding-like cakes made of thick batter and dark cherries. Madison had been waiting and waiting for her clafouti to come out of the rotating oven, when two of the Chinese women had pushed their way in front of her, so they could wait for their clafoutis. A crowd had already formed, everyone peering into the smudged oven window, waiting, hoping they could even find their pan among the dozen rotating shelves packed with clafoutis. People kept stopping the oven, swinging open the door, taking a poke at their pastry. "You're letting all the heat out!" somebody protested. The Chinese women stayed put, did not budge, on serious pastry watch. Then Cindy got into the act and someone, not the Chinese women, said fuck this and fuck that. The women, Xiu Li, Min and Shirley, had looked slapped, stunned. They did not fight back. Alfred, unruffled, had been called over.

Later, in the classroom, Cindy was still complaining loudly about the Chinese students and Wendy said maybe she should "temper" it. "I don't give a fuck!" Cindy answered. It occurs to me that what will be good for the book—drama, flubs, struggle, scenes—will be hard on us.

At lunch Jen's boyfriend, a cute boy in a small pickup, shows up and whisks her off to McDonald's, so it's just Lorrie, Trina and me. I'm grateful to be included. We sit on the chipped cement stairs around the side of the building. I finally get their stories. Trina, twenty-two, is from the Gaspé, so her B&B plan is about going home. She was studying biochemistry at Concordia with the plan of becoming a surgeon, when she dropped out to go to cooking school. "I'll go back to school some day," she tells me. "Three out of the four kids in my family have university degrees—one brother's even working on an MBA at Cambridge—so my family was pretty surprised when I dropped out to do this instead. But I've found what I love. I think about food all the time. I talk about it all the time. This is what I want."

Lorrie, who's ten years older than Trina, has a degree in special-needs counselling, but did Pearson's cooking course with Trina two years ago. "I've always wanted to be a pastry chef, though, even when I was doing that program. I was so jealous of Trina doing pastry this year, so it's a gift to be allowed in."

I like these two women, as I particularly like Jen and Diane. I like nearly everyone so far, although I know to steer somewhat clear of the complainers, the few loose cannons.

Today we've been told there's a meeting right after lunch. It sounds official, even punitive. Will there be consequences for the clafouti scuffle? But when we gather in the classroom, someone turns out the lights and the door opens and we're all suddenly singing "Happy Birthday." It's Wendy's thirty-third birthday and someone has managed to retrieve an ice cream cake from the walk-in freezer, a night-class exam from the week before. It's a sponge cake layered with chocolate and banana ice creams, covered in ganache and studded with sugar cones. I like the combination of crunch and smooth. I've never eaten an exam before.

Back in the Lab, Claudette spreads dark chocolate-coloured gel onto a plastic tray with a metal spatula. She smoothes the glops into a sheet of brown lacquer. It doesn't look quite edible, more like something you'd use to glue tiles. She turns the spatula this way and that. It's the first time we've seen Claudette in her chef's jacket. She's different from the woman who stumbles over the pronunciation of safety and hygiene terms as she reads them (sometimes word for word) off her overheads. This woman has no doubts about who she is. Ardis told us Claudette never took a day off from her job at the Château Champlain when her sons were little. "She was the *Chef*."

Claudette whips a paper cone together, simple as origami, fills it with gel, cuts a nearly invisible tip diagonally off the end and begins to pipe, the tiny thread of gel making delicate, graceful loop the loops. "Don't stop pressing your *cornet*. When you want to stop, you just pause." Her legs are hip-width apart, knees slightly bent, the back-saving way to do back-breaking work. "Fabrice and Edward, they are the best writers," she tells us. "They have a style of their own."

We watch, fascinated. Perfect letters are coming out of a piece of folded paper. *Bonne Anniversaire*. "We are an artist in pastry," Claudette says and straightens up to tell us about a decorating competition she entered back in the eighties. Transferring photos of Robert Bourassa, Pierre Elliott Trudeau and René Lévesque onto the top of her cake, she wrote "Renéssance" in gothic letters. "Either the judge didn't get my word play or she didn't like my gothic lettering," Claudette says, laughing. "I only got seven out of ten points." Maybe the judge didn't like René and his politics, I almost say, but don't.

We have three assignments this afternoon: First, paint our hard-sugar *pastillage* disk in a colour wheel. Then practise piping. Then try to make our bon voyage cake design in brown gel. The colour wheel's fun, but fifteen minutes into the piping everyone's feeling like a failure. I'm at the back station with Avedon and Jen, right in front of a garbage can, and I hear the mutterings of people as they go by and drop their failed *cornets* into the trash. It's hard to get the hole tiny enough. I go through three *cornets*, and still the gel is clumping at the too-big opening.

"I think I'm getting it," says Jen. A few minutes later, she says, "No, I'm not."

The *cornets* themselves are hard to make: take an 11x14 sheet of parchment, cut it in half, slice the halves into two more halves, then fold one half into a perfect isosceles triangle. With the bottom toward you, fold down the top corner over your index finger, and tighten the paper into a miniature funnel. I remember watching students from last year's class making *cornets* and thinking they were magicians.

Lane, who's used to making hundreds of fruitcakes for her neighbours in Kahnawake, comes over to me, clearly agitated, "Am I doing it right?" Her parchment is creased, nearly shredded. Her hands shake.

But Ardis had told us about people shining in one area and not another, about how it all evens out. Shirley, who the Friday before could barely wrap the string around her tart boxes, is brilliant at this. Her letters have an elegant ease. Mine are still mainly glops with an unbroken thread here and there. The good parts are the accidents. Already I am thinking: This is not my thing. I don't even like decorated cakes. What does this have to do with wonderful-tasting desserts?

And then the fire alarm goes off. We file out to the front parking lot, Claudette complaining loudly about the school administration. "They have hard heads. Usually they don't tell me ahead of time and we've got génoise in the oven. At least there's nothing baking this time."

Two fire trucks are parked outside, so maybe it's no drill. The sun and air are warm, a reminder that we're missing the last of summer, that there's another world going on out here. I end up standing next to Avedon. She tends to be quiet, looks a bit lost. She's twenty-five, a bit older than the others, she tells me. Last year she was at McGill studying business when she decided it wasn't for her. Her mother wasn't thrilled about her change of career plans—pastry is not commerce—but Friday's strawberry tarts had made an impression. "She sees now that I'm doing something."

In the locker room later, it's me, Yujie and Xiu Li. We commiserate about the difficulty of learning all the microbiology for the hygiene module.

"It is so hard for us!" cries Yujie, explaining that the baby blue mini-laptop on her desk is a Chinese/English dictionary. "But real, paper dictionary works better," she says. They're confused by something Claudette covered this week: HACCP or Hazard Analysis Critical Control Point, a self-inspection safety system for people in food services that was first developed for the space program.

"But what is space?" Yujie asks. I try to explain, wave my arm at the ceiling, talk about astronauts. They smile and nod politely.

The seven Chinese students did not know each other before, Xiu Li says; they just walked in that first day of class and found six other students who, like them, spoke Mandarin. I wish I knew the Mandarin word for space.

How to describe the space we inhabit for so many hours each day? The Lab is nearly nondescript, big, squarish. The walls are school-beige and there's lots of dull chrome (sinks, stoves, mixers, counters). The space is only about function, with its L-shaped corner for the giant fridges and freezers, the line of gas and convection ovens against one wall. None of the equipment is new. There's a glassed-in office where the teachers have a desk, filing cabinets, a phone, a computer and refuge from us.

There are technically twelve work stations in here, enough for eleven teams of two and one team of three. In the beginning we would cram together, two teams on a counter, bumping elbows and handles. Sometimes this was annoying, sometimes comforting. Claudette, however, has now assigned stations that will apply even on days with our other teachers. Every month each team will draw numbers out of a bowl and we're to work wherever it says. The stations are not equal:

some have stainless counter tops, some are wood, and some (a classy touch) are marble. It's hard to know what to wish for the first time we draw stations. Marble is good, Alfred says, for puff, but lousy (too cold) for bread. Wood's better for rising doughs. All we can do is hope to be at the right station for the right module.

At the end of the line of gas and convection ovens is the huge, rumbling, much-used rotating oven with its dozen, blackened, always-moving racks. I've taken to calling this oven "Lucy" because I can imagine Lucille Ball having a zany "I Love Lucy" time with it... Lucy and Ethel have decided to make a little extra money by working in a bakery. The boss tells them to mind the store and everything is going okay until Lucy decides to make bread, only she realizes she forgot to put in the yeast after she's put the loaves in the oven and then she tries to retrieve them with a broom, but a small fire breaks out...

Lucy is under the one window in the room. Through this small, high opening we can see the colour of the sky if we remember to look up.

It's a rainy morning with tipped-over cars on the highway and empty seats in the classroom. But even with people missing, we're loud. Claudette, who's dressed as if she's heading for the Casino—sequined, sleeveless top with tight black pants—puts her hands over her ears. "I wouldn't want a lot of kids," she says. After two weeks' absence, Rena's back, sitting in her usual corner. She looks pale, wrung out. On top of lovesickness, she's been hit with a sinus infection.

"What does it mean when you see a mouse?" Claudette asks us. "That forty-nine brothers and sisters are nearby!" She's full of other good news, too: flies contaminate everything they land on, carrying cholera, typhoid, polio and food poisoning. And then there's this nice little fact: some bacteria don't die even in the freezer. "That microbe, she's just waiting for better conditions. She's on vacation in your freezer, cross-country skiing."

Today we're studying first aid, which reminds Claudette of a story. "A long time ago I was working in an Italian bakery. It was early in the morning. The baker was talking and talking while he was doing what he'd been doing for fifteen years. Suddenly he's hopping around clutching his hand. We think he's kidding. But no, he got his fingers stuck in the rolling machine. He damaged his fingers so badly, he couldn't be a *pâtissier* any more."

Another story: A student is on a pastry *stage*. His cake knife falls and he grabs it, cutting all his fingers so badly he can never work in pastry again.

So. We've been warned. Claudette has a few more cautionary tips that she flashes on the overhead, obvious things like mopping up spills and not-so-obvious things like keeping a bowl of cold water nearby when working with hot sugar. She ups the terror by showing us a badly dubbed Québécois industrial film of people choking, falling off ten-foot ladders, getting burned in explosions.

I'm thinking about all this when I slip, fall and crash into the wall of the women's washroom fifteen minutes later. There's been water on the floor in here all week. When I limp back to tell Claudette, she's upset, has me go to the office to file an accident report. There is a sense of broken things throughout the building. Half the chairs in the cafeteria are missing half their bottoms. If you land on a seat wrong, you get a sharp edge of plastic up your bum. Such a hard-scrabble place to be learning such refined skills.

Claudette is going over a new monthly cleaning chart when I return. Not only are we responsible for our own equipment and tools, our own dishes and work table, our own sinks, we've now got extra jobs—from oven burners to the Lab's major appliances. My monthly job is to clean the three convection ovens. And, as of the day before, each work station has a job. Ours, number seven, is to clean the backs and undersides of the five sinks. "In a kitchen," Lorrie says, as she lies on her back and scrubs like a fiend, "you are always cleaning." After several restaurant gigs, Lorrie knows about dirt. But judging by the gunk we uncover down there, it looks like the students before us didn't share the same work ethic. Or maybe they just weren't as afraid of Claudette as we already are.

Claudette is warning us now: "Don't come to me at the end of the year complaining that you were always the one who did the dishes.

I won't want to hear it." Another edict: we all leave at the same time at the end of the day. "You can't say: 'My clean-up is done. I want to go home now.' Forget it! You stay and help each other."

All this is being said as she stands in front of the Chinese students. There are already rumblings among some classmates about their breaches of hygiene, about walking off and leaving messes, refusing to wash dishes. Do the Chinese students hear what she's saying? Do they understand what she's saying?

"Welcome to the life!" says Claudette and waves us home.

"I hope we make something I can take home today," I tell Jen, sliding onto my stool. It's Beauch's birthday and I haven't made him a cake. I'm in pastry school and there's no cake. There's no time to make a cake.

"It's my fault!" Alfred says as soon as he comes in. "The crust on the apricot flan wasn't quite cooked enough yesterday, but the pastry cream was good. Well, maybe a bit too eggy. You know," he says, throwing out another non sequitur, "clafouti is very popular in France. They serve it there with a mountain of whipped cream. I forgot to tell you that yesterday. Hey, do any of you know what Maizena is?"

"Honey?" Suzy ventures.

"Don't call me that in front of everyone," says Alfred.

Maizena, it turns out, is the commercial name for cornstarch, which we'll be using in one of today's batches of pastry cream. Alfred wants us to see and taste the difference between pastry cream made with flour and pastry cream made with cornstarch. Both will be prepared in service of our first agenda item—*crème mousseline.*

"Ooohh," some of us cry.

"It's got nothing to do with mousse!" says Alfred. "It's pastry cream with a lot of butter inside."

Today, he promises, we might walk out of here with two cakes: a *fraisier* (sort of a French strawberry shortcake), and a praline mousseline cake. We're going to construct real, live *entremets* with rings and acetate and layers today. I'll have a cake for Beauch now, maybe two, though neither will be the old-fashioned spice cake he asks for every year. He'll have to cope.

I notice that Jen's not tracking Alfred. She sits facing our counter, eyes down, as if she's afraid to move. One of her killer migraines—she's been getting them since she was seven—is coming on. "I can't get too excited about anything," she whispers to me.

I'm trying not to get too worked up myself, but I feel anxiety build as Alfred tells us all we must do today. You need an orderly mind for pastry, I'm realizing. You need a definite, logical mind, the nerves of a yogi and the body of a boxer. I have my strengths, but these may not be among them. And speed? I've never done anything fast in my life. Things seep in deep when they take hold, but I've never been what anyone would call a fast study. Triple earth sign—sun in Taurus, moon in Virgo, rising sign in Capricorn. "My God," one of my old LA friends said after doing my astrological chart. "Things must move awfully slowly for you, Denise." I could use a little air, fire and water this year.

In the Lab, Alfred demos the slicing of a génoise cake into three layers. "Make it five if you can," he challenges us, warning that we must be careful with our big, new and very sharp serrated cake knives. "I don't want to see little drops of blood today, okay? That knife is the most lethal weapon in your toolbox. I'm doing this slowly because my fingers are more important than a cake. What is a cake anyway? A block of sugar and a bit of flour."

What he wants to see is that each team has organized the four components for a constructed cake: *entremet* ring (a stainless hoop), the right-height acetate to go inside the ring, a nine-inch cake board to go under the cake, and a small plastic tray. We'll be building on this tray, fitting the bottom of the ring with a layer of génoise, "punching" it by brushing on sugar syrup, layering this with mousseline cream, and up, up, up with three, four, five layers, until our cake reaches nearly the top of the ring. On top will go a thin layer of rolled marzipan.

"But don't go running to Claudette and tell her I showed you how to make *entremets*, okay?" he says. "This is Claudette's specialty. This is her module to teach you."

Jen and I manage to make two batches of pastry cream without lumps and without scorching the bottom, but at the ten o'clock break she goes home, clutching her stomach, migraine in full nauseating swing. Nadia's usual partner, Madison, is out sick today, too, so suddenly I'm working with Nadia, Michèle and Stinky. These are girls not long out of high school, tall girls, big girls, zoom girls. Except for Michèle, they don't know much about baking either—Stinky told me she bakes only Duncan Hines and thinks they're great.

They're also adorable girls and welcome me into their loud trio. Nadia keeps smiling at me encouragingly. "Come on, Denise," she says. We take turns lobbing softened butter into the mixer bowl where it's quickly incorporated into the now-chilled pastry cream. I'm so afraid of doing it wrong that my butter lumps get smaller and smaller. Nadia's get larger and larger.

Alfred walks over just as the stuff begins to curdle. He leans into the mixer bowl. "The problem is not with the butter or the pastry cream," he says.

"So what is it?" we cry.

"The problem is patience," says Alfred.

"I'm bad at patience," Nadia says.

Keep beating, he tells us.

Eventually it holds together and I am left feeling better than I have all week. Maybe I am good at something. Maybe patience will be my forte. Speed won't be, nor organization. But maybe decades of watching things work out somehow, will count for something. Mostly, though, all those years of home-baking seem to mean bupkis (make that babkas) in pastry school.

We fold finely chopped strawberries into the lovely buttery cream and then we punch and layer, punch and layer. Nadia is moving so fast she puts too much mousseline on the first layer. She doesn't have enough for layers two and three.

Oh well, she says.

At 11:35 Alfred yells out, "Don't make more than one cake before lunch, guys!"

Not a problem.

Over lunch in the classroom Rena tells me about her break-up with her younger, longtime man. She's been so upset she was even considering dropping out of pastry school. But then last Saturday Wendy and Diane called her at home, picked her up, took her out to dinner and convinced her to stay. "I was so touched!" Rena tells me, eyes filling.

Alfred comes into the classroom where he surprises Min, who's leaning deep into the large, top-opening freezer, arms stretched up to keep the lid open.

"You looking for me?" Alfred asks. "You ticklish?"

Min giggles. "I do monthly cleaning," she tells him.

Just the day before, Jing asked me how to lift one of the burners from the stove now that Claudette has assigned each of us a burner—or in my case, knobs—to clean each time we work on the gas ranges. So the cleaning message *is* getting through the language barrier. I only hope Wendy, who's eating lunch at the back counter, has heard Min's answer. Wendy, more than anyone, I've noticed, is critical of the Chinese students. She finds them pushy and aggressive. Interesting, coming from her.

Qiang comes in looking shaken, though his mouth is still smiling. Someone has broken into his locker. And though it's not clear what was taken and Qiang keeps saying, Oh, well! and Okay! everyone is angry for him, and hugely sympathetic. There's a running joke these days between Qiang and Madison that seems to revolve mostly around the word "what?" Now when one says the word, it sends the other into peels. What? What! But no one's laughing now. Who would do something like that to a fellow student?

As we pack up our lunch bags, Jing takes out pictures of her three-year-old son, Grant, and we coo over his cuteness. We are taking little steps toward each other. We're laughing over things no one else would think was funny. We're beginning to hang like a gang.

"I had a weird dream last night," Jen tells me first thing. "There's a king who's trying to catch a woman who wants to be the queen of pastry, but he thinks she wants to rule the world."

"Get out now," warns Andrea.

"See you guys in a month," says Jen, grinning, making the crazy gesture at her temple. She told me a few days ago that, without trying to, she now knows the recipe for pastry cream by heart. "Isn't that scary?" she asked with real alarm.

Alfred's eyes are so bloodshot this morning it looks like he has conjunctivitis. As we were leaving yesterday I asked him if teaching was more demanding than owning a bakery. "Four years ago, when I first started teaching, I had no car and was commuting from the West Island by bus and teaching both days and evenings. I slept from 2:00 to 5:00 a.m. and then got up and did it again," he told me. He has a way of ducking questions. What is his story?

But the red eyes this morning are from a late night at Farinex, the growing giant of a baking-goods supplier in Boisbriand, a suburb north of Montreal, where it runs workshops for professional pastry chefs. Four chefs had come together to create a cake and then demo it for their fellow *pâtissiers*. "We had to sign an agreement that we wouldn't use the award-winning cake in our own shops," says Alfred.

The top-secret cake was created by a chef whose specialty is Bavarian cream, another whose talent is decoration, and two others who contributed the sponge and the butter cream. "After this module, you'll also be able to create a cake," Alfred promises. "With the cream module you'll become very creative, especially with flavours."

For now, though, we are beginners, even if making a *fraisier* three weeks into it seems advanced to me. Today we'll learn two more French-pastry staples: crème anglaise and Bavarian cream. And though chocolate is not Alfred's module, we'll also be working with chocolate for the first time.

"Never, never, never melt chocolate over direct heat," he orders us. "Only melt it in a metal bowl set in a pot of simmering water, a double boiler or *bain-marie*, okay?"

"Okay," we promise, and watch Alfred as he sticks a metal bowl full of chocolate pieces, or *pistoles*, into the microwave, closes the door and punches in the time.

"What are you doing?" Tara cries. "You can't put metal in a nuker."

"You just told us we had to melt chocolate over a *bain-marie*," says Suzy.

"Don't do that, eh?" he whispers, pointing to the humming microwave. "You're not allowed. And don't tell Ardis or Claudette. They're going to kill me." If we should ever need to break the rules, he adds, just make sure the metal bowl doesn't touch the sides of the microwave. "It will start to sparkle."

At the first break, Anna takes Rena—who also looks as if she hasn't slept in days—home. But on her way out Rena asks Alfred how the chocolate will eventually be incorporated into the Bavarian cream. She might be an emotional mess right now, but she's still got some priorities straight.

It's like night and day, yesterday and today, in the Lab. I'm back with Jen, and because we're working in groups of four, we're teamed up with Lorrie and Trina, already like professionals with their moves worked out, their minds orderly as the *mise en place* of ingredients they organize before starting. Just watching them is an education. Their year in professional cooking—not to mention time since working in restaurants—has given them edge, finesse and confidence. They show us how to whip cream by hand—though each has a different technique. "The idea," Lorrie says, "is to incorporate as much air as possible in there. That's what gives whipped cream its volume."

It feels very "pastry chef" to stand there with a huge stainless bowl in the crook of my arm, giant whisk going at the cream like crazy. But the glamour wears off in three minutes when my wrist and shoulder begin cramping, both mind and body screaming, "Are we there yet?" Jen gets there first with perfectly whipped medium-peak cream, the mounds holding their upward shape, not folding over as in soft-peak nor standing at stiff attention as in firm. Cream, we all know, can change personality in five seconds. Overwhip and you've got butter. Underwhip and you've got soup.

"Are you free for lunch?" Cindi, another fifty-something who's enrolled in professional cooking, pokes her head into the classroom just as I'm sinking onto my stool. I'm reluctant to leave my classmates. I've come to like the companionable munching and lazy, easy talk among us. I like unwinding together. We don't really know each other, but we do. Yesterday Wendy, Tamara and Diane were talking cup size in the locker room. (Not measuring cups.) And when Diane caught me a minute later sniffing the crotch of my checks and said, "I know what you're doing!" we both collapsed in laughter.

"Why don't you eat with us?" I suggest.

"This is so much more than I bargained for," Cindi says, climbing onto the stool next to me. "I feel like I know nothing after twenty years in my own kitchen." Cindi is small and blonde, classy, and very West Island. "I was peeling a carrot in class this week and felt like I didn't know how to do it right."

We commiserate for a while about this and about how hard it is for our families to accommodate our new schedule and preoccupation. At some point Cindi looks around at the others in the room and says, "It's hard, isn't it, keeping up and making space for this, finding the balance?" But among the young women at the counter along the wall—Trina, Lorrie, Andrea and Michèle—there isn't one nod of recognition. They don't know. Not yet. There's an awkward pause before Cindi, packing up her lunch box, says, "My mantra is that I don't have to be the best. This is just part of my life. I already have a life."

Or rather, we had a life. I'm glad to be doing this, but I miss my friends. I miss writing and having mornings with Beauch. I miss my house. All my daytime hours are spent in the Lab with its one tiny window, mixers going, water running, days filled with lectures and demos and constant talk and homework and all that I've taken on. A year feels like a long time to be gone from the rest of life.

It's been a hard week filled with bombs-away days. Some days I've been too discouraged to write. It begins Wednesday when Ardis cheerfully assigns me to work with a girl who's come in as a student-for-a-day as I had the previous year, and since Anna is absent and Rena needs a partner, off Jen goes to work with her. I am suddenly separated from my smaller, but sharper, other half.

The newcomer is an odd partner—part innocent, part gabber, part reminder of what I am not doing right. She seems more on top of things than I am, my mind moving into that blank panic I've begun to notice sets in when we walk into the Lab after going over the day's agenda. Then the girl leaves one hour into it, and I am truly on my own.

Ardis has given us recipes for both oatmeal-raisin cookies and hazelnut biscotti. "Initially I thought I'd have each team make one recipe, but then I thought it would be more fun if we all made everything!" Wheee! Ardis says she needs the cookies for some event that evening. We can buy half of what we make; she keeps the rest.

To make things trickier, we are to overlap recipes, starting the second while the first is in the oven. And to make matters trickier, biscotti are baked twice. That makes three oven watches. "It's a cakewalk until this part," Ardis warns before setting us loose. "And you know," she adds, "Claudette is very bad about babysitting your things in the oven."

"Alfred, too," someone offers.

"Yes, I know," Ardis says. "But today you babysit your own biscotti. You write down what time you put them in and you keep track."

"There was a mad fight on Friday at the oven," says Suzy. I am surprised she has brought this up. Do the Chinese students hear or understand what she's just revealed?

"Everything's going to be fine," says Ardis, acting as if hasn't heard a thing about our bad behaviour. "The cookies are going to be fine! No need to panic, okay?"

But it turns out there is. I labour in the back-sink station alone, having lost even more time in trying to chat helpfully with the student-for-a-day while she was there. I am so mad at myself and my out-of-place teacher impulses, mad at Ardis for separating me from my partner, mad at becoming so dependent on Jen so fast, mad at having to show someone the ropes when I can barely hold onto them myself, mad at my faulty memory, mad at my panic. Mad. A bad thought comes: what *am* I doing here?

Meanwhile, I am wasting more time, more movement. There is no KitchenAid at this station, so I have to go round one up from the cart. The day before, Claudette gave us headaches (worse than the ones we already had from manoeuvering our clumsy *cornets* and skooshy gel), by running an engraver at full bore so she could number and letter every whisk, paddle, hook and bowl of twenty mixers. We are now to be accountable for every piece. I stand there, minutes leaking by, trying to find the matching parts, while all around me other teams spoon cookie batter onto trays. What's happened to last week's fun?

Though it looks unpromising at first, the biscotti dough comes together. "Add flour," Rena comes by to say. "There wasn't enough in the recipe." This helps, as well as the suggestion to put the whole hazelnuts into the mixer, too, something I'd never have done at home, folding nuts in by hand at the very end. "I did it wrong," Rena says, "and I had to add the nuts in one by one." One thing about being behind: You get good advice from those ahead. And Rena, after her see-saw love life and sinus infection, now seems to be really back.

When I get home, I notice my lips are completely raw, as if I've been in the desert all day. I have been licking them over and over without realizing it.

Biscotti

1 1/4 cups (300 mL) all-purpose flour
2 teaspoons (10 mL) baking powder
3/4 cup (175 mL) sugar
1/3 cup (75 mL) white bread crumbs
1/2 cup (125 mL) whole almonds with skin
1/2 cup (125 mL) whole hazelnuts without skin
1/2 teaspoon (2 mL) orange flower water
1/2 teaspoon (2 mL) vanilla extract
2 tablespoons (30 mL) orange juice
2 eggs

Egg wash:
1 egg mixed with 2 teaspoons (10 mL) water

Granulated sugar

Sift the flour with the baking powder. Add the sugar and bread crumbs, and combine, using a mixer at low to medium speed. Mix in the almonds and hazelnuts. Whisk together the orange flower water, vanilla, orange juice and eggs. Gradually add the liquid to the dry ingredients and mix for approximately one minute until you achieve a firm dough. Divide the dough into two equal pieces. Roll each piece into a uniform rope of eight inches. Place the ropes on sheet pans lined with parchment. Brush egg wash on top of both ropes. Sprinkle lightly with sugar.

Bake at 375°F (190°C) for about 25 minutes, or until golden brown. Let cool for at least one hour. Then slice ropes diagonally into cookies that are 3/8-inch thick. Place the slices cut-side down on sheet pans lined with parchment. Bake at 375°F (190°C) until the cookies start to turn golden brown around the edges, approximately 15 minutes. Cool on racks. Store in airtight container.

3

Butter Cream 101

It's the start of Module Nine, Whipped Rising Batters: choux pastry (the light and lovely stuff of which éclairs are made), sponge cakes and meringues. I've got a killer cold, as do Michèle, Rena and Trina. Everyone's hacking. Baking fatigue has set in. But Claudette is jolly this morning. "In this trade you have to be enthusiastic even at one in the morning!" she says, and proceeds to teach us the most basic cake on the planet: *le génoise*. Sponge cake, my mother would call it. Génoise looks, even tastes, simple. After all, it's only made with eggs, sugar and flour. But this is French pastry, so it isn't. Génoise is a fragile little thing.

The key is getting the ribbon right. This is what's supposed to happen when the warmed egg yolks and sugar—"warmed, not cooked, otherwise you get scrambled eggs" —are beaten for a long time. How long? Until it's perfect, Claudette says, and goes from team to team checking our ribbons, lifting our whisk attachments and tracing circles on top of our batter. How quickly or slowly they sink back in is what we have to assess. "Give it another shot on medium speed," she tells Jen and me, then demos how to properly fold in the pastry flour, slicing the rubber spatula through the middle of the batter to get rid of lumps.

Génoise

makes two 8-inch cakes

1 1/4 cups (300 mL) cake flour
1/8 teaspoon (1 mL) salt
5 large eggs
2/3 cup (150 mL) sugar
1 teaspoon (5 mL) vanilla

Preheat oven to 375°F (190°C). Lightly butter two 8-inch cake pans. Sift the cake flour with the salt and set aside. In a stainless bowl whisk the eggs with the sugar until fully blended. Then place the bowl over a pot of simmering water (a *bain-marie*) and continue whisking. Whisk until the sugar is completely dissolved and mixture is warm to the touch (not hot, or the eggs will begin to cook). Remove bowl from the heat and beat at high speed (if using a stand mixer use the whisk attachment) until mixture is thick, pale-lemon coloured and cool, close to 10 minutes. Test for "ribbon" by lifting the whisk and tracing a circle on top of the batter. It should retain its shape for 8 seconds. Fold in the flour in a slow and steady stream with a rubber spatula, plunging the spatula deep into the egg mixture. Fold gently, but until all trace of the flour is gone. Pour batter into prepared pans, smoothing tops with an offset spatula. Bake immediately for 20-25 minutes or until the tops are lightly browned and a cake tester comes out clean. Turn the cakes out of the pans onto a cooling rack as soon as they come out of the oven (this prevents moisture condensing wthin the cake). When cooled, cover the cakes with plastic wrap and store in a cool, dry place, or freeze.

For once, Claudette seems pleased with our results at the end of the day. I stay behind to dry and put away my tools. I've been lagging all day, having to walk to the sink, wash my hands, then dry my hands every single time I blew my nose. "You sneeze, you wash. Your scratch your ear, you wash!" Claudette's rules.

"You're not asking for enough help, Denise," she says, coming over. "You're off in the corner."

It's true. "I'm a corner person," I wrote in a journal when I was twenty-one and taking my first university creative writing class. "I've noticed," my professor responded in the margin.

"You do help me," I tell Claudette. "You're such a good teacher. You give the best demos. You are so incredibly clear."

She seems surprised at the praise. "Me, I don't want to be nice," she says. "I want you to learn. But I don't take your problems on me." It's a warning, I guess, not that I'm about to bare my soul to this tough little person.

I lock my toolbox and head off to a radio interview at CBC with Bill Richardson. Five short stories from my first book are to be read by five different actors and broadcast nationally on "Between the Covers" this week. I've waited five years for this to happen and would like to tell someone at school, but really, except for Ardis, there is no one here to tell.

"That's neat," my pastry friends would likely say. But it might create more space between us, a natural age-and-experience space I work hard every day to close up. Besides, with my head cold, I'll sound like a foghorn when I read from the book. Though I might not be asked to read at all. I already know from the pre-interview that Richardson is much more interested in my being in pastry school than in my being a writer.

And he is, quite unashamedly, when we do the interview later that afternoon. He asks me a few questions about the book, but only comes alive when talking about my adventures in the baking trenches. "Does your mother have a good recipe for honey cake?" he asks at the end. (It's Rosh Hashanah.) I'm amused, if a little disappointed. Of course, food makes better radio than fiction. Who am I kidding? But, Bill, I want to say, I do both.

Trying to do both, anyway. The plan had been that I would put the day's notes into my computer every night after Georgia was in bed: what we made, who said what to whom. Notes that would accumulate over the year and then, like a soufflé out of the oven, there it would be—a perfectly baked book at the end of the year.

Here's how it's shaping up: I drag home at 4:30, find out from the sitter, Valerie, what homework has yet to be done. This is turning out to be more and more each night because it seems that although

Georgia really wanted me to hire Valerie last August after interviewing thirty women for this hour-and-a-half gig, she now doesn't want to have too much to do with her. Then I drive Valerie to the métro station (she has no car), drive home, finish up the homework, try to listen halfway attentively to the details of Georgia's day, get supper on the table, do the bath thing, do the bedtime thing, throw the greasy wad of towels, checks, socks and chef's jacket into the washing machine, return phone calls, check emails, and attempt a meaningful relationship with Beauch when he comes home from work at 11:15. Write? Right.

Four weeks to the day since we began pastry school, we meet the last member of the teaching quartet. "It's me, Fabrice!" says a large, greying, bearded fellow perched on a too-small stool at the front of the classroom. "Call me Chef, call me Fabrice, no problem!" A pastry chef for more than thirty-three years, he now teaches here full time and works as head *pâtissier* for a former student, owner of Eileen's Cakes & Pastries on the Kahnawake reserve outside Montreal. A dream catcher is embroidered on his chef's jacket. (But why is a pro like him working for his student? Is there a story here?)

Noticing that some of us are wearing checks without *our* jackets, he tells us we need to be prepared to go into the Lab first thing when he's teaching. "I don't like to talk too much. I'm a worker. With me you make a lot. Next week we make 500 pies for Eileen's for Thanksgiving." He has a high, sweet, French voice. "I'm a gentle man, but you don't respect me and rules of the school, I kick you in the fucking ass."

"I think I'm going to like this guy," Lorrie whispers to me. There's a shocked silence, "fucking ass" hanging loudly in the air, until Wendy asks, "When are we going to Paris?"

Fabrice grins as if he was waiting for this question, stands, unfolds an accordion of photos from Paris, like a guy in a raincoat selling naughty French postcards. "You come to me. You tell me where you want to go: Parees? London? Brussels? Good! I take you."

Everyone knows he's just returned from eight days in Paris with the close-to-graduating evening class, that he's French-born himself and that he got his students into the Barry-Callebaut chocolate showroom, plus into the kitchens of some of the big boys of French pastry, like Joël Bellouet.

But "Parees is not free, 'kay?" Fabrice holds up a bottle of Vichy water: "This cost $7.50 in Parees,'kay? But is easy to fundraise. The evening class, they raise almost $6,000 last April at a Sugar Bush. They do all the cooking. They invite all their friends, all their family and all the school, 'kay?" He seems uncertain about us tracking his mostly French English.

I'm mostly following, but can see from Min, Xiu Li and Yujie seated across the counter from me, that they're in heavy decoding mode. Their heads are bent over Yujie's tiny laptop. They whisper to each other. After Fabrice says a trip to Paris will cost about $1,400 per person before fundraising, he asks for a show of interested hands. Among the Chinese students, only Qiang puts his up.

"Paris!" Jen breathes next to me. Her arm has shot up and so has mine. Parees! as Fabrice says it. I can't imagine a more perfect way to end this year. It's only late September, but if I'm reading the twenty-foot signs right, if this past week is any indicator, we're going to *need* Paris at the end of these eleven months: cafés, les Champs Elysées, French men, pastry shops *au chaque coin*.

Jen sparkles at me: "We'll go together, right?" Fabrice has said something about bringing spouses, but I'm already thinking: no spouse. I love travelling with Beauch, but I want to do Paris with les girls. I want to go on day-long quests for the perfect millefeuille, to drink *alongées* and eat truffles all day. I look over at Trina and she's nodding and grinning at me. So is Lorrie. We're in.

"It's a French city, Parees," Fabrice is saying. "I tell you, the evening class, no one spoke French, now they speak French. Someone says 'bonjour' to you in Parees, you say 'bonjour' back."

But he cautions us again: Paris is not cheap. Each of us needs to start saving our money now, start depositing a cheque for $140 per month to our special class bank account—let's call it Future Chefs 2004, Wendy suggests—so that at the end of ten months we'll have enough. We also need to begin hatching fundraising ideas with the new evening class due to start in November. "You fight with evening group, I kick your fucking ass!" says Fabrice.

More people laugh this time. Min catches my eye across the table, gives me a little smile. Lorrie leans into me and whispers again, "I *like* this guy."

And here's another caution: "Is very important to understand not all teachers are behind this," says Fabrice and there's a sudden, dark cloud overhead, as if the sun has dimmed momentarily in the City of Light.

Who would be against this? What teacher would not think this was a terrific opportunity? We raise our own money, we go with an instructor, we learn more about our craft. I have an idea who the *mais non!* vote might be, based mostly on personality, and on a comment made in hygiene class last week. "Me, I've been to Paris two times. It's a nice place, but so filthy."

An hour has gone by and the Chinese students are looking at their watches. They're not here for Paris. They're not here for more foreign travel. They're here to learn a trade and get jobs. Fabrice has us open our textbooks to Module Six: *les pâtes friables*. Pie crust, is my guess. According to our text, there's *pâte à foncer, pâte sucrée, pâte brisée, pâte sablée*. Fat, flour and water are the main ingredients. Fabrice reads one recipe aloud from the book, then sets us loose in the Lab, saying only, "You make four pies today. Let's go."

But which ones and in what quantities? Is everyone to make one each of the four recipes? This will make one helluva lot of pies, though I remember last year's class saying that Fabrice's recipes for anything fed thousands. And how are we teaming up? In twos or fours?

The next half hour we scurry to gather in ingredients, organize our *mises en place*, try to look like we know what we we're doing. But eventually the bravura collides with the fact that we haven't a clue what to do. We begin to ask among ourselves, pride gone. Fabrice comes over to our table and spells it out as clearly as he's able: three of us are to make one recipe each of the first three recipes in the book, while the fourth person organizes the *mise en place* for the fourth (monster) recipe to be done in the giant Hobarts. Nowhere in anything he said earlier could we have known this.

Lorrie dibs the *pâte sucrée,* squishing the eggs and butter between her fingers with great relish (Lorrie possesses loads of nearly scary, overwhelming energy), while Jen begins on the *pâte brisée,* and Trina starts measuring vast quantities of flour for the big *pâte à whatever.*

I set to work on the *pâte à foncer,* but almost immediately, Lorrie and Cindy, who's working across the counter, begin telling me that I'm doing something, all things, wrong. My *pâte* does seem dry, but just as I'm about to add a bit more water, Lorrie says, no, don't, you can't, it's too late. I wrap the raggedy mass in Saran and stick it in the fridge. Later, Fabrice tells me I should have added more water: "No problem." It seems I'm here to crack my head against the same old lesson: listen to yourself. Failing that, listen to the teacher, though in Fabrice's case this would mean intuiting a lot.

We cut, scale and roll, learning Fabrice's little tricks like stacking the pie crust-filled tins on top of each other with a flourish of flour and a square of parchment between pans, then rotating a half dozen of them in one hand and sculpting off the excess with a metal spatula—quick like a mad chef.

Fabrice has promised us two apple pies to bring home—one made with piles of apple slices, cinnamon and sugar; the other his famous caramel apple pie. "How much brown sugar?" we ask as we mob him at the stove. "How much cream?"

"How much? This much!" And Fabrice laughs as he pours an unspecified amount of thirty-five percent cream and crumbles handfuls of brown sugar into the pot.

But come two o'clock, his pace changes. "Hurry in the oven! Hurry in the oven!" We shove pies into the rotating oven, forget about them, remember just in time, take out half a dozen, shove in half a dozen more.

It's Friday afternoon. We're done in, fried really. I'm blowing my nose once a minute; Trina's hacking up a lung. The flour flies, dusting everything from the tops of our shoes to every whisk and zester in our toolboxes. But back in the classroom at four, Fabrice pronounces himself happy. "You make very nice pies. Now you know how to do."

But the pies I bring home today are nothing to write home about. They taste apple-pie generic. Surprisingly, Fabrice seems to be the only teacher proud of his recipes, the only one to make a big deal about how something tastes. "It's very good, this one. You will like," Fabrice said several times about the caramel apple. But the only truly delicious desserts I've eaten in a month of pastry school are the *fraisier* and the chocolate Bavarian cream. I can still taste the fluffy cloud of that Bavarian. I ate it standing up at our work counter, dipping a plastic spoon into its soft stiffness.

We often eat our "products" like this, standing up, quickly, nearly inhaling them. It worries me some, this standing and stuffing, reminding me of binges of yore. Still, that was solitary and secretive. This is communal, as we compare reactions with the person next to us—don't you think the other recipe for pastry cream is better? can you tell I underbeat the cream? my grandmother's crust is flakier!—then moving right along to the next assignment.

I'm still thinking of the intense chocolate Bavarian when something comes to me. I am here in search of the delicious. Flavour! Texture! Divinity! It's not a professional goal, more an aesthetic one, and not one I would expect most of my classmates to understand. Do I need to rethink why I'm here? I'm having more and more days when I barely remember I'm doing this to gain credibility as a future baking journalist (as one food writer calls herself), days when I forget about the book altogether. Some days I'm just holding onto the giant whisk of a giant Hobart going at top speed.

I'm in search of something else tonight, too. "Bake me a pie!" Fabrice challenged at the end of our first day with him. Each of us is to make a pie and bring it in for our next pie class. I pick up *Canadian Living's Best Chocolate* cookbook and flip through the pie section... Best-Ever Chocolate Cream Pie. I haven't made a chocolate cream pie since I was a young bride in my early twenties. I read down the recipe: heat the milk and cream in a pot, whisk the sugar, eggs and cornstarch in a bowl, temper the egg mixture with some of the hot milk, then return the egg mixture to the pot to boil... Wait! This is chocolate pastry cream. I have been reading recipes since I wore braces, but only now am I starting to see the patterns. Ardis promised us: The way we read recipes will change. The way we bake will change. The method will be in our heads.

I appreciate Claudette's high expectations and hyper-organization. I love Ardis's food science know-how and womanly warmth. Even Fabrice's laissez-faire haze is welcome after a few days with *Le Générale*, as the guy in the food storeroom calls Claudette. But with Alfred, we laugh, we learn, and we come out—does this sound overwrought? have I completely lost my perspective here?—better people.

"Smiling, laughing, dancing—that's the way to live!" he told us recently. "When the baby's kept you up all night, go on vacation. When your back is out, go camping."

But even days with Alfred can turn into upside-down cake. Based on what he's written on the board this particular Tuesday, the load doesn't sound too strenuous: *crème Chantilly*, fondant, Italian meringue butter cream. And he's promised us éclairs at the end of it. "And not mini-éclairs," he says. "I made you éclairs!" He's come in especially early to make the *pâte à choux* shells.

But by 10:00 a.m. they're still not out of the oven. He runs to the Lab every fifteen minutes to check them.

In between, he holds forth on whipped cream. Lifting a container, he reads from the side: "An edible oil product." Alfred looks at us like the world's gone mad. "Where's the garbage?" This is Nutrafil, pure white, completely inorganic, indestructible, and a frequent substitute for whipped cream. Alfred tried Nutrafil in his bakery for a week. "But if I can't eat it, how can I expect my customers to? Where's the garbage?" he asks again, and goes to check once more on the éclairs.

They're still taking their sweet little time in the convection ovens, so he goes on to talk butter cream. We'll learn three kinds this year: the Swiss meringue butter cream we made the previous week, Italian meringue butter cream, which we'll be making today, and fondant butter cream. "I prefer Italian," he says. "So does Claudette. It's glossier and thicker. But I have a pastry-chef friend who prefers

Swiss. Fabrice has his own butter cream recipe, which he makes with whole eggs."

Last week a friend stopped me mid-story about this crazy place. "What is butter cream?" she asked. Her question reminded me that not everyone lives and breathes Italian versus Swiss. Not everyone cares. But it also made me look at butter cream objectively. It's made of egg whites and sugar syrup and butter and shortening, I told her. It's the colour of ivory, a winter white until you flavour or colour it. It's fluffy and pretty, and it tastes like sweet, creamy air. Yes, but what does it do? she asked, surprising me again with how little some of my friends know about baking. (No wonder many think I'm wasting a year.) It's icing, I said. Frosting. It's what goes on a cake. On top and in between layers. She looked at me blankly. It's the glue, I finally said. Butter cream holds everything together. Ohhh, she said.

Perhaps butter cream is *the* question, the way brown stock versus veal stock became the issue at the heart of Michael Ruhlman's *The Making of a Chef*. Ruhlman, a journalist, asked each of his instructors at the Culinary Institute of America to talk about the two staples of culinary life—Sauces 101—and everyone had not just a preference, but a complete philosophy built on that preference.

Swiss meringue butter cream is less dramatic than Italian, it seems. We gently warm the egg whites and sugar over a *bain-marie* before beating them into a medium-peak meringue.

Fondant butter cream is simpler yet, consisting of soft fondant and a blend of shortening and butter. That makes it denser and more obedient when it comes to piping flowers and borders, but I think I'd miss the lift of the egg whites.

Italian meringue butter cream, though, is the mainstay of this program and promises to be a challenge. It's all about timing and temperature. There's butter and shortening to soften, egg whites to whip until just so, sugar syrup to cook until just when, and then all the elements come somewhat dangerously together—boiling sugar syrup poured into whirring egg whites at just the right angle. Thick, white, and shiny is what we're after. And cool. All that napalm heat has to be out of there before we start pitching in the softened butter.

We're to do this in small increments, hoping the meringue has cooled enough not to melt the butter. It won't necessarily look promising at first, Alfred warns, with the volume of the egg whites temporarily gone and the texture curdled. The secret is to keep going no matter what. Something lovely and fluffy and buttery smooth will emerge, he promises.

But what with the slow-baking éclairs and Alfred's long riff on products, we don't actually get into the Lab until after lunch. I hear some grumbles around me: "He talks too much."

At the stove, Alfred demos how to work with fondant, which will be used as the glaze for our éclairs. Fondant looks like Elmer's glue and proves about as cooperative. First you wrestle the stuff out of the container into a little pot. Then you add sugar syrup to make the right consistency for dipping. Then you warm it to body temperature. While I whip the cream and icing sugar for the filling—what's known as *crème Chantilly*—Jen's at the stove cursing. The fondant comes midway up her arm. No spoons are used: this is all done with bare hands to better gauge the temperature. Alfred admits that not all chefs or teachers approve of this hands-in technique. "Typical French chefs don't like to dirty their hands," he says, rolling his eyes. "So they place the spoon just below the bottom lip to test the temperature. This is more hygienic?"

"I'm mad at it!" Jen suddenly cries, and I know not to ask one more time, "How's it going over there?"

The Italian meringue butter cream is still cooling off in the Hobarts and now it's nearly 3:00 p.m. and things go wonky as some overwhip and others underwhip their cream, struggle to fill pastry bags (I still don't know how to fill a pastry bag and not get as much on the outside as I do on the inside), and try not to lose a finger on our giant cake knives as we slice the éclairs in our hands.

It even gets to Alfred, who begins barking orders in a nervous, panicky, new-to-us voice. He's also realized that even with all the éclairs we've sliced and filled, we've so overshot our production that trays of pastry cream and litres of Chantilly are left over. At four we leave with migraines and all the éclairs we can carry.

Italian Meringue Butter Cream

4 large egg whites (1/2 cup, 125 mL) (room temperature for 30 minutes)
1 rounded teaspoon (6 mL) salt
2/3 cup (150 mL) water
1 1/3 cup (325 mL), plus 2 tablespoons (30 mL) sugar
1 1/2 cups (375 mL) unsalted butter, cut into tablespoon pieces and softened
1/2 cup (125 mL) shortening, cut into tablespoon pieces
2 teaspoons (10 mL) vanilla

Combine whites and salt in a very large bowl. Stir together water and 1 1/3 cups sugar in a 3- to 4-quart heavy saucepan until sugar is dissolved, then bring to a boil over moderate heat, without stirring, brushing any sugar crystals down the sides of the pan with a clean pastry brush dipped in water.

When syrup reaches a boil, start beating egg whites with a stand mixer and whisk attachment at medium-high speed until frothy, then gradually add remaining 2 tablespoons sugar and beat at medium speed until whites just hold soft peaks. (Do not beat again until sugar syrup is ready.)

Meanwhile, put thermometer into sugar syrup and continue boiling until syrup registers 238°F (117-121°C). Immediately remove from heat and, with mixer at medium speed, slowly pour hot syrup in a thin stream down the side of the bowl into whites, beating constantly. Increase mixer speed to high and beat, scraping down side of bowl with a rubber spatula, until meringue is properly cooled and forms medium-stiff peaks.

With mixer at medium speed, gradually add butter, then shortening, one piece at a time, beating well after each addition until incorporated. Continue beating until butter cream is smooth. (Mixture may look curdled or soupy before all of the butter and shortening is added, but it will come back together by the time beating is finished.) Add vanilla and beat one minute more.

I take a day off, my first. Today is the deadline for Canada Council grant applications, and being a dedicated procrastinator, I begin today. I write ten hours straight, continuing even after Georgia comes home from school, not even bothering to tell Valerie not to sit this afternoon, typing quietly upstairs in my office, hoping she and Georgia won't realize I'm here. I write twenty pages of this story so far, surprised that between all the demos and baking and lectures, I've been able to take quite a pile of notes, though some are scribbled right on recipes. At least it's not all going by me.

Still, as I run to the post office at ten minutes to nine to get the envelope date-stamped October 1, Georgia patiently trailing behind, I realize I haven't explored enough the *writing* of the book, about how I could bring my fiction-writing sensibilities (grant talk) to a non-fiction book. After years of grant proposals and years of rejections, I landed my first funding less than a year and a half ago: a Quebec *conseils des arts* grant for the book of short stories I'm trying to finish now in my oodles of spare time. I'm feeling, if not exactly lucky, somewhat encouraged.

It's been strange and wonderful to hear my five stories read this week by five fine actors on CBC Radio's "Between the Covers." The stories had grown distant, a bit old, floppy hat, especially when compared to my proximity to the new stories. The actors made them live again.

Hearing them broadcast each night this week, I realize I miss being good, just even respectably okay, at something. I'm not among the stronger students in pastry school, a hard fact to accept. Learning is hard for me, though crazily, consistently I continue to put myself in the way of the new. Six months ago, I thought pastry school was going to be like a ticket to a new town. I could get on a different train just like that and leave behind lectures and marking and student evaluations and all the disappointments of teaching. Now it seems I've swapped those for the disappointments of learning.

When I come back into the classroom after missing the day before, someone crows, "Denise!" I've been missed. I have friends and they missed me. I realize with some surprise that I've missed them, too.

Yesterday Claudette began assigning a team each day to work as her sous-chefs. This means extra responsibilities, such as helping in demos, collecting money at the end of the day for what we're buying. And if the joint isn't clean at 4:00 p.m., guess who stays late? I don't want this job, but it's coming.

Claudette warns us, too, about our (mostly) cozy little teams. "At some point you will begin to have friction. It's already started, I can see!" She puts her hands on her small hips, smiles knowingly. "Believe me, you'll get there. We are like a couple. We can have concessions and then suddenly there are too much concessions, and…divorce!" She is laughing now. Jen and I don't find this funny. We look at each other doubtfully. What could get so bad? You can see frissons of friction between Cindy and Shirley, even between Trina and Lorrie. But us? Never.

"Every time I teach you, I open the parentheses for the trip." It's poetic the way Fabrice begins our second class, though looking at the board, I wonder how wide he dares open the parentheses this morning:

500 pie shells
lemon pie
coconut pie
pâte sucrée

How can we make five hundred pie shells after the trouble we had with one hundred last week? And how will we manage to do anything after making those five hundred shells?

We talk Paris fundraising for a while. Wendy seems full of ideas and experience. Already we're got raffles, Christmas gift baskets, garage sales, bake sales, not to mention the Sugar Bush in April for which Fabrice says we'll need to make 3,000 crêpes. Everything with this guy is in the thousands.

"Okay, I start the Parees project," says Fabrice. "Let's go!" Again, though, he alludes to a teacher ("She," he calls her, then quickly adds,

"Or he...") who will not support our Paris trip. "You respect her position," he tells us, giving up on pretending we can't figure out who this bad person is. He also adds that we need to keep our fundraising simple. "You are studying, too. At the end of the year you will be very tired."

"What about something like a *guignolée*?" says Trina. "That's simple...going door to door, asking for money."

"I go as Santa Claus, and Claudette she go as..." Fabrice trails off, laughing.

"The Grinch," whispers Lorrie.

It's so out there, the differences between Fabrice and Claudette. A clash of styles, I would imagine. I'm coming to value and respect this no-pretense, clear-as-water woman, but is she saying no to Paris or no to Fabrice? How could she be saying no to us?

Min, Yujie and Xiu Li sit listening, chins in hand, waiting through Fabrice's Paris talk and occasional "fuck its." Today is bring-in-a-pie day, after all, and Min seems eager to present her two little pies. "Made with red bean paste," she told me earlier.

Min is the least smiley of the Chinese women; she's married, with an eleven-year-old son. This week, she told me, she and her husband splurged and bought him a piano. "I'm the only one of us Chinese students who has a technical degree, not a bachelor's degree," she also told me. Qiang was a web designer in China, Jing a teacher, Xiu Li an accountant, and Feng is actually working on a master's degree in environmental engineering at Concordia while she's doing this course and working every night in a dépanneur with her husband. The Chinese students are the most educated people in the class. I wonder if West Island Wendy knows this. "They're not very clean," she said in the locker room last week. "I don't think they bathe very often." I was so shocked by her display of arrogance and ignorance, I could only say, "That's not true."

She's not alone in her prejudice. It often feels as if the Chinese students are our scapegoats. Something doesn't get cleaned up: must be the Chinese. Something goes missing: must be the Chinese. It makes me ashamed to be among the "others."

"Okay, let's see!" says Fabrice. It's sweet really, each of us going up, pie pans in hand to lay them before him. He picks up mine—the whipped cream-covered chocolate cream pie that I messed up the crust on twice last night and which kept me in the kitchen until 2:00 a.m.—and makes to put it in Jen's face.

We cut and serve and everyone tries a little bit of every pie. Min's bean curd is, I guess, an acquired taste. I find it starchy, thick, odd. There's apple pie from Madison and a cheese pie from Trina. It's a bit surprising how amateurish our home baking is. Only Lorrie's done something complicated, many-stepped, but the result still doesn't make it on the tongue. I secretly prefer the silky, deep texture of my chocolate cream, though it, too, looks like it was made by someone who doesn't know from a pastry bag. Still, we are full of compliments for each other's efforts. Fabrice is the most complimentary of all: "Very nice, very nice. I appreciate," though it's unclear what he hoped to accomplish with this time-consuming exercise. That there are many kinds of pies one can make?

But the 500 pie shells..."Let's go!" Fabrice orders at 10:45. We're using an old Mohawk recipe from Eileen's Cakes & Pastries on the reserve, and each team of four weighs out staggering quantities of flour, shortening and water. Later it looks like we've been caught in an avalanche.

Pâte à tarte (Pie Pastry)

6 cups (1.5 L) all-purpose flour
2 1/4 cups (550 mL) shortening
1 teaspoon (5 mL) salt
1 1/4 -1 1/2 cups (300-375 mL) cold water

Yield: 3-4 two-crust pies.
(Tip: Line pie pans with leftover dough, cover tightly with plastic wrap, and freeze for future use.)

In a large bowl, measure out flour and salt. Add shortening in medium-size chunks; then, using hands, gently rub the shortening into the flour, breaking it up until mixture is in small, sandy lumps. Make a small well in centre and add 3/4 cup (175 mL) of water and mix with your hands, adding more water gradually, just enough to make a slightly sticky, elastic dough. If it gets too wet, just dust more flour into the bowl. Do not overhandle! The more you work the dough, the less tender and flaky it will be.

Turn dough onto a clean, floured surface and shape into a 12-inch-long cylinder. Cut dough into 6-8 small rounds. Roll one to a 10-inch diameter circle, fold in half, then lift into pie pan; unfold to fit. Gently pat into bottom and sides of pan.

Trina has to be one of the most rock-solid people I've ever met. And she's only twenty-two. I think we all see her this way. Eyes turn toward her for reaction in class, especially when there's a question no one knows the answer to. Claudette and Ardis ask for her help in demos. Sure, she's gone to cooking school and has worked in restaurants, but so have others in here. Besides being quick, smart and capable, Trina is mature, a quality we could use more of around here. Her special status has been established without pomp or envy. Trina herself makes jealousy difficult. She's a big girl, but not at all fat, with black, curly hair and glasses. She has a dry, snorty little laugh. Maybe it's her Gaspesian rearing: no games, no airs. It's just Trina, fair and square.

She's got a new job, she tells me one morning—*garde-manger* at Il Sole, a trendy Mediterranean place on the Main that I would occasionally lunch at with literary friends in another life. Trina's moving up.

She's also getting burned. Looking across at her this morning as she bent over her notes, all I could see was the top of her black cooking cap (patterned with multi-coloured baby seals, hand-sewn by her mother). Trina caught me looking and held up her arm. I saw the bright pink markings of a grill.

"I was reaching into the 500-degree oven for potatoes last night," she said. "We were in the middle of a rush. I didn't feel it till later."

We've gotten so many lectures from Claudette on preventing and treating burns. Just yesterday we heard it from Ardis, who had us cooking sugar as part of the Ingredients module.

"I have a scar on my arm from teaching this lesson," she told us, not smiling for once. "You're going to be taking that sugar to 350 degrees, so the first thing we're going to be talking about is first aid. If you get 350-degree sugar on your skin you'll blister and scar."

First step is to plunge the burned body part into the bowl of cold water you must keep within quick reach when doing sugar work. Then, "You peel off the sugar. The faster you can peel it off the better," said Ardis.

"You freaked out?" she asked, after a few of us yelped. "Good! Fear is a great motivator in learning." And watch where your spoons are dripping, she added. A few years ago, a student asked Ardis to check her sugar, forgetting all about the spoon she had in her hand, forgetting that it contained burning, hot, drippy sugar, forgetting that Ardis was right there.

Ardis held up her arm, the evidence still there.

I spend hours twisted around a revolving cake platter, metal spatula in hand, straining to duplicate Claudette's deft sweep of butter cream along the sides of a cake. Welcome to masking. I try before break and after break, before lunch and after lunch. I try with a big offset spatula, I try with a flat spatula, I try with a small offset spatula. Cindy, Lane and I labour doggedly, then hopelessly, at the back station. Working with Trina and Jen earlier, I'd been right under a vent, and with the heat on the fritz in the school and fall temperatures dropping, Claudette had finally turned on all the ovens and opened their doors.

"Move," she directed me. "You'll get sick from the draft and it's making your butter cream seize up." But in the new station I fare no better, failing again and again to make my surface seamless, smooth as a satin train. Mine is bumps, lumps and missing parts. And that's on Styrofoam. With a real, live sponge cake to slice in three, daub with syrup, then mask and decorate, it's only worse. Start spreading butter cream on a cake and, like Velcro, it picks up every crumb in its path. The more I spread, the crumbier the surface gets. Use two bowls, advises Claudette—one with crumb-less butter cream (the new stuff), the other with crumbs in it to wipe our spatulas in. I space out for a second and suddenly I'm masking my cake with the crumby one.

And I still have to get to the decoration: a shell border around the top and bottom circumferences, plus three roses of varying sizes in pastel shades of butter cream with leaves and stems, which I hope I can muster after one earlier lesson. Then we're to make a paper *cornet* and write Happy Birthday in brown gel.

It gets worse. And then, I don't know how, it gets worse still. I want to stop and cry, but there isn't time. Still, it isn't until my butter cream emerges from the pastry tip in out-of-control globs, until I run out of space and can only write Happy Day, until I see the quite professional results of my fellows—Jen's turquoise-tinged roses, Trina's perfect peppermint-striped borders—that I feel my failure completely. Even Lane and Cindy rally, with Claudette's help, at the end. Their cakes aren't perfect, but they are presentable.

Mine is not even sellable. I put it in a white bakery box as quickly as I can, thinking I'll buy it and sneak it out, but Claudette catches me. "You should have called for help," she tells me. Her face, a professional teacher's face, betrays nothing as she looks at my unhappy Happy Day cake. Lopsided, with a border that is more oval than circular, it is covered with too-bright yellow roses, their petals splayed, already wilted. "I could have fixed it."

What kept me in those final moments from asking for help? Feeling the pressure of time, the pressure of a naturally slow person having to live at higher speeds, I must at some point thought: lost cause.

"Did you make a nice cake?" Alfred and Fabrice ask as I leave the Lab. The two are sitting in the pastry office.

"It was so ugly I had to buy it myself," I tell them. They seem to think this is very funny. "Don't worry," Alfred reassures me.

Maybe it is funny. Lots of things have been funny in the past five weeks.

"It's not a matter of life and death," Suzy reminded me at lunch when she saw how discouraged I was. "And all we can do is our best, right?"

But what if this is my best? I hate being last or weakest. I hate not knowing what I'm doing, hate being the slowest, the oldest. I like being good at things, which is one of the reasons this pastry course is so hard on me. I'm not only the snail among hares, a slow-poke among sprinters. I'm only okay at this, after being told my entire adult life what a great baker I am. It's not as if this will be my métier, but the need to be good is beginning to feel bigger than everything else. Writing well about pastry isn't going to be enough. Now I have to be good at it, too.

The story goes that John Cage, the great out-there American composer, wanted to be listed in encyclopedias in side-by-side entries. And he is: under both MUSIC and MUSHROOMS. I don't know which came first—the desire for double fame or whether Cage was as truly, madly, deeply interested in fungi as he was in fugues. My hunch is he loved both. And he loved the attention.

I'm not going in any encyclopedia, but I understand the desire to be accomplished in several disciplines, to be passionately engaged in several arenas, especially radically different ones. (Oh, I didn't know you bred Chihuahuas in between choreographing ballets.)

This being considered "accomplished" must go to the heart of my desires and insecurities. I remember walking on air for weeks when an otherwise un-enamored boyfriend called me "an accomplished woman." And when Beauch's father told us a number of years ago—this is while we were in the middle of cooking the entire family's Thanksgiving dinner, his dinner—that "there are lots of things you two don't know how to do," I nearly smacked him with a drumstick. And see? Years later, I'm still nursing that offense.

No wonder I try so hard. In the first photos we've taken of each other in pastry school, I can see it: the grim, got-to-get-this look on my long face.

My sis, a psychotherapist, says our folks paid more attention to our struggles than our achievements when we were young. As if they themselves were invested in the work. Everything takes work. If it comes easy, it's not an accomplishment.

One Christmas, my father had an artist friend of my mother write in calligraphy a long quote on persistence for the four of us nearly adult kids. He framed them. I don't remember the words exactly, but it had to do with riding things out. Persistence wins the day. "Talent alone will not. The word is full of talented failures."

But how do we get really good at something? How the hell how? I know that's partly why I'm here, to learn not just about learning, but mastering. I also know that on the mechanical side, I need to practice my boring little butter cream borders at home. I need to not give up or give in. But tonight, after my worst day so far, I just want to go back to something I know, something I can do without thought or strain, though nothing comes immediately to mind. Taking a shower? Sleeping?

4

Life of Pie

It's kind of late to be finding this out, but Beauch doesn't like French pastry. He admires what I bring home, but it's an abstract admiration. Even the two mousse cakes I made on his birthday sat for a week in the fridge before I pitched the uneaten halves. I think about our past visits to patisseries. Was I the only one eating? Was I so wrapped up in my own private *réligieuse* that I didn't notice he wasn't having any? How did I miss this? He likes éclairs. He likes chocolate mousse. But all these meringues and ladyfingers and génoise, even things like crème caramel? He'd rather eat a brownie.

Since I come home nearly every day with a white bakery box bulging with something French, we're getting quite a buildup in the fridge and freezer. Strangely, even I lose interest once that stuff is home. It's as if I can taste the stress, the sweat. Thankfully, Georgia is only too happy to partake. So are many of my neighbours, plus Cynthia, Georgia's bus driver, who has taken over Georgia's after-school care. Cynthia, a large, young woman who seems to cheerfully accept her shape, leaves smiling with a box of pastry every day.

It's not that Beauch isn't a food person. He's written a cookbook that's coming out in December: *Salut! The Quebec Microbrewery Beer Cookbook*. He's the cook in the house, loves feeding us well. He does all the food shopping, enjoys trying out new recipes, and adores eating out, especially at Le Saucier, the school restaurant.

French pastry, however, holds zip appeal. He finds the desserts from pastry school fussy and "just not that delicious." So this turns out to be one food journey we're not taking together, not at all like the production of his cookbook, where we conferred constantly on the desserts I tested and retested. I have Beauch's financial, moral and creative backing this year. He's my base, my reality check (Hey, kiddo, he said last week while editing one of my short stories: You're a writer, remember?) But his eyes glaze over when I tell him how the cream curdled or that Jen forgot to put the timer on for the pies. Twice recently while I was giving him the details of a pastry procedure he put up his hands to form a T: time out. Maybe I should feel lonely on what is turning out to be a solitary trek. But I don't have time to think about my marriage much these days. And besides, I am anything but lonely.

I trade in-law tales with Lorrie, talk broken hearts with Rena, discuss chefs/restaurants/current pastry trends with Trina. Eight hours a day there is someone to talk to. And who else in my life understands the truly crucial difference between medium- and stiff-peak whipped cream?

Even with the pressure, the laundry, the fights, I'm part of something here. I'm a girl again, a girl among other girls (plus Qiang, whom we treat as one of the girls), giggling about boobs and boys while we learn something new. After working for years in corporations, on faculties, with volunteer committees—I'm learning the real, non-corporate, non-buzz-word meaning of teamwork. This is my team.

The chocolate cake of all chocolate cakes—Alfred has been promising us this since the first week of school. He's timed it for the Friday before Thanksgiving. It's a chocolate sponge filled with chocolate ganache (cream and chocolate melted into a blissful emulsion), then covered with a *miroir*, a different ganache that we have something like ten seconds to pour and spread so that it's as smooth and shiny as an ice rink. On top of this go the chocolate flowers—large, nearly abstract forms—that we've made using solid brass dipping shapes (a mere $375 for the set at France Décor, the pastry equipment store. Fortunately, Alfred's letting us use his).

What's the cake called? we ask Alfred. "It's a story," he says.

When he started his pastry course at the ITHQ in 1968, chocolate mousse, chocolate Bavarian, chocolate anything was not all that popular. Then in the early eighties the French chocolate company Cacao Barry came to Canada. It brought its wonderful chocolate, gave chocolate classes, passed on recipes. "That love story is still going on today," says Alfred. After the visit, Montreal pastry chefs began adding chocolate cakes, chocolate mousse, chocolate tarts to their repertoires. Some learned the craft of artisanal chocolate making.

But the name of the cake? we press him.

In honour of finally "discovering" Canada, Cacao Barry named its new all-chocolate cake the Jacques Cartier. "Even now when I run into old customers, they'll say, 'I miss your Jacques Cartier cake,'" Alfred says.

It's an easier, smoother, cheerier day. Until we get to *le miroir*. I pour the ganache over my better-than-usual layers, then start working it to the edges with my little offset spatula. The more I smooth, the worse it gets. I finally have to lay my favourite tool down, leaving one lumpy corner. Even Jen's *miroir* has a blemish. Alfred comes over, peers at my cake.

"Where's the worst spot?" he asks. I point and he puts the chocolate flower with the largest petals right there.

"See?" he says. "It's beautiful."

"Claudette would have had me start over," I tell him.

"I'm not Claudette," he says.

Ganache

makes 3 cups

1 1/4 cups (310 mL) 35% cream
2 2/3 cups (500 g) dark chocolate, chips or finely chopped
2 tablespoons (30 mL) unsalted butter

2 tablespoons (30 mL) unsalted butter
2 teaspoons (10 mL) corn syrup

In a small pot, bring cream and 2 tablespoons (30 mL) of the butter to simmer over medium heat. Do not let it boil! Place chocolate, 2 remaining tablespoons (30 mL) of the butter and corn syrup in a metal bowl. Pour hot cream over chocolate. Let it sit for 30 seconds before stirring. Then gently combine the chocolate and cream with a large spoon until the cream is completely absorbed and the mixture is very smooth. Let it cool completely, stirring occasionally. Ganache will gradually thicken (this may take several hours) and become spreadable.

At break I run into Ardis. Her long red hair is flying free today. No teaching—it's her day off—no net. "I heard one of your stories on CBC Radio last week," she says, beaming. "I heard it as I was driving in to teach, and then again as I was driving home at night." She wants to read the book. I'm flattered. And worried, as I often am when someone from a different part of my life wants to read my fiction. "You're such a cheerful person, but your stories are so dark," I've been told more than once.

I want to be better at decorating, I tell her. "I was so disheartened last week."

"Masking a cake is difficult," she agrees. "Sometimes I think I should teach this module because Claudette is so expert. She's so far away from a beginner."

Still, it's not Claudette's fault I can't get it. "She tough, but fair," I insist.

Ardis sighs. "If only she'd take a day off. Claudette's having health problems, you know. It's her eye. She has a glass eye."

It's not until later that night that this sinks in. I close one eye. How can Claudette do a single thing, let alone mask a cake perfectly in two minutes?

I'm also left wondering: Am I supposed to know this? I love people confiding in me, especially the teachers. Truth is, I've always loved people talking to me, telling me their stories, their secrets.

"Sometimes I'm afraid to tell you things," a friend told me a few years back. "You're so nice, but you take everything in. You have a sharp eye. You see through people." Other friends have prefaced confessions with, "This better not end up in a short story." This year I'm particularly invested in people talking to me. Still, lines can be crossed and it's only October. Claudette's glass eye is a story I probably need to keep to myself.

A few days later Alfred has us stop early—it's only 2:00 p.m.—get dressed and regroup in the classroom.

"I had a bakery for eighteen years," he begins. "Pâtisserie Harmonie was one of the top three bakeries on the West Island. It was a million-dollar business. One Christmas I went out and bought a car with cash. But six years ago this January I went bankrupt and lost everything. I lost my house and my cars. The only thing I didn't lose was the most important thing: my family. I woke up one morning with $13 in change in my pocket. I don't blame it on the Ice Storm, which was going on at the same time. There is only one person to blame and that's me."

We listen, barely breathing, quiet like we've never been quiet. You could hear a cake tester drop. Alfred must have decided it was time to tell us his story, the story he's hinted at and we've guessed at, but never known for certain. It may look tacky, but I start taking notes, trying to keep my eyes on his face.

The main problem, Alfred says, is that he never took a day off. "I never closed the door." He would arrive in the middle of the night, have his favourite 3:00 a.m. breakfast of apple pie and ice cream, and get to work. If he took a break during those eighteen-hour days, it was a catnap on top of bags of flour. Eight years passed before he took even a single day off, and on that particular day a former pastry teacher called and asked for his help. He also began taking courses to become a teacher here. It was too much.

"You lose control, you go into a depression. Then you start taking the little 'candies' to feel better. You feel great, but you don't know what's going on. That was the beginning of the end."

Alfred's eyes are red. If he doesn't burst into tears, I might. But then he nearly smiles. "It's probably a sad story," he says. "But it's a rich story, too."

Rich because some important lessons were learned, and he wants us to learn them less painfully than he has. "If you want to open a bakery you need to know one thing: What is it you really want to focus on?" Alfred began with bread, cakes and pastries. Eventually he added chocolate and ice cream. "You have to work three or four things at a time at least. You have to standardize your recipes. And you have to be exceptional."

And forget trying to do this out of your home, he says. "I disagree 100 percent with starting a home-based business. You are wasting your time."

Do a business plan, do marketing surveys. Does your neighbourhood need a bakery? Who do you want to bring in? Whoever your clients will be, you have to welcome them all, he says, "the rich, the poor. I had three hundred 'bosses' a day."

Wendy, who's either gutsy or insensitive or both, breaks in: "Would you consider starting again with a new partner?" (Is she thinking of dumping Diane and going with Alfred?)

Three years ago, Alfred was offered $100,000 a year to be a partner in a patisserie. He said no. "The only people I would trust in business now are my wife and kids," he says. "One of the saddest answers I can give is that I don't trust anyone."

He sees we're stunned. "I don't want to scare you. I only want your success. When you open your shop, call me. I'll consult for free."

It's nearly time to go now and his eyes are sad again. "You know, in the old days, thirty to forty years ago in Quebec, there would be a church and there would be a bakery right next door. After 10:00 a.m. mass, people would come out of church just as the bread was coming out of the oven. This is what I was born into."

Fabrice talks Paris again. "This trip is not 'official,'" he reminds us. The spirit of Claudette fills the room, even though it's her day off.

But it doesn't have to be Paris, Fabrice tells us. It could be Greece. Greece? I'd love to go to Greece, but I thought this was supposed to be about France and French pastry. We take a vote: France and Italy are the top two choices. And instead of Paris, maybe Lyon, says

Fabrice. "Lyon is a great food city. Florence, too." Maybe *he* wants to go somewhere other than Paris. He says the f-word again and Min covers her mouth, giggling.

Wendy, who's volunteered to be the secretary for Future Chefs 2004, writes down the trip rules as Fabrice lays them out:

We must all participate in the fundraising events, even if we're not going on the trip.

If we have to cancel out of the trip at the last minute, we forfeit our individual portion of the fundraising money.

We pay into our Future Chefs account between the 15th and 21st of every month.

We will go on the trip at the end of May, pushing our grad date up by a week.

We will not go to Claudette to ask for anything regarding this trip.

"Thou shalt not kill," Lorrie adds to me in an aside and we choke back laughter, thinking of a few people already under consideration.

Fabrice wants to include one last rule: the students who don't go to Paris will have the chance to do a local culinary trip. Last year he took the day class to Quebec City for two days. "They dance and sing all night. I never saw them like that."

The subject of accommodations comes up. Suzy wants a bathroom in her suite. Anna wants to go on the cheap. Two of the bigger personalities are ready to take each other on, but it's 9:30 and we've got pies to make. Eileen's Cakes & Pastries needs pumpkin pies for Thanksgiving, and guess who's making them?

Fabrice is a good guy, but I'm less and less sure about him as a teacher, even his ability to communicate in English. It's okay for a couple of hours, but not whole days, to be in this unmapped place. We make massive amounts of Fabrice's *pâte à tarte* recipe, then pumpkin filling in the giant mixers—not a pretty sight—plus a huge number of tartlets and I don't even know what else.

At lunch outside in the still-glorious sunshine, I ask Jen if she knows what's on for the afternoon. "Probably make a thousand pies," she yawns. Later, as we roll and roll, Fabrice strolling among us saying,

"Good excellent let's go," it seems she wasn't far off. In the mad blur of boxing all those pumpkin pies at the end of the day, Michèle drops a whole pie on one of her shoes.

Lorrie's on the smoking patch (not for the first time, apparently) and is hyper and directive. "Am I coming on too strong?" she asked me this afternoon when I said something sarcastic. I told her I would silently lift my spatula when I wanted her to back off, but that in the absence of instruction from Fabrice, her help was "mostly welcome."

The more complete truth is that I'm finding it both helpful and hampering to work with her and Trina in our teams of four. They're fast and smart and experienced. But they also tend to do everything and not give Jen and me the space to do things on our own. I've never made a recipe of butter cream by myself, for example, which is going to make the exam—coming soon—scarier than I want it to be. I'm also beginning to notice Jen does practically no dishes, so she also gets to do more of the real stuff.

Cindi from professional cooking told me at lunch she's growing a bit weary of teenage company. "The kids are searching for a life. But we already *have* a life, Denise." I nodded, feeling thankful to have an adult across the hall who understands. "You and me, we're layering. This is just another layer," she said. This seems like exactly the right word, though it's an awfully thick layer, like a too-generous topping of too-sweet marzipan.

Chicken and potatoes bubble in vats on the stove today. Strange and sort of wonderful to be surrounded by the smell of chicken and salmon instead of chocolate, eggs and butter. Real food. We're experimenting with savoury pies in prep for Pie Day on October 31st, our first big fundraising event for Paris.

Though we've made Fabrice's dough recipe more times than we'd like to remember, Jen and I make a flub right off, forgetting to add the water first to our giant Hobart. Fabrice comes over and dumps in the litre and a half of liquid, spraying flour, shortening and water up and over the bowl's edge. The goo is everywhere, on the floor, on the stolid legs of the mixer. Jen doesn't make a move to clean it up.

Fabrice puts an arm around my shoulder. "This is how you learn. By mistake, okay?" And I realize again that pastry school's steep learning curve—make that a sharp right angle—is best summed up by, "Well, I'll never do *that* again."

Still, I think I like making pie crust and rolling pie dough more than anything else so far. I'm not even gaga for pie. But I like sectioning off chunks of cool dough with my *corne*, my dough slicer, then dusting the marble table with jets of flour and rolling and turning and dusting and rolling and turning and dusting, an ever-thinning circle emerging with the pressure. Big roller, small roller, it doesn't matter. Let's go.

Back in the classroom, day's end, Fabrice gives us a heads-up. Someone in cooking has complained about pastry students not being *en forme*. Specifically, some of us are not buttoning our chef's jackets all the way up to the neck. I look around at my classmates. Madison does wear her checks low, and occasionally someone forgets theirs at home and has to wear jeans for the day, but mostly we're compliant. The tattling rivalry between cooking and pastry has begun.

"What is it?" someone asks. "Why are we looked down on?"

"Chefs are the rock stars," says Lorrie, shrugging.

And pastry chefs are what…the roadies? The groupies?

Ardis passes around a bucket of cocoa butter, encourages us to dip in. "Yicky, right?" she confirms to those bold enough to taste. We're in Ingredients this morning with everyone's favourite: chocolate. "Hey," she says, "do you know what Christopher Columbus said after having his first taste of hot chocolate? 'Wheee! You can travel all day without feeling tired!'"

So chocolate *is* a drug. Apparently, though, what most of us love in North America is not the pure thing. "When you say you love chocolate, what you really love is chocolate with sugar," Ardis says. When chocolate was first introduced to the New World, it was drunk as cocoa mass mixed with water. Later, brilliantly, the Dutch added milk and sugar.

When we get to the chocolate module in February, we'll be learning what Ardis believes marks a true pastry chef: tempering, the process of melting what's called couverture chocolate through six different chemical processes. It's what gives chocolate that lovely, shiny, hard surface. But tempering can be frustrating, she warns. "You'll get out of temper along with your chocolate. But to me, learning to temper is a basic."

We're not there yet. For now it's chop, melt and go. Using compound chocolate—lower quality than couverture, but which doesn't need to be tempered—we'll be making truffles today. Everyone except Cindy, who claims she's allergic to chocolate, cheers.

I've been in love with chocolate since my parents popped the first Barton's truffle into my mouth at age three. Barton's truffles were small, two-tone squares of deep, dark velvet one could buy in small shops in Manhattan in the fifties and sixties. They were sophisticated, European, so different than a Milky Way. For the next thirty years chocolate was friend, lover and favourite binge food. I wasn't especially discerning. If it was brown, sweet, melty, down it went.

My mother made a simple chocolate cake during my teen years: cocoa, oil, eggs, flour. She'd cut it into chunky squares and put it before our family of six. "Flash," my father called me as my hand moved from plate to mouth. Even as an anorexic seventeen-year-old, I allowed myself a minute portion of my mother's famous chocolate ice-box cake (which I now know was really a chocolate Bavarian). Later, as a young wife, I made chocolate mousse, chocolate fondue—it was the seventies by then—and brownies by the panful.

When my first husband and I split up in 1980, my three-year-old daughter, Ariel, and I moved back in with my parents. I was thirty-four, at loose emotional ends, and doing public relations for a Catholic hospital in LA's inner city. The place was run by an order of exuberant, street-wise, business-savvy nuns. My favourite, Sister Janet, added to the sisters' bottom line by making supremely fine fudge and selling it in the hospital's gift store. St. Mary's Hospital was probably as appreciated for its fudge as for its emergency room and welcoming presence in that hurting neighbourhood. Sister J's fudge certainly brought me solace as I sat in my windowless, tiny office writing press releases. It also added to my bottom line: a male co-worker began calling me Fudgebottom.

Sister Janet knew I was into baking and began selling me chocolate at cost—huge, luggy bags of Guittard *pistoles*. I had a Plan B then, too—True Confections, a dessert catering business I would run out of my mother's kitchen. I'd specialize in flourless chocolate desserts and chocolate truffles—Chruffles, I trade-named them. For six months—late at night, after work, after Ariel was in bed—I'd work on recipes, packaging and *my* press releases. I began dropping off boxes of Chruffles as samples to local patisseries.

I still see myself in my mother's yellow and avocado kitchen, mixer going, lights blazing. It's nearly 2:00 a.m. I'm melting chocolate, licking my fingers, exhausted and so happy.

Sadly, I made less than $100 in those six months. I began to see that if I didn't greatly increase my speed, my production, and my investment in equipment, I would soon go broke. I also gained twenty pounds. Newly single, chunky and desperate, I joined Overeaters Anonymous. There was no going back.

Still, for years after, especially when truffles began to catch on, filling display cases, creaming the market, when I began to tire of the corporate world and long for something sweeter and more fun, I would wonder if I hadn't given up too soon, hadn't made a really big mistake.

Of course now, after Alfred, after Claudette, I'd do it totally differently. Forget Mom's kitchen, forget licking my fingers.

"I'm missing you a lot!" Claudette greets us. She's decided she prefers us to the evening class. "You complain less," she says, before launching into a few complaints of her own: We're not cleaning the burners properly, our rolling pins are too big to be stored in the Lab lockers, bowls are being left wet on the shelves.

She can't help herself. For Claudette, to teach is to correct. Thankfully, she also has the ability to hear herself. She stops suddenly and laughs. "You know me. I'm the policeman."

It's all Whipped Rising Batters today. No decorating, although there's a decorating exam coming up too soon. "It's a lot," she admits, waving at the agenda on the board: Swiss meringues, *succès*, sponge cake, *pâte à choux*. "We're going to have our hands full." She skips fast through the first two recipes, claiming they're review, though how can something be review when we've done it once?

First, though, Claudette wants to talk about the Pastry Olympics, the country-wide competition that begins at the first levels in schools like ours. Ten promising students will be chosen and coached ("I'll push you like crazy," she promises) for the city-wide competition to be held here at Pearson on January 14th. Then come the regionals, also held in our school—it rotates year to year—a month later. That winner goes on to the provincials in Quebec, and from there it's the pastry finals in Winnipeg. There's one catch: only someone twenty-three and younger can win. If you're older than this you can still compete; you just can't win. Why so young, I wonder? Our class has some really talented people in their thirties, even forties: Rena, Diane, Qiang, Min. Am I personally disappointed? Not for a moment. The Pastry Olympics sound terrifying.

I ask Trina if I can trail her through the process—it's a given she's among the select—and she sort of says yes. "I'll keep out of your way," I promise. "I'll wash your dishes." I already know there will be plenty of those. Contenders are required to make six desserts from start to finish in six hours—tiny éclairs, millefeuilles, and a completely decorated birthday cake among them.

Which brings us to today's agenda. *Pâte à choux* will not only be among the challenges in the Pastry Olympics, Claudette warns. It's also on our Whipped Rising Batters exam. The ingredients—butter, flour, sugar and eggs—couldn't be more basic. The method—which I might get in my head eventually, but which might forever elude my hands—is pure complication.

First, we warm five eggs in their shells in a tub of hot water. Then we melt the butter in water on the stove. Then we dump all the flour into the simmering water, causing it to rise in a protesting, atom-bomb cloud. We frantically stir the mixture, still in the pot, still on the heat. We stir and stir until the bottom of the pot is dry and we have a dough ball.

Turning this into a metal bowl, we add the now-warmed eggs, one by one. We do this by hand, with a wooden spoon, until our arm is about to fall off and our shoulder needs traction. We add egg by egg, one, two, three, incorporating each completely before adding the next. We slow down the addition of egg, drizzling in mere drops of the fourth (beaten) egg, stopping only after frequent tests, which involve drawing our finger through the middle of the dough, like Moses parting the Red Sea. How quickly the sides of the dough collapse and how much—this is our signal. Too much and the *pâte* becomes overly shiny and we're sunk. Move quickly, Claudette barks. *Pâte à choux* has to be piped warm.

She goes from team to team—too wet, too stiff. There's some perfect point and most of us are close but either not quite there or already beyond. I am my usual timid self, afraid of making a mistake and moving like a snail. I feel my dough: not even lukewarm. I still don't know if the texture's right, but the temperature sure isn't. Quickly, clumsily, I scrape the sticky, tepid stuff into my pastry bag.

Then comes the hard part. We're to pipe three-inch-long cylinders—lengths marked in pencil—onto the parchment. At first, the *pâte* doesn't want to come out at all, then it doesn't want to stop. I don't have shapes. I have ooze. Claudette comes over. "Your dough's cold," she pronounces, grabs my bag and makes three perfect éclair shapes on my parchment. Zip, zip, zip.

I'm ready to add *pâte à choux* to the list of things I'll never, ever make when I get out of here. But then my éclairs come out of the oven, puffed and shiny under their egg-yolk glaze. The shapes aren't perfect, but the taste/texture is a cross between sweet popovers and Yorkshire pudding—eggy, light, crisp. I can barely stop at four. After weeks of moderate consumption, *pâte à choux* might be my downfall.

Pâte à choux (Choux Pastry)

1 cup (250 mL) water
1/2 teaspoon (2mL) salt
1/2 teaspoon (2mL) sugar
1/4 cup (50 mL) unsalted butter (cut into small pieces)
1 cup (250 mL) all-purpose flour
4-5 eggs

Egg wash:
1 egg beaten with a pinch of salt and 1 teaspoon (5 mL) of water

Preheat oven to 425°F (220°C). In a small saucepan, boil water, salt, sugar and butter. Be careful to not allow too much evaporation. Remove from heat and add flour all at once. Stir vigorously with a wooden spoon. Put the pan back on the heat, continuing to stir until the mixture forms a ball, sticking neither to the sides of the pan or to the spoon. When pressed with your finger, ball will bounce back slightly. Do not overcook.

Put the mixture into a stainless bowl and begin adding the eggs, one by one. Mix with a wooden spoon until each egg is fully absorbed. Add the first four eggs like this. Test to see if this is enough by drawing a line through the centre of your dough. If the sides close slowly, you have probably added enough egg. If it doesn't close, add part of another beaten egg. Test again to get the correct consistency.

Lightly butter and flour a sheet pan. (Or use a sheet of parchment.) Using a large star tip, fill pastry bag quickly with the dough and begin piping 3-inch cylinders on the parchment paper.

Bake at 425°F (220°C) for 15-20 minutes or until the choux are light golden in colour. Then reduce oven temperature to 350°F (180°C) and vent the oven door for another 15 minutes. If pastries sound hollow and feel crisp, they are done. (The centre should be just a little moist.) Remove from pan to cooling rack as soon as baked.

"I'm here to show you some pie fillings," Alfred says. "It doesn't matter what you've learned so far. Him it's him, me it's me." Alfred could be seen as treading on Fabrice's turf in today's riff on creams, fillings and glazes, but he doesn't seem concerned.

What does concern Alfred is that when he came in early to make the dough for our pies, he doubled the water by accident, then had to add more flour and shortening to compensate. "I'm really mad at myself. It looks okay, but now it will be a bit too elastic," he says. That after thirty years he still makes mistakes like this is immensely reassuring. I try to tell Alfred this later, after he's brought his mistake up a third time, but he doesn't seem comforted. He's still mad at himself, almost bewildered.

Another ambitious agenda is written on the board: two kinds of apple pie, cherry pie, chocolate pie, date squares, coconut squares and yet another batch of Italian meringue butter cream.

"It's not a busy day if it's well planned," says Alfred.

"It's not," says Lorrie, turning to tell me this from her stool. "It's perfectly doable." Where's my spatula when I need it?

She happens to be wrong. As we begin assembling the five *mises en place*, peeling apples, draining sour cherries, cooking pastry cream for the chocolate pie, I'm plagued by the other items on the agenda that (with good planning) can't be left until later. Should I also be starting the butter cream and the date bars now?

"I'm completely lost today," whispers Jen, who's now in charge of the chocolate cream pie. She's assembled all the sugar/cornstarch/flour containers for the fruit pies at the back of our counter, but when I check the weights, they seem way off. Time flies by as I check and recheck. Lorrie leaps around next to me at the counter.

I'm supposed to be working with two different juice mixtures, one a "slurry" of cornstarch and cherry juice, a cloudy pink liquid. The other...well, who knows what it is exactly and how it's different. They look the same to me, though the second one has less juice in it. Jen is fuming at the stove over chocolate cream that's not happening, while Lorrie and Trina seem to be travelling through space as they attack their recipes.

"I'm losing my mind," I finally tell Lorrie, who tries to explain the theory behind slurries, how they thicken and give substance to sauces.

In the end I grab one of the two mystery mixes and throw it into a pot with the sour cherries and turn on the heat. Whatever was in the container never amounts to much of a thickener, the cherries sitting in a lovely, deep-red juice, not a sauce, all afternoon.

The day stays like this—too many things to remember, scads of dishes, one demo following another, too many things to be made in not enough Hobarts: wash, empty, fill, wash. At 2:45 the Italian meringue butter cream still hasn't been made. "We have to do it," says Alfred, with a quake in his voice. "It's for Claudette." I actually make much of the butter cream on my own, throwing caution and 120-degree sugar syrup to the wind.

At 4:15 we limp out of the Lab wondering where we've been. Today I hate this. I hate the pressure, the chaos, the personalities. I'm not even very happy with Alfred.

Up at 5:00 a.m. to study for the MAPAQ food hygiene exam. ("We're really worried about bacteria now," said Georgia last night, checking the fridge thermometer.) Claudette, who's brought in Halloween candy for us, says she, too, had only four hours sleep. She's talking a mile a minute, whisking transparencies on and off the projector so quickly there's no time to read the sheets.

In the Lab, as I squish my way through another bag of *pâte à choux*, Claudette comes over to help. The outside of my pastry bag is so sticky she has to hold it with a J Cloth.

"Oh, well," she says, "you're here to learn." Except for her eyes looking a bit tired, she's the same peppy generalissimo.

"I don't believe you slept only four hours," I tell her.

Later, standing still for the first time in nine hours, I sample a piece of chocolate sponge with Lorrie and Trina. We confer as usual on its properties.

"Hmm," murmurs Lorrie. "Surprisingly moist."

"Goes down like a dream," I agree.

"Are you guys standing around playing with yourselves?" Claudette demands, coming by.

"Do you know what that means?" asks Lorrie.

"Yeah, sure," says Claudette, and grabs me from behind in a hug that feels surprisingly affectionate.

"It means masturbate," says Lorrie, watching Claudette's face.

"I know," says Claudette, who drifts off in the direction of a voice calling her name.

We say we're afraid of her, that she's tough, uncompromising, rigid. But we demand her help constantly. We lean on her, hard, calling her to our side every few minutes. Claudette! Claudette!

It's a military operation, a choreographic spectacle, a Cecil B. DeMille production. It's Pie Day, Friday, October 31, first official fundraising event for Future Chefs 2004. In ten hours twenty-four people who didn't know how to turn on the rotating oven nine weeks before will make 700 pies, the grand total of our marketing efforts inside and outside the school. Beauch alone has taken orders for more than a hundred pies at *The Gazette*.

By 8:00 a.m., we're standing at our assigned stations, Fabrice's old radio blasting out pop tunes from a top shelf. (By ten, we've heard Coldplay four times). Lorrie has drawn up a work plan for the day, and just this once, I'm grateful for what she calls her "anal tendencies."

She's organized us into teams of four, each under a *sous*, or assistant, chef. I've lucked out, landing in Tamara's group. I already know her to be one of the cooler heads in class. She's also smart, funny and refreshingly insecure.

Lorrie's plan is actually brilliant, with each group concentrating on one of six pies: apple, apple and ham, chicken, salmon, sugar, and lemon meringue. I'm in the lemon meringue brigade, which turns out to be the best of the lot because we get to make pies from start to finish. While the teams making salmon pies, chicken pies and apple pies are endlessly, ceaselessly, rolling out top crusts for their pies—we made all the bottoms the day before—we get to multi-task, opening myriad boxes of Sheriff lemon pie filling mix (who has the time to squeeze a million lemons this morning?) and whipping up mixers of meringue.

Good cheer and optimism reign through the morning. *We are doing this.* I call Beauch at home to bring over our apple peeler/corer/slicer. Michèle has brought hers in, too, so two people at least can tear through the crates of apples, while six others do it by hand. Apple peels, potato peels fall to the floor, chunks of chicken, flour. We're on a roll. We'll clean later. Tamara never loses her sense of courtesy: "Would you mind washing this pot now, Denise?" she asks.

A dozen boxes of pizza arrive at noon and we eat in shifts, fast, starved. I sit in the classroom with Trina and my team. Fabrice joins us and we talk Gaspé roots and genealogy, trying to put pie out of our head for half an hour.

Back in the Lab, Fabrice shows us how to make spiky tops with the meringue, using the tips of our spatulas. There's no time today for lovely lattices made with pastry bags. Cindy plops meringue on each one. "This is like warm, fluffy come," she says to me and throws back her head to roar.

It's looking good. Until it isn't. Mid-afternoon the truth begins to show. We are running as fast as we can, but we are still running behind. In Tamara's group, we shovel just-baked apple pies into stacks of made-up bakery boxes being assembled by the flying hands of Anna and Avedon. Staff and students from the school begin lining up outside the Lab's swinging door, waiting. Pie now. Time is going, but we're still buoyed by the order and good will that have prevailed until now.

And then a little after 3:00, Claudette comes into the Lab and with a few words lets it be known there is going to be a problem. She needs the Lab at 4:00 p.m. for her last exam with the evening class. This is, in fact, their last night after a year and a half of pastry school. It's another unfortunate collision: not only is it Halloween and those of us with kids will have to leave at some point, but this is the evening class's adieu.

I don't actually see Claudette—there isn't time to even turn around—but after this the mood changes. The clock is telling the truth: we're never going to be able to get 300 more pies covered, baked and boxed. Fabrice mans the rotating oven now, whisking apple pies (our biggest order) in and out. Even he looks grim. I'm at the end of the table closest to the oven so I begin taking still-hot apple pies from the racks and putting them in boxes with the lids left partway open so they don't get soggy.

When Beauch comes to pick me up at 4:30 to drive the hundred-plus pies to *The Gazette*, the apple peels are thick around our shoes. We stick to the floor. The Lab is a flour-coated, chicken-gravied, mash-potatoed, apple-crusted hell.

We make a dozen trips to our van, realizing we've never worked out the logistics of transportation. The chicken pies slosh in their boxes. The tops of several slide right off, the filling dripping through the thin cardboard onto the boxes beneath them, into the carpeting, the upholstery. We pile pies into the trunk, on the back seat, on the floor.

Looking around, I see that half of my classmates have mysteriously disappeared; the other half are boxing like maniacs. It feels like desertion to leave.

"Go, go!" says Rena, who's been keeping track of the various orders. Fabrice nods. There are 106 pies in my van and a kid at home expecting some kind of Halloween.

5

Creaming

The Monday after Pie Friday Michèle can barely keep from crying. Nadia, sitting next to her in the classroom, hands her a tissue. When Michèle finally arrived home last Friday evening after sitting an hour and a half in traffic, with her hundred pies in her trunk, she discovered many of the chicken pies had folded in half.

"And no one was home!" she tells us, voice breaking. "I had to empty that trunk by myself." Many drippy trips to the kitchen and back, she sped off to her job as a waitress in a Chinese restaurant. "Where the hell have you been?" her boss yelled.

"So I yelled back, 'Go to hell!'" says Michèle, who can't stop the tears now. "I'm really emotional. Sorry, guys."

What she's especially upset about—this doesn't fully come out until our next class with Fabrice—is that some of our classmates left early that day. Not technically early—it was four o'clock—although it was clear by then we were in crisis.

"I had to leave," Suzy says in defense.

"You're part of a team. You don't leave until everyone else leaves," Lorrie snaps.

"You don't know what goes on in my life," says Suzy.

"It's a pie module. We're here to make fucking pies," says Tamara.

I put up my hand, not sure of what I'm going to say, just knowing I have to say something. I tell them how the *Gazette* people went wild over our pies and how much we've accomplished in such a short time and that even though it's easy to get combative, we have to stick together. "We need to not be so hard on ourselves and each other," I say and am surprised to hear my voice break.

"Working hard is not funny," Fabrice says, deciding, it seems, to enter the fray, at least elliptically. "You are a slave." He tells us he has no days off for the next two weeks. He teaches here, he's head pastry chef at Eileen's Cakes & Pastries, and weekends he's at the University of Sherbrooke working on his teaching credential.

"You never see me bad, right?" he asks. "It is very important to keep a smile. Be positive. Keep your smiles, girls!"

For once, Fabrice almost has the right words. "Now my career goes down"—he makes a sloping movement with his arm. "I am not sorry about that. I am happy to be teaching you. Me and Alfred we go down. You are aiming for the sky. But you have difficulty to smile, you come see me."

Michèle isn't ready to smile just yet. She's still weeping quietly. "Sorry, guys, it just made me so mad to see people leave their dishes. It was such a mess here!"

Fabrice confirms this: for the first time in five years, the cleaning guy had to pass a scraper over the Lab floor that night. But Fabrice doesn't want anyone feeling guilty this morning: Based on our great sales—we made a profit of $2,400—he wants to know if we're up for another pie fundraiser for Paris.

No one says anything right away or even nods, but eventually Trina says, "Sure."

"Why not?" says Lorrie.

We can't count on extra help, though. Fabrice has asked the other teachers in the department to pitch in, but, according to him, they've all said, "You started this project. It's your problem." (Hard to imagine either Ardis or Alfred responding this way.) Personally, I don't want to talk Paris just now because I'm beginning to seriously wonder about something: Will we even want to go on a trip with each other in seven months?

Claudette has approached Jen about the Pastry Olympics. "At first, I said no," Jen confides to me at lunch. "I told her I don't feel like I know enough. I'm too slow."

"But you made nearly perfect *pâte à choux* the first time," Claudette had pointed out.

Jen tells me this with a pink, anxious face, but she's clearly pleased. Tentatively, she's placed her name on the list with Trina, Lorrie, Rena and Michèle. More and more, I'm convinced Jen has what it takes. I'm glad she's my partner, even if she does duck the dishes.

Yesterday as we weighed out ingredients for pound cake, I made a confession of my own: I don't like Madison calling me a "nice little lady."

First, I tried to explain to Jen, I hate being dismissed as "nice." And "lady" makes me feel old.

"But you don't act old," Jen said. "You act like..." I could see her searching for a good number. Thirty? Forty? She stopped. "And don't you want to be thought of as nice? Plus," my four-foot-ten partner looked me up and down, "you *are* little."

I seem to have the rep already as being "the nice one." Feng and Yujie told me in the locker room last week: "You are so nice to us! We like you very much!" Which sadly says more about the way others in our class treat the Chinese students.

Until this week, I thought the central, defining question in French pastry was butter cream. That butter cream was the thing that revealed the truest, deepest proclivities of a pastry chef. But I think I was wrong. I think it's meringues.

We've officially learned French meringues with Claudette. But meringues are an easy-to-fail endeavour with her, leaving me wondering how I've made successful Pavlovas for nearly thirty years. Claudette is adamant: you must "respect the steps," waiting for the egg whites to achieve volume before adding all the sugar in. You go teeniest sprinkle by teeniest sprinkle, and even then it's too fast. (Rena has encouraged me to just walk away from my mixer. "If you watch those egg whites, you're sunk.")

But when is enough enough? According to Claudette, who runs from team to team decreeing the meringue ready or not, most of us don't wait quite long enough to add in the sugar and then we beat the whites at too high a speed. I feel like an impatient little failure every time I make meringues now. Though once out of the slow-baking convection oven, they always taste sublimely, gloriously, the same. I love their crunchy, devastating sweetness, like eating baked snow.

But then Alfred shows us French meringues. "I hate to get involved in Claudette's method or Fabrice's method," he says. "Just write down that this is Alfred's method." As he starts the mixer on low to break the membrane of the whites, he explains. "Let it mix while you're doing other things. Give it a couple of minutes." Only then does he pick up speed, changing to medium. "The action of the whisk creates foam and now I'm ready to work." Bit by bit Alfred begins pouring in the sugar, until the whites come up to medium peaks. "*Il faut serré des blancs*," he tell us in a rare moment of French. "You have to unify, solidify your whites."

But here's the subversive part: Alfred adds in the second half of the sugar by hand. Not by hand with a spoon, but by hand, his hand. He rolls up the sleeve of his chef's jacket, rises on his toes in a perfect *relevé* and plunges his entire arm into the fluff, folding the sugar in with large, deep movements. He looks up at us dreamily. "I love that sound, hearing the friction of the sugar against the bowl." Some of us wince at the sight of his hairy arm in something edible, but I forget this when I bite into the baked meringue later. The crunch of sugar is in there. I love it.

Meringues, I'm coming to see, don't just make the chef. They *are* the chef. Claudette's French meringues are as silkily crisp as her platinum bouffant hairdo. Fabrice's meringues are made with a cup of meringue powder from a box. They're quick and they're pretty. But they taste like a short cut. They taste lazy. Alfred's meringues are hard-won, earnest, snappy and irresistible.

When I run into Alfred the day after, I tell him how much I loved his meringues, that I prefer them, in fact, to everyone else's. He practically blushes and, standing there in the hall, explains the whole technique again as if I hadn't heard it the day before. "That little bit of sugar between your teeth in a French meringue, that's important to me. Pastry is all about sugar. So don't dissolve it, don't make it go away. Keep it in there so people can feel it!"

Alfred's French Meringues

8 egg whites (1 cup, 250 mL)
1/2 cup (125 mL) icing sugar
1/2 cup (125 mL) granulated sugar
Pinch of cream of tartar

Preheat oven to 175°F (80°C). Fit your pastry bag with a medium-large star tip. With a whisk, mix the two sugars together. Beat the egg whites until foamy, then add cream of tartar. While still beating at medium speed, sprinkle in about 1/4 of the sugar. When the meringue begins to stiffen and to increase in volume, sprinkle in half of the sugar you have left. Again, let the volume of the egg whites come up. Do not be in a rush!

Once the meringue forms stiff peaks (or until it doesn't run when the bowl is turned upside down), stop the machine and fold in the remaining sugar by hand in a slow, steady stream. Fill pastry bag with meringue and pipe immediately. Bake for 1 1/2 hours or until completely crisp. Do not let the meringues take on colour. Cool on racks.

There's a rumour circulating that Fabrice, not Alfred, will be teaching the bread module.

"Can I speak with you?" I ask Ardis in the middle of making *pâte sucrée* with Fabrice.

"Sure," she says, and leads me into the pastry office, closes the door. But not before I see the alarm in her eyes. I've been wrestling with this for a week. I need to speak up *and* I need not to be seen as a prima donna. An old struggle.

A few of us have already appealed to Alfred: "You're the bread guy. We want to learn bread from you." But while he's disappointed, too, he's told us, "I can't get into this."

"We all love Fabrice," I begin with Ardis, stretching the diplomacy perhaps, though I realize that this is true. I do love Fabrice. I love them all. "But if Alfred is the undisputed 'bread guy' as you told us that very first day, why isn't he going to be teaching us bread?"

Ardis nods because it does make sense.

"I want to understand bread, not just make a million loaves of it," I explain, apologizing for putting demands on the program, for acting more like a student than someone who's taught and knows the difficulty of scheduling. "I just feel that I need to defend my education here."

"I'll see what I can do," she promises.

Less than an hour later, she's in the classroom, asking Fabrice if she can speak with us.

"Every year," Ardis begins, "we teachers take bets on when the first friction will happen, when the honeymoon is over. Usually it happens sometime in October. It took you guys longer, but you made up for it this week."

Ardis is smiling, but there's nothing soft in the smile. Apparently, people have been running to her all morning with tears, complaints and tattle-tales: so-and-so didn't stay to help clean up after Pie Day, someone else is upset that Claudette has asked Rena and Anna to accompany her on a career day, especially as they're the ones who have been absent most. Someone else is complaining about inequities regarding Paris. And then someone—no names—called someone else a bitch this morning. No wonder Ardis looked braced when I said I needed to talk with her earlier. What's *her* beef? she must have wondered.

"You're all under tremendous pressure here," she continues. "We're pushing all this information, all this learning, into you and you're trying to get it. We teachers are here twenty hours a week; you're here nearly double that."

But—and Ardis has never been more clear—this is no excuse for bad behaviour. No fighting. No bad manners. No name calling. We get along or else. We behave or we're out.

A few afternoons later, as we're washing the burners and knobs of the gas ranges and hoping to go home half an hour early, Fabrice realizes no one has made the *pâte à tarte* for the tops of our apple pies, required for next week's pie exam. Jen and I must be standing still for a moment too long because we get chosen to make two mother-size recipes of pie dough.

"Yeah," says Jen, "let's dirty what we just cleaned." Still, with fetching and measuring help from Trina, we manage to make both batches in half an hour. "See how you two rock now?" Trina says.

In the new spirit of cooperation, Tamara comes over in the last stages, empties the second bowl and takes care of washing the Hobart. At 4:00 p.m. the entire class leaves the Lab together. Workers unite!

"I hope you're going to write the bad stuff, too," Nadia says to me after our collective tantrum. Like a number of my classmates, she sometimes asks how the book is going.

"You can say anything about me you want," Lorrie tells me. "Anything. I know I can be difficult. I won't be hurt. Just be honest."

I'm glad everyone knows I'm writing a book about this year of ours because I wouldn't want any rude surprises later. Any lawsuits either. And I'm grateful that my classmates are open and keen and seemingly unself-conscious with me.

But the pressure's on, too. How do I tell these girls of eighteen that it takes a long time to write a book? Some, I think, expect it to come out as we're graduating in June, kind of like the graduation program. "Don't forget to invite me to the launch," says Nadia.

A few things have to happen first. I have to pass all twenty-two modules—from puff to pies. Like everyone else. I have to fundraise for Paris. Like everyone else. Raise a kid and keep a marriage going, like at least a few women in here. Plus get out alive, or at least without requiring back surgery or landing in the Douglas psychiatric hospital with a panic attack. Then I have to patch these crazy notes together. I found bits of a conversation between Suzy and Alfred on a recipe for lemon curd yesterday.

And then there's the small matter of the other book. The title, *Any Day Now*, is a nasty little joke these days. "Bad girl!" a close friend said to me this week when I confessed I was still working on the stories for the new collection. I felt slapped, mad and misunderstood, like a very bad girl, or at least, a very bad writer.

The stories are pretty much done, but the editing, the reworking, is not. I'm still months away from sticking the whole lot into a mailer and sending it west to my publisher. Where is it? she emailed this week.

Something came to me tonight, though, as I sank down at the computer. It was late. My chocolate-stained towels were agitating in the washer again. Back sore, feet the same. It's a collision—intense kitchen life all day, an arena sometimes too real, and then meeting up with my little fictional friends at night. But it's rich, too, like a crème caramel made with thirty-five percent cream coated in a deep mahogany sauce that slips out of its ramekin onto a white plate. Voila! A life.

There's a queasy feeling in the air as we gather for the pie exam. We've had three theoretical exams that involved memorizing facts. This one requires getting our hands to do what our minds remember. What little confidence I had was shot the day before when I blew a batch of pastry cream. Lumps—cooked-in lumps of cornstarch that defied the whacking of spoon, whisk and mixer—riddled what must have been the twentieth recipe of pastry cream I've made since this all began. Day One beginner's stuff, and I messed up.

Jen is worried about other things: "I've got the recipe for pastry cream in my head now and I can't get it out."

To add to the stress, Fabrice has changed the rules at the last minute. We will make all the crusts ahead so we won't be evaluated on pie crust at all. (I check our syllabus again: the module *is* called *Pâtes Friables*.) No, we will be tested on what has never been emphasized in this module: beauty. We are to make two or three apple pies, pick the loveliest and show it to Fabrice for grading. Then we will painstakingly cut five different kinds of fruit and create a "beautiful" design with them on a fruit tart. *Oui, Chef, oui, Chef.*

I'm so nervous, I go down on my knees by the side of the bed in the early morning, make the sign of the cross as we enter the Lab's swinging doors an hour later. "It won't help," says Nadia, laughing.

I end up at the table next to her, not a good person to pace myself by. Speedy Nadia is cutting out leaf shapes to decorate the tops of her apple pies while I'm only figuring out that there aren't, in fact, any already-made pie shells to work with.

"You roll," Fabrice tells me, looking surprised that I don't know this. But I thought...

He's brought in his old radio again, tuned it to CJAD, and walks among us, massaging tight shoulders. When "We Are the Champions" comes on, he sings out, "You are the Champions!"

The *pâte sucrée* doesn't turn to ash, the adorable leaf cut-outs stick, and the pies themselves—towers of sliced apple under taut crust as they go into the oven—only partly collapse in the baking.

But we don't have time to congratulate ourselves because there are baskets of kiwis and berries to cut, arrange and glaze for our tarts. When I show my (I must say so myself) pretty, bright tart to Fabrice, he wraps his large arm around my shoulder, looks down at me and says, "You are a wonderful woman." As Beauch points out later, "He didn't exactly say anything about your pies."

Later at le Brasserie des Rapides, the neighbourhood sports bar I've never set foot in before, fifteen of us toast Jen on her eighteenth birthday. She sips half an inch of her now-legal Molson, but whispers to me, "I really only like Budweiser."

We eat poutine and other atrocities and plot future fundraisers. We've decided we have to find a way to pay for Fabrice's and Alfred's Paris trips, too. It will be our surprise to them. I walk home at three, only mildly guilty for not having used the extra time to write.

Another test done, another module passed, though it's doubtful how much any of us know about *pâtes friables*. I've brought my exam home with me and cut into it before I even get out of my coat. The apple pie is still warm, and damn, it's good.

Up until midnight making a late birthday cake for Jen. It's a bittersweet chocolate cheesecake, and according to Claudette, who tries a piece the next day, "It's much better than the cheesecake they're serving in Le Saucier today."

I look doubtful.

"No, I mean it," says Claudette.

"A compliment from Claudette on a cake you've made?" says Trina, who overheard. "I'd think that was pretty rare. I'd prize that."

Something's happening. Bent over my Mother's Day cake with its mommy and baby duck motif, classmates come by to compliment my design, my execution, even my butter cream borders.

"It's only your second time masking a cake," Claudette adds. "Not bad, Denise." Later, after I forget to put the cherries in my Black Forest cake and have to dismantle three gooshy layers of génoise and Chantilly, Claudette says, "You shouldn't be discouraged, Denise. You're doing well."

I can twist a sheet of parchment into a *cornet*. I can make a respectable butter cream border. I can mask a cake without destroying it. And ten weeks in, I no longer go completely blank when I walk into the Lab. This could be called progress.

For our last class in Ingredients, we've each chosen an ingredient to research, bake with, and present to the class. The range is wide—from Diane and Wendy's apple banquet (soup, salad and sauce) to Michèle's riff on maraschino cherries (served on a Pavlova) to my primer on using olive oil in sweet baking.

After telling me for two weeks that every time she thinks about standing in front of the class she feels like throwing up, Lorrie presents a brilliant treatise on wedding cakes from different cultures, even duplicating a Greek motif on tiles of royal icing.

We're full by now, but the show keeps going. Andrea's brought in her Polish grandmother's perogis. "I could eat them every day," she says, frying some up for us.

Nadia is next with trays of canoli.

"Of course, I'm Italian," she says.

"No!" someone says.

"We eat panettone even after a big meal," she tells us.

"No!" we moan, as she describes a typical Italian banquet: antipasto, salad, pasta, granité, main dish, and then "a sweet table at midnight." (Sweet table at midnight. I'm supposed to be paying attention, but my mind gets stuck there. What a great title. If I ever have the time to write a short story again, maybe I'll use it...)

Tamara, whose presentation is on rose water, tried to get her grandmother's recipe for Turkish delight, but the grandmother—a survivor of the Armenian genocide who ended up in Baghdad—has recently reverted to her girlhood tongue, Turkish, making it impossible for the rest of the family to communicate with her. (Another short story.) "Roses taste the way they smell," says Tamara, as we bite into her best guess at Turkish delight. "It's not exactly like my grandmother's," she murmurs.

It's all fascinating, but the most interesting talks are done by the Chinese students, who introduce us to new foods and techniques. When it's her turn, Xiu Li shows us how to make Chinese dumplings. You bring the dumplings to a boil in water. Then you add a cup of cold water and bring them to a boil again. You repeat this two times.

Why? we ask, and Xiu Li is quiet. "I don't know," she finally admits. "My mother did this way." We hoot appreciatively. Different cultures, same mother. After she's done passing out the samples that we all respectfully try, we clap and cheer, though no one is smiling more than Xiu Li. This little band of Poles, Gaspesians, Italians, Hungarians, English-Canadians, Trinidadians, Mohawks and Chinese are travelling somewhere together at last.

Stage: the for-real, boss-hovering 6:00 a.m. experience. I want to close my eyes every time someone mentions the word. But there's no way to duck the subject now that it's only a couple of months away, no way to duck this part of the program: three weeks in March, four in the summer. Three hundred hours in a patisserie, restaurant, grocery baking operation, caterer or pastry factory. It's a module like all the others. You don't pass your internship, you don't graduate.

But you have rights, too, Ardis reassures us. "If it's just free labour, it's a bad *stage*. You're there to learn."

What if we hate it? What if the boss treats us badly, makes us do nothing but wash dishes or scrub the floors instead of piping out meringues and *pâte à choux* like we've been trained to do? "Call me first before you walk out," Ardis says.

"Don't burn your bridges," Trina tells us.

"Yup, everybody knows everybody," says Lorrie.

After years of setting up internships, Ardis says she has a pretty good idea of what's important to employers: arrive on time, be respectful (*Oui, Chef! Oui, Chef!*) and don't quit without at least a phone call.

There's a new evening class, now that the last one has graduated. They're slower than us, reports Fabrice. But they're older, "very smart," he says. "Some engineers in there. Very nice group."

"What does that mean?" asks Tamara, who's growing bolder by the day. "We're going to embarrass ourselves?"

"We're young and dumb?" Lorrie asks.

Fabrice talks Paris in the springtime. He's adamant about the other teachers not getting any of our fundraising money. "Last year nobody trust me. The direction push me, support me, but the other teachers they say, 'You crazy. You lose your name, your time.'" I need a translator this morning. The direction? Does he mean the administration? His name? His reputation? And how could the other teachers take our money? Isn't this a mite paranoid?

"But I make the trip! I go!" he finishes.

Later in the Lab, it's the usual fun as we try to follow our chef's vague instructions for cheesecake. But no one seems too bothered today. We'll figure it out as we go. We have so far.

"Did you have an exam yet? A practical exam?" Alfred asks.

Sure, we say. Pies.

"No, I'm talking a serious exam," says Alfred.

Ahhh, Alfred, we say. But we know he's right. In a few days we'll be taking our first serious practical exam, a Quebec Ministry of Education exam on Creams, Fillings and Glazes. And today we're going to see how much we really know. This is a trial run, a practice, with each person doing all four items on the exam: coffee mousse, lemon curd, crème caramel and Italian meringue butter cream. We will be given the recipes without instructions, just like on the exam. We will not be allowed to bring in even one note, just like on the exam. The method must be in our head.

"What's the failure rate?" asks Wendy.

"I've seen some people fail with 92 percent," says Alfred.

We screech.

It's not the total that counts apparently. Each of those four items must receive a passing grade of 80 percent. We could, theoretically, get 100 percent on three items, flub the fourth, and have to do a retake. Alfred will also taste everything we make. "I have a week to digest it," he says, trying to make us laugh. "I'm still full from last year."

He goes dessert by dessert, telling us what to watch out for, starting with the hardest, the coffee mousse. "Here comes your nightmare," he says. "It will be your nightmare today and it will be your nightmare next week. Because you're doing a much smaller recipe for the exam, it will create major problems."

Next, the Italian meringue butter cream. "You dump everything into a bowl and there you are," Alfred jokes.

I laugh, thinking of all the necessary stages: beating the shortening and butter together in the mixer, then washing the mixer bowl and whisk meticulously so there's not a bit of grease that could flatten the egg whites, separating the eggs, making a sugar syrup, starting the whipping of the whites when the syrup reaches 110 degrees, carefully adding the syrup when it reaches 120 degrees (not a degree higher) while the whites are beating at medium speed; then when it's cooled, adding in the shortening and butter, bit by bit, until the butter cream holds its own.

"You laugh, Denise," Alfred says, "but I've seen people do this." And he tells us the story of his final exam at the ITHQ.

He and his partner in the two-year program were being tested by a jury of Montreal's top pastry chefs. His partner dumped all the ingredients—unbeaten egg whites, butter, shortening, granulated sugar—into the mixer.

"I said, 'What are you doing!'" Alfred remembers.

"I'm making Italian meringue butter cream," his partner answered.

"That's how stressed out he was," Alfred tells us. "This guy's still in the trade and he's still nervous."

He's tried to relax us with this story, but as soon as we get into the Lab, nerves take over. For starters, there are twenty-four of us and only half that many mixers. It means sharing, being patient, and getting all four items made individually. I don't know how to work alone, I realize. I only know how to do any of this in a team.

The next five hours are punishing. Cooperation does not reign. With the clock ticking and equipment scarce, manners go. Even Trina loses it at some point. We dash from stove to counter to oven, trying to get our timing down. If you start with the crème caramel, you can get it in the oven while you begin the many-stepped mousse. Then you can put together your *mise en place* for the lemon curd and the butter cream. But wait! All the mixers are taken. Eventually everyone hits an air pocket. I never even get to the butter cream.

Which does not instill confidence for the actual exam three days later. While I wait outside the Lab with my group—we've thankfully been broken into four staggered groups over two days—I try to quantify the fear I'm feeling. I hate to fly. No, this is worse than the worst turbulence. I'm afraid of heights. I'm afraid of public speaking. Nope, worse.

My legs and hands are shaking so much as I try to put together my *mise en place*, that I have to stop and hold my hands for a few seconds. If you can do this, you will be able to do anything, I tell myself. Nothing will ever really frighten you again.

That thought gets me moving. I make the first three items on the exam without major mishap. But the butter cream has me worried. I let the sugar syrup go too high—125 degrees Farhenheit instead of 120, which would mean taffy instead of frosting. Into the garbage. As I'm adding the butter/shortening on my repeat attempt I notice there are crystallized bits of sugar syrup stuck to the whisk. When I taste the butter cream, I feel the slightest grain on the roof of my mouth. It's not butter-smooth.

I look up. I'm the last one in the Lab. Everyone else has done their exam and departed. Alfred, whom I've only been slightly aware of for the past half a day, comes over. He takes a spoon to my crème caramel, lifting it to his mouth, closing his eyes. The scrutiny is slow and real. I've never seen him so serious.

"It's grainy," I tell him when he slips in a spoon of butter cream.

"It's lovely," he says a moment later. "What do you want? Perfection?"

Overall, I get a 92 percent. I lose marks on my coffee mousse, which I thought was pretty good, but he claims is "a bit spongy."

So I've passed. No retakes. But I've been left with an awfully big promise to myself: If you can do this, you can do anything.

"You miss me?" Claudette asks.

"Yes!" we crow.

"You lie," she says. "You had some peace, eh?" She's talking so fast, I'm already pooped.

"I'm strong today, yes?" and she flexes her arms for us.

Another mad cake day: trays of sponge, cheesecakes, Swiss cakes, *bûches de Noël*, plus the marzipan decorations for our Christmas *bûches*.

I consider myself a cheesecake veteran, but both Jen and I read the recipe wrong and put in a pound of cream cheese instead of a kilo. Claudette notices our cheesecake batter is lower in the pan than everyone else's.

"Take it out," she says.

Out?

"Yes," she says and walks away.

Moping, Jen and I ladle the filling back into the mixing bowl and add the rest of the cream cheese. It doesn't all come out of the pan. There's a thin layer of thicker filling that has already seeped into the graham cracker crust. Lorrie told me she had a cake decorating teacher in Toronto who greeted every calamity with: "We fix! We fix!" We sort of fix.

Five of us have volunteered to stay late this afternoon and help the evening class with their first Paris fundraising pie event. At four, Michèle, Lorrie, Jen, Trina and I begin folding boxes. At 4:10, the evening class begins to wander in. They say "Hi" to us shyly, then stand around talking quietly in small groups. Where's their fire? Where's their panic? We're building towers of boxes, up, up, up on the long counter. They slowly begin cracking eggs.

"They don't have your speed yet," Fabrice has told us. But we were fast from day one. Well, not me, though I am catching up. I decorated today's Swiss cake in less than half an hour from jam layer to chocolate sprinkles.

I might be old enough to be everyone's grandmother, but as we rock to Michèle's ghetto blaster this afternoon and fold boxes at the speed of light, I'm so glad to be exactly here.

Viennois Cheesecake

Crust:
2 cups (500 mL) graham cracker crumbs
1/4 (50 mL) cup sugar
1/4 cup (50 mL) melted unsalted butter

Filling:
4 8-oz bricks cream cheese (2 lbs, 1 kg) cream cheese
1 1/2 cups (375 mL) sugar
1 1/2 teaspoons (7mL) vanilla
6 eggs
1 teaspoon (5 mL) each lemon juice and lemon zest

Topping:
1 1/4 cups (300 mL) sour cream
1 tablespoon (15 mL) sugar
1 teaspoon (5 mL) lemon juice

Butter a 9-inch springform pan and preheat the oven to 350°F (180°C). Melt the butter for the crust in the microwave. Place graham crumbs and sugar in a small mixing bowl, mix together. Pour in the melted butter and mix well until crumbs have a sandy texture. Press the crumbs into the bottom and up the sides of the pan. Bake the crust for 7 minutes.

In the bowl of a standing mixer, use the paddle attachment to soften the cream cheese. Add the sugar slowly until incorporated, then add the eggs one at a time, mixing for approximately 20 seconds after each addition. Add the lemon juice and zest. Pour into partially baked shell and bake in the oven for one hour. Remove the cake from the oven and let it sit for 15 minutes.

Turn the oven temperature to 400°F (200°C), and make the topping: in a small bowl with a spoon, mix the sour cream, sugar and lemon juice. Pour over the filling and bake for another 5 minutes. Remove from the oven and let the cake thoroughly cool before placing it in the refrigerator overnight.

6

And a Merry Little Yule Log to You

Michael Ruhlman called bread another country in *The Making of a Chef.* After a couple of months in the Culinary Institute of America's cooking kitchens, he wrote of the bread kitchen: "The differences between cooking and baking were so deep, so acute—and I was so unprepared for them—that the work of the [bread] kitchen confounded me. I didn't get it. I *couldn't* get it."

Ruhlman could also be describing the differences between pastry chefs and bakers. Alfred has already told us, "Bread is not pastry. Bakers are not *pâtissiers*. And *pâtissiers* are not bakers."

What are you? we asked.

"Give me flour and a rolling pin and I'm happy," he said. "I'm a batch and bench guy, a *tourier*, someone who makes croissants, puff, Danish. I'm not a bag guy." (As in pastry bag.) I heard Claudette recently say, with just a touch of condescension: "Alfred is a baker." She obviously is a *pâtissière*, a bag lady.

I think I'm more of a baker, but since beginning the bread module this week, I feel as if I've washed onto a barely familiar, somewhat hostile, shore. It's all about yeast, temperature and timing. And maybe temperament, too.

And yet if there is one thing I would like to master this year, it would be bread. I've made bread—white, wheat, rye, beer, even somewhat perfected a cheese-stuffed Georgian yeast bread, called *khachapouri*, from my daughter Georgia's native country—and I've mostly enjoyed the process, even if a lot of my loaves over the years would have made better doorstops or roofing material. Bread making is an earthy, hearty art, useful in a way that learning how to write Happy Birthday in perfect script with piping gel isn't. I can already see myself next year: sprung free from pastry school, upstairs writing, smelling the baguettes I've effortlessly made baking in the oven.

A-P flour .... 1000 g
Fresh yeast .... 10 g
Salt .... 14 g
Shortening .... 10 g
Water .... 650 mL + 25 mL

"The first baked good man ate five thousand years ago was bread," says Alfred from the blackboard.

We wanted him, we got him. Alfred will start us off on the bread module with our first baguettes and three days of theory. "I will try to give you everything I can," he says. "Some days we'll be making seven different kinds of bread. When you know how to work a timing chart that won't be a problem."

The more recipes you make, the more you need a timing chart, he tells us. It's our anchor. He remembers one morning when he was too sick to go in and start his breads at Pâtisserie Harmonie. How were they going to manage? "But then one of my sous chefs said, 'I've got Alfred's timing charts. No problem.'"

A timing chart is low-tech: a sheet of paper, with columns for each bread to be made across the top, and each of the many steps written down the side: in mixer, out of mixer, first punch, scaling, shaping, in proofer (a steambath with shelves for reliable, even rising), out of proofer, in the oven, out of the oven. Each item has a time written next to it. This is the only way to keep your sanity apparently, but looking at Alfred's sample timing sheet for today makes me dizzy. Baking is chemistry, but bread is math and I've never been great at math.

The other half of the module we'll have Fabrice, which means we'll be cranking out a whole lotta loaves. (Beauch is happy about this. Enough with the meringues.) But what about the exam? Wendy asks. "Whose methods should we use, yours or Fabrice's?"

Alfred thinks a minute. "Mine," he says. Does Fabrice know this?

But time's short and he's eager to talk flour power. The differences between bread flour and all-purpose flour are negligible, according to him. "It's the differences between the all-purpose flours that are interesting," he says, and I remember that Alfred once tested flour for Robin Hood. There are twenty-five kinds of all-purpose flour, but for our purposes we're only concerned with three: domestic, which one can buy off the grocery shelves; regular, which is from the Prairies and is used by most bakeries; and strong flour, which is used to "push" weaker flours such as rye and multi-grain.

And finally, no more instant or active dry yeast. We'll now be working with fresh yeast, great smelly blocks of it, learning its needs and idiosyncrasies. Where and when the yeast goes in the mixer is crucial, Alfred tells us. Using the big Hobarts with the hook attachment, we'll start by dumping in the room-temperature water, then the crumbled yeast, which will sink in the water before it begins to bubble, then the flour, then the bit of shortening. And last, another small shot of water and the salt.

"You must memorize one thing: Never have the salt touching the yeast. It will kill it." And Alfred has another no-no: "I don't want to see anyone eating the fresh yeast today. If you do, you'll be in the john for the rest of the day, trust me."

"We'll try to control ourselves," says Suzy.

In the Lab, we layer the ingredients in our Hobarts, kneading the dough for seven to eight minutes with the dough hook. I've never much liked kneading by hand, often pooping out before the requisite fifteen to twenty minutes. But with a professional mixer and hook attachment, it's as strenuous as pushing the buttons on my timer.

"Then you take a little piece of your dough"—Alfred reaches into a Hobart—"and if your dough has been properly kneaded, you should be able to see through it." He stretches the lump until it's taut, holds it up to the light.

Next he tosses a smidge of flour into the turning mixer so the dough won't stick to the bottom, lifts it from the bowl as if it were a new baby, and gently places it on the wood counter before easing the dough into a stainless bowl also dusted with flour.

But what to cover it with? This is not a small issue. Not plastic wrap—"Useless. It sticks to everything." Not grocery bags or garbage bags; they've all been treated with chemicals. "Garbage bags are for garbage and my breads are not garbage," says Alfred. No towels or wet rags either—"The rags will absorb the humidity from the dough." And definitely don't put dough on top of the oven where, again, it will dry out.

We're to leave our dough on the counters and cover them with the huge, untreated, clear polyurethane bags Alfred has special-ordered for this module. "Bread is very fragile," he says.

Part of its fragility is caused by the vagaries of temperature. When we start assembling ingredients, their combined temperature needs to register 240 degrees Fahrenheit: water, 100 degrees; flour, 70; room temperature, 70. When we take the dough from the mixer it must be between 80 and 82 degrees Fahrenheit.

But how can we tell? we chorus.

"Are you walking around with an instant-read thermometer all the time?" I ask.

Alfred nods, then shakes his head and mimes testing the air with one raised finger, then shoving his hand into a bag of flour.

"By feel?" I ask.

"Yes," he says.

This *is* another country, a place with strict rules, yet where intuition is all. I want in.

After a long lunch and more theory—there's no hurrying bread—we return to our resting dough. It's doubled in size, but not for long. Alfred shows us how to press the gas out of the yeasty mounds until they look hopelessly deflated. Another thirty-minute rest, though, and they've risen again, ready to be scaled and shaped.

"What are we going to make today? Baguettes? Belge? Parisienne?" Alfred asks. "Okay, we're going to make submarines," he decides suddenly. "You'll come out with eight small breads."

We section off dough with our dough cutters, surprisingly sharp as they slice through the stretchy mass. I love the way this feels, so different than sectioning off pie dough with plastic *cornes*, though I love that, too. We weigh the eight lumps on our scales, adding and subtracting morsels so they all weigh the same. In a bakery this is crucial; every customer needs to get the same amount for the same money.

Alfred shows us how to "round up" our eight subs so that they become little domes on the cornmeal-sprinkled baking trays, then how to score them with an extra-sharp knife to get that real bakery look. Then it's another hour's snooze under the plastic tent.

How do you know when bread is fully baked? someone asks when it's time to finally put our buns in the oven. "Baked bread looks beautiful and golden," says Alfred. And it makes a sound. "It cheeps like a little bird: tweep, tweep. The bird doesn't speak English, only French. It *is* a French bread."

At home that night, Beauch greets my eight loaves like long-lost family: "Finally!"

French Bread

6-7 cups (1 kg) all-purpose flour
1 tablespoon (15 mL) fresh yeast (available in most Italian groceries) or 1 teaspoon (5mL) instant yeast
2 teaspoons (10 mL) salt
2 tablespoons (30 mL) shortening
2 2/3 cups (650 mL) water
cornmeal for dusting

In the bowl of a stand mixer layer in this order: water, yeast, 3 1/2 cups (500 g) of flour, shortening and finally, salt. Using hook attachment, gradually add as much of the remaining flour needed to form an elastic, smooth, not-too-dry dough. Knead with the hook attachment for ten minutes, until dough is slightly sticky to the touch. Toss in a small handful of flour to keep the dough from sticking to the bowl. Gently lift the dough and place in a lightly floured bowl. Cover with untreated plastic bag in the oven (unheated) with oven light on. Let dough rise for 1 1/2 hours or until it has doubled in size. Remove from bowl and on a lightly floured surface, gently press the air out. Form into four long baguette shapes and place on a baking tray lined with parchment and sprinkled lightly with cornmeal. Preheat the oven to 375°F (190°C). Cover loaves with the plastic bag and let rise again for 45 minutes. Using a very sharp blade or knife, make three diagonal slashes across the tops of the loaves. Dust them with just a sprinkling of flour. Bake for 30 minutes or until golden and hollow sounding when tapped on the bottom.

Monday mornings still find me in a state of stun, a barely bearable mix of fear and anticipation. It reminds me of the feeling I would get on seeing the Montreal skyline after a visit home to LA during my first year of living in Montreal. Can I do this? Do I have it in me to do this some more?

Beginning the week with Claudette is especially daunting.

This particular Monday, she's got us making four recipes, two of which she admits she hasn't made herself. They're for six-step, ten-step, hundred-step modern *bûches*—complex variations on the traditional Yule log—recipes she was given the week before at a Farinex workshop for professional *pâtissiers*. Three and a half months into pastry school we're expected to make them, too. I think this time she overestimates us. But it's Christmas. The chefs at France de Lys have already made 30,000 *bûches de Noël*. Let's go.

The instructions alone take more than an hour, a long, long time considering Claudette's rapid-fire delivery. But the recipes! Jen and I are assigned a vanilla bean-infused Bavarian cream with a tunnel of intense berry sorbet surrounded by *joconde* (nut-infused sponge) and a piped layer of *dacquoise*, a meringue made with both blanched and unblanched almonds, pistachios and a hint of coconut. Other teams are combining ganache with cinnamon, orange butter cream with rum and caramelized bananas. Pastry school has never smelled or tasted so good.

It's a long, focused, satisfying day. The logs are beautiful to look at and incredible to taste. We sample each other's work, eyes rolling with pleasure. At the end of it, Claudette calls us together. We've done okay, she says. "But you need to get your speed up. You need to get better organized. It's December." And she proceeds to tell us how her classmates at Farinex were done by noon.

Ever hear of a twenty-year difference in experience? For once, I am seriously pissed at her.

The next day is Georgia's Christmas concert at school. I've informed Claudette that I will be coming in after lunch. She might have missed her sons' events when she was head pastry chef at the Château Champlain, but that's not my way. Some things I don't sacrifice. But as soon as I walk into the Lab after the concert, feeling already out of step, I'm sorry I didn't just go home afterward.

Concerts at my daughter's school are emotional events. Parents sit on folding chairs in the gym, straining to see kids in wheelchairs act in Santa skits, sing Christmas carols through their speech boxes. We cheer and clap—a fluttery, silent wave with both hands raised for the deaf kids—but we also cry. I've just had a piece of my other world and I'm in no mood to suffer the petty demands of this one.

Claudette is pushing like mad, tossing out sarcastic remarks as people knock themselves out trying to finish the day's agenda of fruitcakes, Boston cream pies, truffle cakes and marzipan decorations for our traditional yule logs. She says something to me about being late or missing a lot—I don't hear exactly. Classmates shoot me low, warning looks. Stay out of her path.

I can't take this punishment today. If I don't get a vacation soon, I'm going to kill someone. I'm not alone. Everyone looks tired, fed up, pale from lack of sun and too much flour. Everyone is itching for some time out.

But before we can get out of here we have to take the bread exam and survive the bread practice, both with Fabrice. Alfred has done all he can to prepare us. Still, I've never made the two items on the exam from start to finish. I've made parts of them, and even then it was in a team of four.

Eleven a.m. on practice day we're deeply absorbed in hot-cross buns and savarins (ring-shaped baba dough), waiting for things to rise or punching down things that already have, when Michèle and Nadia tear into the Lab, screaming, "Get out of the building now!"

I hear them, but keep separating my dough into buns. A false alarm probably. Nothing's more important than this dough. I look up now and then to see if there's reason to panic. My Chinese classmates work steadily around me.

Michèle comes running through again: "Get out! We've got to get out!" An alarm, not the fire alarm, goes off.

Getting it finally, we drop the dough and run, not even retrieving our coats from the locker room, colliding with a pushy, panicky knot of bodies—students from cooking, butchery, dental hygiene, hairdressing—at the back door. And then—frigid air. It's minus fifteen degrees Celsius out here. We walk-run as a group up the driveway to the street. And then, unbidden, we form a circle, the least-dressed at the centre, the most-dressed on the outside. Michèle, Nadia and Rena, who'd been buying coffee in the cafeteria when they heard people screaming to evacuate, managed to retrieve their coats. They shield us with their bodies. A pair of gloves are handed into me. "Denise, you look so cold!" someone says, as I pull my white turtleneck up over my chin, unroll the sleeves of my chef's jacket. Someone—I can't see well—throws a coat on someone else's back. We shiver, huddle, laugh. But the laughter feels close to tears. Such friends.

We keep looking back at the building: so far no billowing smoke, no explosions. It's clear after a half-hour that no one outside knows what's happening inside. It's also clear we might be here for a while. And then it dawns on me that my van is parked just down the block and that my keys are in my pants pocket. Six of us scamper down the street—six people in white jackets like inmates from an asylum—clamber into the ice block of a van, turn on the heat and drive back to the school. Most have already left for the mall a few blocks away. A good place to get warm, says Fabrice, who's standing on the street. I drop off my passengers at the Brasserie, then return to school. By now only Alfred and a few others are still outside.

"It was a bomb scare," he tells me, smiling and shrugging in that Alfred way. "Someone called the school this morning and said, 'There's a bomb in your school.'" Then he gets serious. "It's becoming a really tough school."

I drive the few blocks home—Beauch is surprised to see me burst through the door at this time of day and in only my uniform—and gather up all the coats, mitts and scarves I can. By the time I get back to the mall, the class has already split in three: Michèle and her gang are having lunch in the Brasserie, Tara and a few others sit at the mall tables eating casse-croute fries, while Yujie, Feng and the other Chinese students Christmas shop at Dollarama. I offer up my armful of winter gear. "Ahh," says Tara and kisses me.

Just as I'm feeling warm for the first time in several hours, someone gets a call on their cell phone. The all-clear has been sounded. I find Yujie and the others in the dollar store and drive us all back to school. In the classroom, Ardis confirms that this was, indeed, a bomb scare. "The first ever in the history of the school," she tells me later, looking spooked. The administrators had all been in a meeting when they were suddenly hauled out.

In the Lab, in our absence, our dough has continued to do what dough does. In the proofer, in the oven, on the counters, it rose and kept rising. We spend the next hour scraping dough from every surface. So much for a test run.

"Can we try again tomorrow?" we beg Fabrice.

"No time," he says, looking genuinely sorry.

But he does make time to celebrate a birthday. Today, even with a bread exam practice and a bomb scare, Trina is turning twenty-three. But where's Lorrie and the birthday cake every loyal partner makes? Lorrie hasn't come in this morning, though she'd told me the day before she was baking Trina a cake.

"That's so unlike Lorrie, to miss something like this," I said to Trina earlier.

"Oh, I wouldn't be surprised if she didn't stay home on purpose," Trina said. "Just out of spite."

"But you guys are such a team," I insisted.

"Not really," Trina said.

Shortly after we uneasily return to the classroom, Lorrie sweeps in with cake and present in hand. She'd arrived earlier as we were all running for the mall and ended up spending the next hour in a warm car talking psychology with the head of the cooking program.

Trina dons the somewhat dented "Party Girl!" hat and button that now rotate from birthday girl to birthday girl.

"You're a very classy friend," I tell Lorrie after she gives Trina a small, elegant photo album for her pastry portfolio.

"Thanks for saying that," Lorrie says. She's heading home before another wave of intestinal flu hits.

"Won't you miss us this afternoon?" I tease her.

"Not really," she says.

Friday, Alfred has been promising all week, will be Junk Food Day: pizza, doughnuts, cinnamon rolls, and although challah doesn't really qualify, he's thrown that into the day's agenda, too. It's our last day of bread with him—a whiz-bang of a module, which has produced a freezerful of whole wheat, nine-grain, brioche and baguettes. He promises it will be a relaxed eight hours.

We've brought in our own pizza toppings. Wendy chops mushrooms and green peppers; Cindy and Lane fry up bacon; Min, Qiang and Feng organize Chinese sausages, vegetables and spices. To speed things along, Alfred has us working in teams of four again.

We're an eager bunch, Trina, Jen, Lorrie and me: "I'll get the yeast!" "I'll get the milk powder!" "No, that's okay, I'll be right there for the salt and sugar, I'll get the milk powder!" We end up with two portions of salt and no milk powder for the crucial mixing moment at the Hobart.

Somehow the pizza dough comes together, but no one's considered the havoc of two dozen monster trays competing for space in the deck ovens. Instead of sitting down to enjoy our pizza lunch *ensemble*, we eat in shifts, standing at our work stations, slicing off pieces of too-doughy crust topped with too-mild sauce. But there's no time to critique, because of what's left: most of the day's agenda. I keep looking at my timing chart, but it's wishful thinking at this point. I have no idea what to do next: braid the temperamental challah, which has already sent Jen into fits, or start shaping (weighing, rolling, slicing—a big process) the cinnamon buns, which are due out of the proofer in five minutes according to my timing chart. Dough doesn't wait. It screams NOW.

Then Lorrie and Trina begin arguing about something and Jen throws some sheets of parchment on the floor saying "I can't do this!" and all I can do—otherwise I really *might* kill someone—is sink my hands in hot suds and begin washing the mountains of dishes no one else seems to see.

"I have a kid who has tantrums. I can't deal with a partner who has them, too!" I whisper to Lorrie.

"Did you tell her?" asks Lorrie. "You need to clear the air."

Their air clearing earlier doesn't seem to be doing them much good. Trina, who's usually so good at hiding her stress, is huffing and puffing. "Can you guys start the doughnut dough?" she asks Jen and me. Testy.

Doughnuts. I have entirely forgotten the doughnuts. A wave of futility and hopelessness presses down so hard, I nearly sit on the floor in the flour and cry. I cannot do this.

But this is pastry school, an alternative universe. An hour later, I'm at the stove frying up doughnuts. Gloriously golden loaves of challah cool on the portable racks. Expertly iced cinnamon buns sit on the work tables. It's some kind of magic. Human magic.

Min brings me over a slab of her wonderfully seasoned Chinese pizza, studded with bits of corn and sausage. "For you," she says, "because you like." I guess she's forgotten I'm a vegetarian.

I offer her a slice of my now-cold cheese and mushroom. "It's very boring compared to yours," I say.

"That's okay," she says.

By four, even Alfred looks like he needs a vacation some place far, far away. I pass Diane as we put away our clean bowls and she rolls her eyes at me. In the early weeks of pastry school she would wink and smile as we passed each other on the way to get ingredients. The look then was complicit, understood. Now, too.

A big dump of snow has been predicted for the following Monday. Sunday night I listen to the radio, and again Monday morning, a schoolgirl's hope in my chest. But no, it's business as usual for both school boards. After Georgia's bus leaves, I take off on foot for Pearson, the snow so deep I'm climbing and sliding more than walking. I'm sweating by the time I arrive, late as usual. I hope Claudette will be late, too, since she drives in from far north and east of the city. But no one is here—the Lab is dark, the classroom, too. A heater problem, the lone person in the administration office tells me. No school today.

I spend the day at home working on short stories. They're connecting where they need to connect, fading to black where they need to end. And for the first time in six years I think maybe, possibly, *Any Day Now* is nearly done.

It's the usual spinning teacup ride as we make Sachertorten and gingerbread, lemon pound cake, carrot cake and marzipan decorations. With Claudette it's always five items minimum.

At some point I'm behind her as she speeds to get something from the storage room and she spins around and asks, "So, Denise, are you still enjoying our pastry program?"

She asks the question so warmly that I give back an unreserved "Yes!" Not that this isn't essentially true, but it's somewhat more complicated than this, including my feelings about her. Her mood all day is jollier, sweeter. We stay intensely busy, but it doesn't feel grim. We're so upbeat we mostly forget there's a bread exam in two days.

("A bread exam? That's so cute!" one of my non-pastry school friends said to me on the phone this week. Cute? Cute! Where's my spatula when I need it?)

It will be a piece of cake, Alfred and Fabrice have reassured us. A cinch. No rewrites. In other words, we're all going to pass the bread exam. Between them they have decided to cut the recipes from four to two: savarin and hot-cross buns. Neither of these are bread per se, but we are so relieved not to be working on four recipes at once, not to be filling out a timing sheet times four, monitoring four willful, independent mounds of dough, that no one says a word. To hell with learning. We've absorbed all we can for now.

Still, I'm nervous the day of the test, getting up early to study my not-always consistent notes on the two recipes. But it isn't until Fabrice comes into the classroom, where six of us are waiting for the 9:30 exam slot, that I begin to seriously worry. Even Nadia's eyes are darting, flashing fear, as he tells us to copy a timing chart, *his* timing chart, not Alfred's, on a separate piece of paper. We end up doing this twice, confused about what he really wants.

Once in the Lab, though, I calm down as only getting down to work calms me. The hot-cross bun dough rises on cue. Even the medieval torture machine (aka the degasser) doesn't stick to the dough as I scale it.

But the paddle attachment doesn't seem to be doing the job on the savarin. Of course it's not—I'm supposed to be using the whisk attachment, Jen tells me. (You'd never know this was an exam by the tips and promptings going back and forth. Claudette or Ardis would fail us on these grounds alone.) By the time I get properly attached, I look down and see that all this beating with the paddle has turned my dough a nice, silvery shade of grey. It's the colour that happens when the beater comes into too much contact with the bowl, a kind of stress injury. It looks toxic. And it is; not death-causing, but enough to give someone a case of the heaves.

I call Fabrice over. "Yes," he says. "It's grey."

Should I start over? I ask, knowing starting over in bread is nearly impossible. "No, no," he says. "Continue. We pitch after."

My savarin*s* rise and turn golden in the oven.

"Very nice," Fabrice says when I present my six best hot-cross buns and the lovely poisonous savarins. "In the garbage."

At least this time, he doesn't say, "You are a wonderful woman." But he has to pass me, that's the promise.

As usual, I'm bringing up the rear, and as usual Jen has left me with the mama's share of dishes.

"What module do we have you for next?" I ask Fabrice, from the sink, trying to make conversation. I want him to know I am grateful for his generosity. Technically, he should have failed me.

"Not until April," he says, and starts in on "that pain-in-the-ass Claudette" who hogs all the fall and winter hours so she doesn't have to teach past April. He's muttered about her before, but now there's real anger, real frustration in his voice, none of which he hides as he stands at my table.

I murmur my sympathies, though I have no idea how to respond. I admit to him that I'm not especially looking forward to having Claudette for the entire month of January. It's prep for the Olympics and we'll be with her week in and week out.

"Talk to Ardis," he keeps saying. "She's very professional. She will listen."

I don't want to bring Ardis into this. I don't want to get in bad with anyone. I'm aware again of my split personality: good listener and writer with prurient curiosity: Go. Stop. Tell me more. I really shouldn't be talking about this. I give people such mixed messages. I want the dirt, but I don't want it to dirty me.

And then Fabrice says something that sends me flying. "I told her, 'The trouble is, Claudette, you don't fuck in Parees!'"

Am I hearing this right? Is this just Fabrice? I kick you in the fucking ass?

"She bring her problem in here," he says, again with surprising bitterness.

Is this just another man thinking that all a woman needs is a good fuck and then she won't be any trouble? But this comes from Fabrice, my teacher, someone I've thought of as a basically good man.

I remember his admonition when our claws came out after Pie Day: "No matter what goes on at home, leave it at home. Never lose your smile, girls." That's his moral code. What's happened to his smile?

Only sixteen of us show up for our Christmas party, the day before vacation. People are already scattering. I'm off to LA Trina's going home to the Gaspé, my *bûche de Noël* in tow. I accidentally rolled my yule log the wrong way, then couldn't figure out why mine was so hugely thick and everyone else's long and slender. "A lumberjack log!" Trina pronounced it and bought it for her large family's Christmas dinner, saving me further humiliation, Claudette's exasperation, and having to buy it myself.

We're in civvies this last morning. Cindy's wearing blue eye shadow and Lane's in a clingy metallic top. Lorrie ties the ribbon from Trina's gift in her hair. There's food for a crowd: Cindy's Island chicken, nearly black in its barbecue sauce, Lorrie's crab dip, Trina's *tourtière*, Wendy's now-famous lime/apple jello. I've stayed up until 2:00 a.m. to make *khachapouri*, which I now wish I'd re-warmed in the oven. Only Trina says it's good.

Of the Chinese students just Jing and Yujie are here, Jing looking uncomfortable until Yujie arrives. Jing gives me a packet of delicate, laser-cut bookmarks from China, Yujie a Christmas card:

Dear Denis,
Can't forget in that cold day. It's you passed me back to school.
Thank you very much. You are so nice. I like you.
Merry Christmas!
Yujie

I notice later that it's actually a birthday card. Yujie was the one person who stayed behind to help me clean up a few days before, insisting, when I protested, "I am your classmate!" My Chinese classmates understand that word differently than someone like Wendy, whose near-racist comments are becoming harder to tolerate. Wendy's mostly nice to me, often giving me a lift home after school. But sooner or later I will have to say something, lift or no lift. Yujie, Jing, Feng, Xiu Li, Qiang, Min, Shirley—they are so far beyond someone like Wendy. And she's not likely to catch up.

But today, our last day before Christmas break, we eat each other's offerings, tease each other, relax into one another's company. We have no timing chart, no impossible agenda on the board, no bones to pick.

Fabrice, Ardis and Alfred join the party. (Claudette, apparently, isn't coming in just for a party on her day off.) Rena has thought to buy each teacher a bottle of wine, gifts we've all pitched in for. All month I've been thinking, we have to do *something*. But it seemed beyond my strength to coordinate. While the *khachapouri* was rising the night before, I wrote what I hoped were pithy, personal and grateful notes to my four teachers on the back of overpriced, pop-up Christmas cards.

By eleven, we're out of here, Beauch picking me up for a special early matinee of the third *Lord of the Rings* film. He confessed last week that he's been finding me "singularly focused" lately. Middle Earth seems about as far away from pastry school as one can get. It's a good place to begin a vacation.

I've packed my fat pastry textbook, my checks and chef's jacket, even my little hat. Home for the holidays, I am going to impress my LA family with what I've learned so far. I've set myself an ambitious agenda: chocolate mousse (using the six-bowl, pull-your-hair-out bombe method), *gougères* (Swiss cheese puffs), meringues, génoise, apple pie, maybe even a sour cherry pie. It's Christmas, after all.

But that first afternoon, standing in my mother's kitchen while my parents and siblings and nephew kibbitz in the living room, I feel at a loss. It isn't just the kitchen—it's not my kitchen, though I've baked in here hundreds of times—I can't seem to get a rhythm going. I start with the mousse, try to assemble my *mise en place* as I've been taught: whites in a separate bowl, cream in the litre measure, chopped chocolate (roughly weighed on my mother's postal scale). I reach for the vanilla, realize I've forgotten to take it out, put the eggs back before I've broken them. I am so slow, so uncertain, so the opposite of grace, precision, confidence and economy.

What have I actually learned in the past four months? I take my chef's jacket off and work in my T-shirt.

"How's it going?" My youngest brother, a foodie, pops his head under the hanging cabinets. "Cute hat." He looks like he might laugh.

"It's hot," I say and pull it off. I'm just Deni home from Montreal, messing up Mom's kitchen again. Maybe I'll just make the mousse.

Three years before, my mother was terribly sick: lobular breast cancer that had spread to seven of the sixteen lymph nodes the doctors had biopsied. She was in rocky shape from fall into spring, two rounds of increasingly toxic cocktails dripped into her every three weeks.

Christmas cookies were the last thing on her mind when we arrived in early December, mid-chemo cycle. Beauch was doing a week-long try out at the *Los Angeles Times*. If it worked, we'd move to LA for six months to lend my parents a hand.

I set to work in the kitchen. Okay, so there wouldn't be cookies for the scores of friends and neighbours my mother baked for every year, but at least there'd be cookies in the house. On one of my mother's good afternoons, she could bite into something sweet with a cup of tea. Cookies would help. Cookies always helped.

My mother makes certain cookies each holiday: almond crescents made with icing sugar and pounds of butter and crushed nuts, then dredged in more icing sugar. Mexican wedding cakes, my friend Bea calls them. Russian tea cakes, according to my Russian cookbook. Bakers in the US call them snowballs or (more descriptive) melting moments. Of course, my mother's baking heritage is Hungarian, where they're called *mandulás patkó*. Almond crescents are international, universal, a Christmas given, a family favourite and no one makes them better than Jacky Roig.

What else? Spritz with a creaky, old German cookie press I'd loved to work as a kid. Little Hungarian nut rolls made from a cream cheese dough; another Hungarian delight called coronation cookies (from the famous Mrs. Green), made with brown sugar and tons of butter; a relatively new favourite called chocolate sparkles, with a pound of chocolate and no flour. Altogether, my mother makes a dozen different kinds of cookies each holiday, all kept on the washer and dryer in the utility room in stacks of Tupperware containers, wax paper between the layers. As kids, even as adults, we'd sneak back there to quietly pop a lid and shove in a cookie or two. In my bingeing days I made a lot of trips to that room.

I didn't make any of the Jacky classics that Christmas. Maybe it was the thought of my mother's face when she saw my too-large almond crescents. Hers were always delicate, small as a baby finger, befitting a Hapsburg princess. I would start small, then losing patience and a sense of proportion, shape them larger, larger, larger. "Why are your cookies so big?" she would ask. (*Why are your eyes bigger than your life?*) Not a reprimand, just curiosity. Why? My mother needs to know things.

So I couldn't make her cookies that Christmas. They'd never measure up. Instead I made amaretti. I was fresh from a long visit with Bea in Vancouver and she'd made these soft/crunchy morsels while we were there, a recipe from her mother's Italian kitchen. The amaretti called for an astonishing whole bottle of almond extract, which somehow worked. I'd also found a luscious-looking recipe for a chocolate bar cookie in the *Los Angeles Times*—you made the batter, then put it in the fridge for twenty-four hours, baking it the next day. Weird, but interesting.

It had been a helluva visit by day three. Georgia had come down with the stomach flu the very first night (a gift from her kindergarten class), and my mother, immunity shot, caught it mere hours later. She told me later that the force of the vomiting was so great, she'd cracked her head against the bathroom wall.

And this wasn't the worst of it. One of the components in the chemo was causing an unbearable itch. She couldn't sleep, couldn't think. My mother is an on-with-the-show woman. What's next? What can I do? But now she was moving so slowly. I watched my father watching my mother and that broke my heart more than anything.

Beauch was gone from noon to ten by the time he negotiated the freeways downtown and back, so Georgia was on my watch most of the day and evening that week. That left only late nights to make things better. I finished baking the first night around 1:00 a.m., feeling happy for the first time since we'd arrived.

The next night, everyone in bed, I preheated the oven. Those chocolate bar cookie things were finally ready to bake. But when I opened the oven door a half hour later, I nearly screamed: inside was the plastic bowl of my mother's Cuisinart, melted like a Salvador Dali clock onto the oven rack and onto the bottom of the oven. It was too hot to pry off. Cursing quietly, I waited for the oven to cool down a bit, but by then the plastic had formed itself into a grey, greasy sculpture. It was hard as stone and immovable.

What was the Cuisinart doing in the oven? I'd forgotten that my parents often put their pots and pans and other big kitchen items in the oven after washing them, the pilot light giving off just enough heat to dry them. I turned on the upper oven—thank God there was an upper oven—and slid the wacky chocolate things inside, now feeling more depressed than I had since we'd arrived.

In the morning, several things were clear: my parents were going to need both a new Cuisinart and a new stove. Cookies had not saved the day. They had, in fact, given my parents lots of new things to take care of and spend money on at a time when they needed all their strength and energy. The night before we left they sat us down and gently, firmly said, "Guys, we can manage on our own. We don't want you to uproot your life in Montreal to come here even for six months. We'll be fine."

Two months later, I received an incredibly heavy, small package in the mail. My father had mounted the melted Cuisinart bowl—which now looked like a great, shiny booger—onto a varnished wood plaque, with an engraved brass tag underneath: *Le Cuisinart Rôti*—DRB (Denise Roig Beauchemin) December 2000.

7

Olympic Fever

Tense faces all around. I see this as soon as I climb on my stool. We hardly make eye contact. Even the greetings between my buddies, Trina, Lorrie, Jen, are muted. So I'm not the only one dragging my feet back here. At break, Avedon, Tamara and Andrea confirm they're not overjoyed to return either. Still, no one has topped Madison for resistance: She called Andrea yesterday to see if she wanted to go to the movies today. Madison forgot it was the first day of school. Oh, that.

Not that anyone seems ready to quit. We're too far into it, gotten too many burns, crammed for too many exams. We're back in body, if not in spirit.

It was glorious not being so single-minded for two weeks, to let other parts out. I have to don a bit of a persona to do this. But it's also a physical reluctance. Coming back means putting out and putting out, being tired all the time, pressure without end. It's such *hard* work. And this month it's all Claudette, all the time.

There's the Pastry Olympics we've been hearing about for months. And the toughest module of the year: *Petits Fours Frais*, or, as it's listed in the program brochure, Small Fancy Cakes. I don't do small, as my mother can attest. And I'm getting better at fancy, but not that much better.

"The Module Eleven exam is the hardest and longest exam," says Claudette, who looks more refreshed from the break than we do.

"It takes ten hours over two days. People say I stress them when I tell them about the exam on the first day of the module. But..." She shrugs. We've been warned. We can't afford to ease back in. Starting now, everything counts.

It's bitterly cold the first week back, minus thirty at night, the coldest January I can remember. By 4:15, when I swing my backpack on, mummy up with scarves and leave by the back door, the sun has dropped low on the other side of the building.

Inside, the temperature is humid, thick with expectation and extra long to-make lists. The only word: Olympics. It hangs in the air as dream and threat. Our six future, hand-picked Olympians—Jen, Trina, Michèle, Diane, Min and Rena—struggle with their Olympian load: coffee Carolines, millefeuilles, fruit tartlets, birthday cake, *pâte sucrée* and chocolate mousse. Every day it's the same items, but each day they're to be done faster and better. The rest of us are expected to bake the same agenda, but Claudette's attention isn't really on us.

On the third afternoon of this regimen, Trina comes over. "Have you measured out your ingredients for the mousse yet? If you haven't, you can have mine. I can't do it," she says.

"Are you feeling sick?"

"I just don't have the heart to do it," she says, and her eyes fill with tears.

"Do you want to make the mousse with me?" I ask. "Though that might actually be more stressful than working alone," I add, hoping she'll laugh. She doesn't seem to know what she wants to do.

"Why don't you just get out of here?" I suggest. "Have you seen *The Return of the King*, the new *Lord of the Rings* movie?"

She considers this for only a moment. "I can't leave. I'll stay, but I can't make the mousse."

We begin working together, me doing one thing, she another. I'd almost forgotten how many steps the bombe-method mousse requires. It takes two people. And then, as I'm making the Italian meringue, dashing between mixer and stove, trying to keep an eye on the sugar syrup, trying to monitor Trina's stress level, I find Jen crouched on the floor. "I don't know how to do this," she weeps.

In the end our mousse turns out okay, but Jen's curdles. When Claudette's back is turned, Jen dumps the extra-large bowl of mousse in the garbage can. "I can't even make a mousse," she cries.

The next day Trina's back to her normal, on-top-of-things self.

"Is pastry tougher than cooking?" I ask. She's next to me at the stove, both of us working our fondant over low flame.

I've asked this question of Trina and Lorrie before. And they've both always said quickly, unequivocably, "Oh, no cooking school's much tougher. That's *really* stressful."

This time Trina doesn't answer so fast, furrows her wide brow as if trying to pin down the differences for herself. "Pastry demands such precision," she finally says and I see on her face a newfound respect, a little awe.

Chocolate Mousse

Bombe:
10 egg yolks
1/2 cup (125 mL) sugar
1/3 cup (75 mL) water
1/4 cup (50 mL) corn syrup

Chocolate mixture:
1 cup (250 mL) bittersweet chocolate
1 cup (250 mL) unsweetened cocoa powder
1 1/4 cups (300 mL) unsalted butter, softened

Italian meringue:
5 egg whites (5/8 cup, 150 mL)
1/3 cup (75 mL) water
1 cup (250 mL) sugar

1 cup (250 mL) 35% cream

Whip the heavy cream in a metal bowl until it reaches soft peaks. Refrigerate. Melt the chocolate over a *bain-marie* (double boiler). Remove bowl from heat and whisk in the cocoa and softened butter. Set bowl aside.

Prepare the bombe mixture: bring the first measurements of water, sugar and corn syrup to a boil; meanwhile whip the egg yolks at high speed with a stand mixer, using the whisk attachment. When candy thermometer reaches 243°F (117-120°C), pour mixture into the still-beating yolks, beating at medium speed until incorporated. Continue beating until bombe is pale coloured, cool to the touch, and the whisk, when lifted and moved in a circle, leaves a "ribbon" on top for at least 8 seconds. Pour bombe mixture into another bowl and set aside. Take whipped cream from fridge (mousse will "seize" if the cream is too cold when incorporated later).

Prepare the Italian meringue: Melt second measurements of water and sugar over medium heat in small pot. When candy thermometer reaches 230°F (110°C), start whisking the egg whites in a stand mixer with the whisk attachment. When whites are at medium peak and when candy thermometer reaches 243°F (between 117-120°C), quickly but carefully pour syrup into the still-beating whites at medium speed. Beat until medium-stiff peaks form and meringue cools. Set aside.

Combine the bombe mixture with the chocolate mixture a bit at a time. Lighten this mixture with one-third of the Italian meringue. Fold in the rest of the meringue; then fold whipped cream into the mousse in thirds. Do not overfold.

After four days of Olympic fever, Alfred standing at the front of the classroom in his hairnet is a beautiful sight. We're beginning a new module with him, as well: puff pastry. But it won't be a puff piece, he warns. We have to be here every day. "One day you make the dough, the next day you shape it." He'll be strict on the exam, too, "but not too strict."

And then he says words we don't often hear in this room, "I want you to enjoy this module."

I've already taken a peek at our text as preparation: "Puff pastry is composed of many layers of dough and fat. In the heat of the oven these layers are pushed apart by steam, causing the dough to rise or puff dramatically—hence the name. The French name—*pâte feuilletée*—refers to the other remarkable characteristic of this dough, which is the appearance of these many layers." Apparently the first puff was a mistake: a chef forgot to add butter to a tart dough and then tried to fix things by rolling it into the dough later, folding the dough over itself. He had a happy surprise when it came out of the oven.

The secret of puff pastry is learning to control the rolling pin. "You have to be the boss of your dough," says Alfred. Puff isn't about a whole lot of recipes—we'll probably only use one or two. But we'll be cutting this dough into all kinds of shapes and using it for everything from palmiers to apple turnovers to cheese sticks.

Once again, it's about procedure. First, you dump the flour (a mix of all-purpose and cake) onto the work counter. Then you blend flour and butter between your fingers until you have a coarse, sandy texture. This technique is known as *sablage* and coats the shortening so the water can penetrate. Then you make a well in this mixture, pour in the water and gradually incorporate the flour, turning, turning, adding, adding. I love the sandbox feel of this, and the way it seems impossibly messy at first, then miraculously neat as it comes together.

"You know *détremper,* right?" says Alfred. "This is *détrempe,* the preparation of the dough."

We look blank, shrug.

"You made pies. You made a thousand pies," he says, incredulous.

"That doesn't mean we learned anything," says Tara.

"We learned how to produce," says Suzy.

The raggedy dough goes in the fridge for at least fifteen minutes. Meanwhile, a large amount of cold butter and a stiff white substance called SPS (special pastry shortening) get softened in the mixer and formed into a six-inch block, or *paton*.

This is prep for the next step: *beurrage*. After rolling our now chilled dough into a long rectangle, we're ready to incorporate our butter brick inside it.

There are several *beurrage* methods, but Alfred wants to make sure we learn the classic method today, which involves making a cross incision in the dough, then rolling it into a cloverleaf shape and placing the *paton* in the centre. The four "leaves" get folded over and then you're set to roll. This is the main puff method used in the trade, though Alfred prefers the easier roll-in method. "But then I'm always different than everybody else," he sighs. "I like smearing the butter in."

"You schmear it," says Suzy in her best Yiddish accent.

"Schmearage," says Alfred, laughing.

Whichever method we begin with it all ends the same—rolling the dough (the bossy part) into the largest, most symmetrical rectangle we can. From here we do single, double or triple "turns." The more turns, the flakier the dough. Also the more difficult to work with and the more time consuming: each roll and fold requires a half-hour rest in the fridge.

"This applies to all"—and Alfred does a sweep of his arm and a comic pirouette of his compact body—"puff pastry. And remember: Double turns do not equal two singles!"

"I have no idea what you're talking about," says Wendy. None of us do, but it's always this way at the start of a new module: new terms and new techniques. Puff will also involve a new piece of machinery, one I've walked by so many times I've stopped seeing it, stopped even wondering what it was.

"Meet the dough sheeter," says Alfred. The sheeter, which stands at the back of the Lab and looks like a folding conveyor belt, still has a dusting of flour on its surface. "There's flour everywhere in this module. It's in the air," says Alfred. "You need a lot of flour to roll out puff. We'll be cleaning all the time." This includes our dough, which must have the excess swept off with a pastry brush between turns. Leftover flour will turn our dough grey. After my bread exam I know what that means.

"It's pressure. Let's be honest," says Claudette, briefing us the day before the Olympics. "You have to maintain the same speed throughout the day. And don't panic. When you panic, it's all over."

She's written the Olympics schedule on the board. In six hours these items must be completed:

Pâte sucrée (let rest)
Rolled puff pastry (let rest)
Pastry cream
Pâte á choux (coffee Carolines)
Rolled tartlets
Chocolate mousse
Chantilly
Finish products
Birthday cake—decoration

"I'm kinda scared," whispers Andrea, who's not even one of the contenders. Like those of us not competing, she'll be assigned certain hours to wash dishes at two of the stations. But even this might be stressful. What if you mix up people's pastry tips? What if you can't wash fast enough?

Claudette has us making vast quantities of things in preparation for the competition, assigning Lane and Cindy twenty-two pounds of butter cream in the largest Hobart, a mixer none of us has ever used. Even Trina's eyebrows go up.

Tomorrow our six Olympians compete against each other. Next month, the winner and runner-up will compete against the winners from Montreal's four other pastry schools: the ITHQ, Calixa-Lavallée, Pope Pius X and Jacques-Cousineau. The winner of this second round will go on to Quebec City to compete with other regional winners. Last stop: Winnipeg.

"In Winnipeg, there's a big parade and ceremony," says Claudette, eyes shining. "It's a big, big story."

On the big day, the contenders stand stiffly and silently at their stations. No talking allowed. There's only Claudette barking hygiene cautions: "Put your milk and eggs in the fridge! Get your spray bottles of sanitizer ready. A lot of time is passing!" Despite putting in long hours of after-school coaching, Claudette's never looked more alive.

Ardis creeps around with a clipboard, smiling encouragingly at all assembled. But as one of the three judges, she's also evaluating, checking *mises en place*, hygiene protocols. When things get going she'll be noting technique and procedure. Taste will count later. For these first six hours, it's how these Olympians get to the taste that's important.

Jen is at station eight, Rena's at nine, Trina at six, Min at four, Diane at three and Michèle's in station one where she usually works, what I've come to call Bum Butt Alley because there's so little room between the counters. Today she's got plenty of room. Armando, a pastry grad from the previous year, is at station seven. Since the Olympics are only held every two years, he wasn't able to compete until now.

"Hi," Rena says in a low voice, walking by the sink. I'll be washing her dishes. And Jen's.

"How are you?" I whisper, looking around, not wanting to get her in trouble.

"Trying to keep smiling," she says, and smiles. Yesterday she told me, "I'm just doing this for the experience."

I stand at the sink, waiting for things to begin, taking notes.

"I see you're taking notes, too," Ardis whispered earlier. "Though I'm sure my notes are very different from yours."

Then suddenly, bodies are in motion, eggs are cracked, milk brought to the boil, pans greased. From my post at the sink I watch as Jen hurries from the stove with a steaming pot of pastry cream. Rena begins filling her pastry bag with *pâte à choux*. Jen runs her finger many times through her choux batter to see how it's collapsing (or not). Rena cuts her *pâte sucrée* with the round cookie cutters, the crusts for the fruit tartlets.

I'm struck by a wave of admiration. From September to this! From brownie mix to millefeuille! I'm proud to be washing their dishes.

I've forgotten to give Jen my large whisk, something I promised yesterday. I duck into the tool cabinet, unlock my tool box. It takes me a while to get her attention. But when she spots the whisk, which I've raised a little way in the air, she gives me a smile.

"How long do they bake for?" she whispers, after she's put her *pâte à choux* in the rotating oven.

Until they're done, any of our teachers would say. Pastry school is about running to the oven every minute. Thirty minutes? Thirty-five? "I can't remember," I whisper back.

It feels almost calm in here, though that could be the enforced silence. The Lab has never, ever been this quiet: *Did somebody take my knife? Claudette, come quick! Oh, crap, my pies are still in the oven! Hot stuff! Alfred, help!* I miss the voices. I can't tell what people are feeling. Faces are blank, hands busy. The seven contenders stop only to bend over their recipe booklets.

Jen takes her slab of puff pastry from the oven. I'd forgotten about the millefeuilles, worrying instead about the mousse and Carolines and fruit tartlets, the birthday cakes demanding flawless roses and shell borders. How can it all get done in time?

Armando winks and smiles at me as he goes by with a tray of pastry cream to be paddled and piped. I've been watching him, the new face. He seems gracious, kind, helpful, like Qiang, like Alfred, like Fabrice. Whatever happened to Victor, the mad, mean pastry chef from Ralph Lombreglia's "Inn Essence," my favourite short story of all time and my main reference point for male pastry chefs? I think of that story and character often. "Inn Essence" opens with the worrying return of Victor, just released from a psychiatric ward after chasing a busboy with a knife. Now he's back running the restaurant's pastry kitchen, only somewhat subdued and patchily medicated. By the end of the story the Thai waiters have locked him in the walk-in fridge for everyone's protection. Otherwise there will be "bloodfall," as one of the waiters says. Victor makes our guys—even foul-mouthed Fabrice—look like cream puffs.

Rena's just scorched her pastry cream. "I'm screwing up," she says cheerfully as she turns first in one direction, then backtracks, realizing the plastic wrap is on the table behind her, not in its usual place across the Lab. She laughs, shakes her head.

Rena is still laughing as Claudette walks over.

There is absolutely nothing to laugh about, says the look on Claudette's face. This is the Pastry Olympics. And in that moment I see who Rena is and who Claudette is. And I see that I, too, would rather enjoy myself than be perfect. Is this what I have come all this way to find out again?

When the winner is announced at the end of the day, after everything's been scrutinized, tasted, critiqued, we're careful not to look too glad or too sad. For those of us rooting for all our brave friends (most of us probably), it's a complicated and necessarily quiet moment. Trina looks happy, Rena surprised; the other five smile faintly.

"You won by quite a margin," Ardis tells Trina in private later. Calm, competent Trina is our champ. Rena came in second, Diane third, Min fourth, Armando fifth, Jen sixth, Michèle seventh. Trina and Rena will go on to Round Two next month.

It's easier rolling and turning our butter-filled puff the second time around. Less butter squishes out the sides, thanks to Alfred's roll-in method, used (inexplicably) by less than five percent of pastry chefs. But I should know by now: If it's hard, it's French pastry.

For roll-in you schmear the butter and SPS over two-thirds of your large rectangle of dough, then fold it into thirds like a business letter. We're all happily smearing away, but when I look across at Min, she's making a *paton*. She catches my eye, pats her little bundle, smiles. "I like this way very much," she says.

Today we're also shaping last class's puff dough, which has passed its requisite rest in the freezer, forming it into apple turnovers and my favourite of favourites: palmiers, heart-shaped pastries crisp with butter and sugar. With strong tea, it's my breakfast of choice.

"We use just a little bit of sugar," says Alfred and dumps a big handful on the table. "I don't like sweet, so just a little bit, okay?" and he adds two more fistfuls of sugar to the first. Grins. He places a slab of puff right onto the sugar and begins rolling. He rolls until the dough is almost the width of the table, then takes the roller docker to it. "Ah, the sound of my life!" he says, the docker brrrrring against the wood, a steady tat-tat-tat as it moves across the dough like a spiky paint roller, pricking as it goes. He cuts the dough into strips, then coils the strips into skinny heart shapes and places them on baking trays. Again, they must rest to prevent shrinkage.

"Excess shrinkage. This is the worst thing that can happen to you," Alfred says and rolls his eyes suggestively. There's bawdy laughter from at least a few of us.

When the palmiers emerge from the oven they have grown large, golden and beautiful, caterpillars to butterflies.

It's not just that I love palmiers. I think I love puff. I think I've found my thing. I get lost in the repetitive pleasure of rolling these slabs of buttery dough, applying pressure to the centre, then to the left corner because it's round instead of square, then to the right to even things out. I like the geometric quest of this rolling and the way our big rolling pins glide, covering so much ground in a single push and pull.

Jen and I agree: this is the best. We've granted Alfred his wish. We're enjoying ourselves.

As we're packing up, Fabrice comes in to rally the Paris troops. Enthusiasm, he knows, is lagging. Jen is having financial doubts, Andrea has announced she's now saving her money for Cuba, and Anna says she'll never be able to get off work. For all my hope and desire, I've only deposited $50 in my Future Chefs fund. What we need, says Fabrice, is another fundraiser. He's reserved the Lab for two Saturdays before Valentine's Day so we can mould (and sell) a thousand chocolate hearts. Nobody cheers.

It's our first day with Ardis in two and a half months and it's Chinese New Year, a joyful collision. Min has brought in gifts for many of us, shyly presents me with a silk scarf printed with orange lilies. The Chinese students have also brought in everything they'll need to cook us a special New Year's lunch, including the ingredients to make vegetable dumplings for me and Diane, the non-meat eaters. (Feng confesses later that she was up until 2:00 a.m. preparing. "You shouldn't have!" I exclaim, but Feng just smiles.) In the Lab, she and Min demonstrate how to roll the edges, not the middles, of the dough circles. Diane and Wendy are in the thick of the demo, helping, asking questions. For today, unity.

And a shifting of gears as we start yet another module and another steep learning incline. This one, though, has got everyone cranked: chocolate, substance of choice. We've been looking forward to this module since September. "I'm so excited!" says Lorrie, bouncing on the stool next to me.

But the story behind chocolate isn't so sweet. It is, in fact, a brutal business, says Ardis, wanting us to know this from the start. Cocoa pods come from the poorest parts of the world: Africa, particularly Ivory Coast, Indonesia, South America. Those with nothing, often enslaved children who've never even tasted chocolate, who don't even know what chocolate is, pick the pods. Though she's been trying to buy fair trade chocolate through cooperatives where growers are paid a fair, living wage, the school board has told her it's too expensive. "I'll keep trying," she says.

For now we'll be working with chocolate made by the big French chocolate producer, Cacao Barry. But working with even the best chocolate means learning to temper it, a skill Ardis believes is essential. "Ninety-nine percent of *chocolatiers* in this city don't know how to temper. This will give you a leg up."

And it's not a misnomer, she says, laughing. "I expect all of you to lose your temper at least once in this module. Learning to temper can be frustrating. It can take you a couple of hours in the beginning. But take your time, don't worry, and everything's going to be just fine. I've never had a student who didn't temper on the first day." Still, she adds, "I might as well tell you now. What am I fussy about? Everything!"

"Is your middle name Claudette?" asks Wendy.

Ardis half winces, half smiles. "Maybe. For this module anyway. But remember: This is chocolate. This is fun."

There are several tempering methods—some are cheats—but Ardis wants us to master the two-thirds/one-third method of "seeding" with beta prime chocolate (or couverture). She draws complicated diagrams on the board. "Basically, you're rearranging molecules," she explains.

When we bring a bowl of chocolate to forty-five degrees over a *bain-marie*, or double boiler, we're not only melting the *pistoles*; we're destabilizing the molecules. The goal is to bring the temp back down to thirty-two degrees by adding bits of couverture. This is the only way to achieve the hard, shiny look of professional chocolate. (So *that's* why the almond bark I make at Christmas always ends up looking dull by the next day.)

We won't be gauging our chocolate's temperature with thermometers. Some pastry chefs do this, but here we'll be melting, seeding and testing our chocolate based on what we see, feel and deduce from tests done with small squares of parchment paper. In the demo mirror, we watch as Ardis melts two-thirds of her chocolate over a *bain-marie*, then adds in the other third. "You have to fight to get those last few bits incorporated," she says, pushing insistently with her rubber spatula against the walls of the stainless bowl. She stops to dip a two-inch square of cut parchment, takes it out, lays it on a tray, studies it for a minute.

"Every once in a while, I temper on the first shot. But usually it takes me at least ten minutes." She bends to look at the parchment again, holds it up, points to a barely visible streak. "Nope," she says, "not quite. If your chocolate is in temper it should be without streaks and harden within two minutes."

She reaches across the counter for what looks like a hairdryer. "This is a heat gun. What I'm about to do is called 'giving it a shot.'" Ardis aims the nozzle at the bottom of her bowl, roars it up for mere seconds, dips the parchment again.

"Voilà!" she says. "Shiny, no streaks and it's hard!"

Because tempering chocolate is not easy, Ardis has a ritual for this first day: every time someone tempers, we stop and clap for them. The usual whizzes—Tara, Michèle, Suzy, Trina, Rena—do not temper first. Lane, Shirley and—surprise!—I do. I temper even before quick, natural Jen. As my classmates temper—everyone eventually does, just as Ardis promised—we continue to clap.

We temper a second time—chocolate, unfortunately, only stays in temper for a short while—and again I manage it. Hard, clear, shiny—I have all that. I also have no idea how I did it. It's a delicious mystery, though. Jen and I nibble *pistoles* all day.

"You know something?" Alfred says to me a few days later outside the Lab's swinging doors. He looks around to see if anyone's listening. It's 4:15 and the place has cleared out as it does every afternoon—in a five-minute blur of checks, bodies and slammed lockers. I'm often the last to leave. "You know something?" Alfred says again, and I can see he's considering his words. "Jen," he says. "She has something."

"She's good," I agree. "She's a natural."

"I was pulling for her in the Olympics. But it was pretty much already decided who would get it," he says looking at me significantly.

"Really?" I murmur, hoping he'll say something more.

"Jen has something...special," he says.

"What does it take to become a really fine pastry chef, Alfred?" It's a question I've been meaning to ask all our teachers.

"Passion and devotion," he says without hesitating, as if he was giving the recipe for French meringues: egg whites and sugar.

Maybe it's because of the Olympics. Maybe it's because we're nearly halfway through the course, but I've been studying my classmates more than usual lately, wondering who's got it.

A couple of years ago, Claudette decided to make teaching videos for the more advanced modules. They're home movies—shaky camera and lots of white noise—but I find with a module like Eleven, aka maddening small cakes, it helps. The videos star Claudette, looking crisp and professional, if a little self-conscious. They give us something visual to hang onto and go back to. I've even taken to watching them at lunch. My memory is now so layered with instructions for so many cakes, mousses and doughs, that I need constant reminding.

The one we watch today is the intro to *petits fours glacés*, those adorable two- by three-inch French cakes with the smooth pastel icing. In the Lab we find out that they're really just génoise cut into impossibly small slices—Claudette makes us measure them with rulers, warning that anything more than a centimetre off in any direction will cost us on the exam—then sandwiched with butter cream and covered with pastel fondant, the same sweet glue we used to top éclairs.

The pouring of the fondant is a production requiring strong arms, quick hands and here-goes-nothing bravura. After lining up all the miniscule cakes in a perfectly straight line on a rack over a large tray, you pour the pot of warm fondant in a large and grand (but not so grand that you don't pour straight) gesture over the waiting cakes. Then using the small offset spatula you fill in all the missing places double quick because fondant sets fast. Every centimetre has to be coated, or, yes, there will be hell to pay on the exam. If you can breathe while you're doing all this, more power to you.

Every team is assigned a different flavour. Jen and I get coffee. Jen doesn't like coffee; she doesn't drink coffee. She's disappointed. We arrange to swap at the end of the day with another team doing vanilla petits fours. But it doesn't matter what flavour you get, we discover after a hard day with rulers and too small or too tall cakes. There's only one flavour for petits fours: cavity sweet. I squish one into my mouth at day's end. The first bite is heaven, but already I know I won't be able to finish the whole thing. By the third bite, I think I feel a coma coming on.

Claudette had been planning to show us how to sculpt miniature cats out of marzipan, a break from pouring fondant, a treat at the end of the day, but a few people groan about starting a new project so late in the afternoon.

"Okay, go home," says Claudette.

"I'm disappointed," I tell her on my way out. "I wanted to make a cat."

Claudette shrugs. "I didn't want to make people stay if they didn't want to. I just didn't feel like fighting it today."

She looks so disheartened, I say something about my own teaching, my own reluctant students.

"I wanted to be an accountant, you know," she tells me. "But my parents didn't think I was smart enough. They thought that with my eye problem I should do something else, something easier."

"I don't think this is exactly easier," I say. "And this is very hard on the eyes."

"I guess," she says and shrugs again. But then she smiles and the edge is back. "Hey, the only reason I became a pastry chef was to prove to French male chefs that a little French-Canadian woman could do it!"

I thought I was done with really bad days, that at this point no matter how much I might mess up or fog over, I'd have some technique, some experience, to fall back on. But the last class in January is, I believe, the worst day ever.

It's our first time with mokas, those three-by-four-inch frosted gateaux that look like dollhouse birthday cakes. I'm already calling them "the dreaded mokas."

There's the usual measuring and cutting to the centimetre, the usual layering with butter cream. But then there are all the sides to worry about. Mokas, depending on their flavour, are coated with sliced almonds or nuts or coconut. Claudette shows us how to lift a row of half a dozen cakes onto our largest offset spatulas and lay them into trays, where they get the car wash treatment with nuts or coconut. But if one stray almond slice lands on top before it's decorated with a perfect butter cream border, woe unto you. Points will be subtracted. Lives will be lost.

My génoise crumbles; my butter cream lumps. I am having a dicey time. Just as I am leaning toward Jen to ask for advice, Claudette walks by and says for all to hear, "I know why you're always behind, Denise. You talk all the time."

I am back in Grade One, the chatty little girl who only wants everyone to love her. I do what I would have done in Grade One. I put down my spatula and head for the girls' room to cry.

8

Bread and Chocolate

The day before the Olympics, Round Two, the Lab's in full tilt. We make six different kinds of muffins for our visiting judges and contenders. To prepare for all those competing cakes, we make big, flat sponge. We make high, round sponge. We set up the seven contenders' carts with all they will need: flour, fondant and a hundred other items. By two we're cleaning like fiends, reaching into the recesses of stoves and fridges where no sponge has gone before.

Claudette maintains a jovial mood throughout the day. "These Olympics must be stressful for you," I remark between tasks.

"Only at the beginning and the end," she says.

The contenders are at their stations. The rest of us stand at attention, our sinks already filled with suds and disinfectant.

One contender wears a hijab, the white fabric draped under her gold chef's cap and around her neck. It's softly beautiful against the tailored lines of the uniform, though I worry about the ends getting caught in a mixer.

Only Trina and Rena, the home team, appear sure of themselves; everyone else seems tentative. The start bell goes just as the girl in the hijab realizes she doesn't have a rolling pin. I run to get mine out of my locker, a loan for the day. I feel for her. What a way to start.

We almost didn't start at all. The electricity was out when Claudette arrived at 6:30 a.m. "We'll just have to push everything back until it's fixed," she told Ardis at eight when the power still wasn't on. "We'll cancel the evening class if we have to." ("But the evening class is taking their Module Nine exam tonight," Ardis tells me later. "The Olympics are extra-curricular. The exam is curricular. Wait! I said to myself. What's more important here?")

Luckily, at 8:15 the electricity surged back.

I'm stationed at the far left sink again, washing for one of two contenders from Calixa-Lavallée, and one from Pius X, a school that has no pastry program, only a basic dough module as part of its cooking program. Both women seem uncertain, moving slowly, measuring out butter as if for the first time.

Then I notice someone I hadn't really seen before, a dark-haired young woman in a bona fide chef's hat. She's at station four, right across from Trina, and already rolling her *pâte sucrée*, forming it into cylinders, tucking it into the fridge. In her deft, sure movements, in both her economy and attack, I see that she is the competition.

Three men in chef's jackets prowl around with clipboards, looking over the women's shoulders, peering into bowls, checking things off their lists. One, a beefy young man with a nice smile when he smiles, I know to be a chef from Farinex; another is an older *pâtissier* who owned a bakery on Mont Royal; the third is a teacher from the ITHQ, or l'Institut de tourism et l'hôtelerie du Québec, who seems to know contestant number four. Is she his student? I catch a glimpse of Claudette peering intently from the window of the pastry office.

So it's women performing and men judging. What does this say about our profession? (Maybe any profession.) I feel a little protest rise.

Trina turns to look up at the clock. It's 9:04, a little more than a half-hour into the Pastry Olympics. "Whew!" she says so loudly I hear it across the room. She shakes her head.

The girls at my station are moving as if in a dream. They need a foot at their backs, a spatula at their bums. They need Claudette.

Everyone else is on pastry cream: at the stove, at the counter whisking eggs and sugar, spreading the custard in plastic trays lined with plastic wrap. Watching Trina working her pastry cream with her whisk, smoothing it with her rubber spatula onto the tray, I see again how physical this is. It's in her head, but it's also in her shoulders and legs and wrists.

Contender number four is already piping the *pâte à choux* for her Carolines. She's doing it steady as a machine, perfect, two-inch sticks. Meanwhile, the girls from my station are still at the stove making pastry cream. They finish at almost the same moment and there's a sudden pile-up of pots and whisks in my sink. The dreamy Pius X girl in the tight black pants goes back to her table, where she keeps looking at the recipe booklet, pausing, looking again. She excuses herself to go to the bathroom. Five minutes later she's back, eyes down. She's completely lost.

The judges keep circulating. One cups his hand under a mixer bowl, gauging temperature. Two peer at Trina's first fruit tartlets.

Qiang comes to relieve me at my sink, so I can now watch like a spy from the back corner of the room. Claudette told me I had to observe from here if I wasn't washing dishes. It's a different—bad—view. I can see only the backs of people. I watch Rena's arm expertly folding in the parts of her chocolate mousse, watch her hand dip into it with a plastic spoon, but I can't see her face to see how it tastes. I see her arm tuck the bowl into the under-the-counter fridge.

A judge comes by and motions her to take the bowl out. He takes a spatula to it, lifts a mound, lets a few blobs fall back into the bowl. His face registers nothing but study.

By 10:30 one thing is clear. There are—despite the my-way-or-the-highway approach of some of our teachers—different ways to slice a *pâte sucrée*, or anything else for that matter. Contestant number four cut her *pâte sucrée* into one-inch slices, then stuck all the slices back into a ball, softening the cold dough faster than is possible when it's in one chilled lump. Next, she poked two holes—not one, as we've been taught—in the bottom of the choux for easier filling. Brilliant.

The girl is from the ITHQ, Claudette confirms, stopping to talk for a minute. We watch the young woman. Even her hat is intimidating—tall, beautiful, like pleated organdy, a commanding admiral's hat. Though she is still a student, she is wearing a professional chef's hat. "They have a lot more time to practise at that school," Claudette says, sounding for the first time defensive about her efforts with Trina and Rena. I tell her about the two women at my station, that I could tell they hadn't been trained by her.

"No fire," I say.

"Ahh," she says and puts her arm around me.

How's it going? I ask.

"I can't look," she says and returns to watch from the pastry office.

How's it going? I ask Rena who's stopped for a bite from the smorgasbord of food Wendy and Nadia have brought in, a grab-as-you-can lunch for contenders and dishwashers. Rena grins, gives me the thumbs up. I'm happy to know this, though we both know it could change in a moment.

I've slipped onto a stool near Tara, but I still can't see enough. Then I spot Trina striding down the aisle, her tray of millefeuilles held high over her head. Her cheeks are pink; no, crimson.

"She's nervous," says Tara under her breath. And she tells me that after watching the judges swarm Trina's station and check things off on their clipboards with non-committal eyes, Diane—disappointed at coming in fourth in last month's primaries—is now glad she didn't win. "I couldn't have done this," she'd told Tara. "There's a reason for everything."

An hour later, Trina stands doubled over her work station, not even lifting her eyes to the clock. Miss ITHQ is pulling fondant—the glue that does not necessarily hold things together—out of its plastic container, wrestling it into a small pot. Even she can't do this easily. Trina keeps her head down. Miss ITHQ remakes a *cornet*, seems to be picking up speed.

At lunch a judge had remarked to Claudette, "That girl from the ITHQ is good." Ardis winces when she tells me this. "I have a feeling she's going to win," she says.

The girl in the hijab is wandering around, looking disoriented. I know that look. I wear that look probably more than I care to admit.

But I also know it doesn't belong in a competition. I'm surprised. Calixa-Lavallée is supposed to have a pretty good pastry program.

Trina's still bent over her table. Rena's eyes are fixed on tiny slices of fruit. The girl across from her, one of the students from Pius X is only now rolling out her *pâte* for the millefeuilles. Trina and Number Four filled and glazed theirs an hour ago. They're a thousand layers ahead of her. This is beginning to make me crazy. I feel the clock ticking in my head, in my hands. I want to shake that girl.

Trina's upright at last and rolling something between her palms, hands in the air. Marzipan for the roses on her birthday cake. Last week in a practice, she sculpted a bouquet of yellow buds, nestled half a dozen sugar violets among the blossoms, circled them all in the palest yellow shell border, and wrote *Bonne Fête* in a script that dipped and curved in all the right places. It was a cake so beautiful it made me want to cry. "That's why she's in the Olympics," Tamara said on the way home that night.

And that's why I'm not. Lorrie thought I should give it a shot. "Come on," she urged me a couple of months ago. "Put your name in. How can you write about something unless you're doing it yourself?" That, of course, has been my argument to my friends all year, but I don't appreciate it being thrown back at me.

"I'm too old to be considered," I said, knowing this wasn't the issue.

"Diane's almost forty and she's doing it for the experience," said Lorrie.

"Just being in this course is enough challenge for me," I finally said. "I really don't need the extra stress, Lorrie."

"It would be good for you," she said.

"You're not entering," I said.

"True," she agreed.

Still, it's impossible to watch today's competition and not wonder, Could I do that? I see the questions on the faces of my fellow dishwashers. Could I produce steadily hour after hour? Could my body, my ego, my patience hold up? Because this is what comes clear by noon: the Pastry Olympics is about not choking, especially not choking when you feel most like choking. As in pastry as in life.

It's okay not being Olympics material. Even Julia Child called herself a home baker. Still, I'm not prepared for the appraisal I get from Nadia and Wendy when I step into the classroom to sample their lunch spread. "Nadia and I were just talking about you," says Wendy. "And we were just saying that you are one of the nicest people we've ever met. And that you will make such a perfect..."

I find myself waiting for anything—writer, chef, friend, teacher.

"Grandmother," says Wendy.

It's been a tough day on the personality front. "You're so passive and docile," Tara told me while we were watching our classmates earlier. She meant that as a compliment, she reassured me. My classmates have an odd take on who I am. Granted, it's a girl's take, a generational take, but today I'm feeling sensitive with all this tension and uncertainty in the 350-degree air. How can they see me as having no edge at all? Today I feel as edgy as my fourteen-inch cake slicer.

At 2:45, Number Four is still masking her birthday cake; the bottom, I notice, flares out slightly, not a good thing. Rena's performing micro-surgery on hers, placing the decorations on top with the tip of her smallest paring knife. The judges have their knives out, literally, running them through chocolate mousse after chocolate mousse. One of the girls from Pius X hurls her whisk into the sink of dirty dishes. Things are not going her way. Trina leans into her cake, pressing the paper *cornet*, writing. Rena walks by, makes a slit-my-throat gesture. Number Four hasn't even begun to do the lettering on her cake. The girl in the hijab sculpts flowers from carmelized sugar. She seems to be rallying. Miss ITHQ (aka Number Four) snips the tip of her *cornet*. Rena slips on white gloves to do some final tinkering. Trina, too, pulls on white gloves, a trick Claudette must have shown them. Of course, no fingerprints. Number Four's having trouble with her piping gel. (Don't I know.)

At 3:15 I catch Claudette staring out from the pastry office window. She's watching in spite of herself. At 3:16 she's at the front of the room.

"Stop," she says, looking more tired than I have ever seen her. And it's over. Everything that's been made is carefully carried into the dining room, where each contender gets her own table and a chance to display it as attractively as she can. Trina's and Rena's tables look professional and complete, Trina's millefeuilles fanning out elegantly on a silver platter. The yellow flowers on Rena's cake look even more perfect than ones she'd made in her best practices. One of the girls from Pius X puts out only her birthday cake and Carolines. Either she's ashamed of her other items, or more probably, didn't get to them.

The judges drift from table to table, dipping in teaspoons and murmuring among themselves. And the winners are... First place: the other young woman from Calixa-Lavallée, someone I barely noticed. Rena comes in second, Trina third. The big competition, Miss ITHQ, places fourth. The girls from Pius X, I hear, are in tears, angry at their school for sending them into such competition so unprepared.

How did someone so unspectacular win? Maybe her mousse was deemed creamier, her pulled-sugar flowers glossier. Clearly, finishing every item—Trina was the only one who did—wasn't the deciding criteria. Nor was sculpting the most graceful roses. Nor wearing the tallest hat.

Trina, however, is nonplussed. "I am so relieved," she tells me at the end of the day. "I can't imagine more nights practising for the *next* competition."

A week later, Rena, whose drive to win I'd placed at low to middling, confides that she had really, really hoped to come in first.

The next weeks push us deeper into this deepest of winters. And into puff, chocolate, and croissants and Danish—yet another new module. There is also the increasingly firm push to find our first *stage* placement. Ardis is trying not to add to our concern, but every time the subject comes up, it sounds worse: "If you get fired from your *stage*, you're out of the program," she warns this week.

"I'll tell you another *stage* story," she says. "I had a student who desperately wanted to be a pastry chef, but his attendance was the pits. I kept warning him, but he kept telling me, 'No, no, no! When I'm paid to do this, it will be different. When I do my *stage*, it will be different.'"

Ardis stops to see if we can figure out what happened. Yup. Missed days, late mornings. "What you're like here is what you'll be like in your *stage*," she concludes. Which for me means slow, but earnest. Knowing how nervous I am, Alfred suggests I do my *stage* with a woman who runs a dessert catering business called Sweet Sisters. She makes cheesecakes. "She's very nice," he says. "She hugs everybody."

Nice, not nice. How am I going to manage in a cake-cranking business where every minute wasted, every border smooshed, costs? It's a cute idea (for a book or an *I Love Lucy* segment), but no employer is going to want someone of my age and speed. I'm toying instead with the idea of testing recipes for a cookbook writer who also runs a baking website. I'm not planning on going into the commercial end of this business, after all. I'm going to write about it. And besides, I don't want a huge challenge for those three weeks, just a medium-sized one. As Cindi from the cooking program put it, "I feel like I've been running a marathon all year. Now I just want to walk." She's found a small caterer down the street from her house in Pointe Claire for her *stage*; she literally can walk.

Truth is, I'm yearning to be done. I love my classmates, even the ones I sometimes can't stand. I love our teachers. I've learned so much about baking and teamwork. But I am ready for the unremitting pressure to be off. The previous Friday I choked for the first time on an exam: Module Twelve, traditional desserts. The test: to (perfectly) slice, mask and decorate two cakes—Black Forest and a birthday cake—back to back. I'd been dizzy all week, plagued by a recurrence of BPV (why it's called *benign* positional vertigo I'll never know), a chronic condition I've had for fifteen years. Crystallized particles get stuck in the inner ear canal—I've got rocks in my head, I tell people—causing extreme vertigo in certain positions. My world was rocking.

The medication I'd been taking to steady things had dulled my reflexes and left me lightheaded. Every time I bent to put something in the under-counter fridge, I'd have to clutch the counter to get back up.

"Make sure there are no crumbs showing, or you'll end up doing a rewrite," Tamara whispered as I took my assigned station in the Lab. She'd been in the earlier group, was just about done with her exam. I envied her intensely in that moment.

A crumb-free cake? In my current wooze?

But onward. That's what this year is about. Don't look back, don't hesitate, don't think. Let's go. I summoned all my knowledge, my nerve, my scared energy, my fear of failure and... I couldn't clear the hurdle. I sliced the chocolate cake for the Black Forest, but my hands shook. I began masking it with the Chantilly cream, but used the wrong spatula.

In even the toughest exams something else has taken over before, lifted me out of my fear and self-doubt. Even when I made mistakes, I was propelled, held aloft. This time, although I miraculously passed, I never left the ground.

Black Forest Cake

Makes one 8-inch cake

Cake:

1 1/8 cups (275 mL) cake flour
1/2 cup (125 mL) shortening
1 cup (250 mL) sugar
1/3 cup (75 mL) cocoa powder
1 1/2 teaspoons (8 mL) baking powder
1/2 teaspoon (2 mL) baking soda
1/2 cup (125 mL) milk
1/2 cup (125 mL) milk
4 eggs

Preheat oven to 350°F (180°C) and butter and flour three 8-inch cake pans. Beat the shortening and flour in a stand mixer with the paddle for about five minutes. Add the sugar and dry ingredients and blend for about five minutes. Add the first portion of milk in a steady stream. Scrape the bowl and blend for five more minutes. Change the paddle for the whisk attachment. Whisk together the second portion of milk milk and eggs and add slowly in thirds. Whisk well between each addition in order to properly incorporate the liquid. Scrape down the sides of the bowl as needed.

Divide batter evenly among the three pans and smooth tops. Bake for 20-25 minutes. Test with a cake tester for doneness. Cool on racks. Unmould cakes when cool.

Syrup:
1/4 cup (50 mL) sugar syrup (see recipe below)
1 tablespoon (15 mL) Kirsch (cherry-flavoured) liquour
1/4 cup (50mL) reserved syrup from canned Bing cherries

Chantilly Filling:
3 1/4 cups (800 mL) 35% cream
1 cup (250 mL) icing sugar
1 1/4 cups (300 mL) (1 can, 398 mL) canned Bing cherries, drained (reserve syrup to make sugar syrup)

Decoration:
2-3 cups (500-750 mL) shaved bittersweet chocolate
10 maraschino cherries with stems

Sugar Syrup:
3/4 cup (180 mL) sugar
1 cup (250 mL) water

Combine in a small pot. Bring to a rapid boil. Set aside.

Place the first cake layer flat side down on a large plate or cake board. Moisten lightly with Kirsch-flavoured syrup. Spread 1/3 of the Chantilly and half the Bing cherries on bottom layer. Place the second layer of cake, round side down, on top. Moisten second layer with syrup, spread with 1/3 of the Chantilly and the rest of the Bing cherries. Add last layer of cake, round side down. Spread a thin layer of the Chantilly on the sides and a thicker layer on top of the cake. Smooth uniformly. Scoop small handfuls of chocolate shavings and press into the sides of the cake. Cover completely. Decorate the top with drained maraschino cherries.

Hopes had been high that Alfred would teach the croissant and Danish module. He's a bench guy, after all: puff, croissants, bread. "When I had my bakery you could almost squeeze the butter out of my croissants," he told us, adding with a snort, "The lousiest croissants I ever ate were in Paris. Heavy, bready, no taste of butter."

If I could learn how to make a really fine croissant, I told Alfred, I would feel I had arrived. A croissant befitting my Hungarian heritage (croissants were invented in Budapest in the late 1600s, when the city was under siege by the Turks). A croissant comparable to the wondrously flaky crescents—light, but intensely buttery, crisp yet yielding—made by Le Duc de Lorraine, the patisserie that won top place in *The Gazette's* Best Croissant in Montreal contest. Yes, he agrees. Those are the best.

But instead of Alfred (who has maxed out his teaching hours), Ardis has brought in someone new for this module: Pierre Thivierge. A tall, friendly, completely lovely man who owns a thriving patisserie on the South Shore, he's got a world of experience. But not, unfortunately, as a teacher. There is no agenda on the board, no introduction to the module on the first day. Eventually Pierre writes a recipe on the board. We run amok in the Lab for the first hour, trying to figure out what to do.

Then it begins to dawn on us, singly and collectively: croissant is a lot like puff, only with yeast. There's butter to soften and incorporate into dough. There's folding and waiting and rolling. We are building here, one skill on top of another, each one adding to our understanding of the next. We don't have a world of experience yet. But we are far from beginners now.

Class after class, we temper. Sometimes it happens fast, sometimes not. Chocolate is an ongoing mystery.

Ardis teaches us the *tablage* method of tempering in the third class. It's the old-fashioned way, she says. Melting the whole kilo of couverture at once, you then pour three-quarters of it onto a (scrupulously clean) marble or metal table and begin energetically scooping up the chocolate around the edges with a *corne* and spatula—"Get out all the spatulas and *corne*s you own!" she instructs—then folding it towards the centre. You scoop and fold until the chocolate begins to thicken, then add the whole lot back into the pot with the remaining one-quarter. It's beautiful to watch Ardis do this dance with chocolate and *cornes*, but it's hard to pull off. The one-third/two-third method is a piece of (chocolate) cake compared to this.

Tempering isn't the only repetitive part of the module. It seems we spend hours dipping tiny ganache squares into our (for now) tempered chocolate, spend hours polishing the trays of moulds, hours preparing them with the first lining of chocolate, then filling them with mint ganache or hazelnut praline before sealing the bottoms with the thinnest layer of tempered chocolate. We also spend a lot of time dipping our plastic spoons into those fillings. The orange white-chocolate ganache sends me over the moon. (My checks miraculously still fit, evidence of how many calories must get burned up in a day. I haven't gained a pound.)

Chocolate, we're finding, requires utter concentration and endless patience. And vast quantities of hot water to melt it once it's hardened onto bowls and spatulas. Often Jen and I—caught up in tempering or not tempering—forget about our dishes until class is nearly over. By then the hot water is gone. Washing our dishes takes a long, long time. "Chocolate is so dirty," remarks Alfred, watching us as he preps for the evening class.

And capricious. Will it behave and cooperate for the exam? We're all jittery. Taking place over two days, the exam requires that we produce twelve perfect moulded chocolates (no bubbles, no scratches, no dents) and twelve perfect dipped squares of ganache for presentation to Ardis. "Just be perfect!" she says.

The days of the exam I have one of those box-of-tissues-a-day colds. Mucous pours out of me. Every time I blow my nose, I must walk to the sink, wash my hands, dry my hands, walk back to my table and begin again. Those are the rules. If Ardis sees me blowing and not washing, I'll lose points.

I must blow my nose fifty times before I take my finished chocolates to Ardis on the second day. For the first time, I have a few bubbles in my moulded chocolate creams.

"I don't know what happened," I sniff.

"Go home, Denise," she says. She lops off a few points, but I pass. Even though my head's so stuffed that I can't taste a thing, I take my exam home as reward.

It's the last day of February. There are still four and a half months of pastry school left. But this is our last day with Alfred. It has to do with his contract and the number of teaching hours he's allocated, Alfred tries to explain. He's used up his time with us and must now work with the evening class, teaching *them* bread and puff. I know this is only fair, but couldn't we maybe have him for a short module at the end? It doesn't look likely, he says.

The last week with him is an explosion of puff. We make salty pretzels—"A favourite to snack on with a little coffee, watching TV at night. But you can never, never stop," says Alfred.

We make sweet pretzels, dipped in apricot glaze "for a bit of shine," then dunked in fondant. "Something else to snack on at night," he sighs. "If they reach home. In my shop these were all gone in two hours."

We make ham rolls.

"Ham and cheese?" asks Tamara.

"No," says Alfred. "This is not Tim Horton's."

We make cheese sticks and pinwheels and puff-covered cocktail wieners. We make Alfred's version of spanakopita.

"Hey, let's make baklava," says Anna.

"No," says Alfred.

His "no" never hurts. It's just there, good-natured, benign.

We decide to hold an Alfred Appreciation Day. I stay up until 2:00 a.m. the night after the chocolate exam making cannelloni. Min, Jing and Feng bring in their Chinese specialties. We pitch in for a beautiful Italian cookbook. Rena writes in fuschia chalk on the blackboard: We will miss you, Alfred!

His last day is also the puff exam. I get my first 100 percent, my *vol-au-vents* puffing into perfect little baskets as they're supposed to. And then it's just him and me in the Lab at the end of the day. We talk about my classmates, about our Paris trip, about his sons. His youngest is in professional cooking this year. His oldest, he says, has never really recovered from their bakery's bankruptcy.

Beauch and Georgia come to pick me up a little after four, and as we drive off, Alfred stands at the back door, waving to us. When I turn around, he's still there in his tall toque, waving. The image stays with me for days.

We're not really saying goodbye, he reminded us all week. "I'm going to be right here. I'm not going anywhere."

But it won't be the same, Alfred, we kept saying. It just won't.

9

ALL THE WORLD'S A *STAGE*

We moulded and sold hundreds of chocolate hearts for Valentines. We got a tidy sum from our great pie bake-off, plus a successful Christmas basket draw. Soon we'll be gearing up for our big Sugar Bush in early April, which should net us another few thousand dollars. So what happened to Paris?

We're still fundraising, but for what and for whom now? Jen is definitely not going, is lending all her trip money to her boyfriend so he can start a business or pay off a student loan. I'm disappointed by this news and tell her so, though my feelings about the "loan" I keep to myself. She's too young to be saddling herself with a guy who needs money, too young to be saying no to adventure. There's declining enthusiasm among my other friends, too, people I was really looking forward to doing Paris with—Tamara, Trina and Lorrie.

And what about everyone else? None of the Chinese students are going on this trip, except Qiang who keeps asking me what's been decided. His wife needs to know so she can ask for the time off from work. Then there are people, like Cindy, who never planned on going, but who still have to work all these fundraising events. Fabrice keeps saying that "the others" will have a trip, too. But that also requires planning. And how will we divide our money with the evening class, who have now done two fundraisers themselves and seem at this point more committed to going than we do?

Fabrice is a sensitive man; he must feel the dip in our drive, the friction that's growing between those going and those staying, between the day and evening classes. He pops in at the end of a class with Ardis to rally the troops and inform us that the London to Rome itinerary is a no-go (I don't even remember this particular configuration—London for pastry?) unless we're willing to spend $1,800. What we can do instead, he says, is a week in Lyon with an optional stopover in Switzerland and then on to Paris. On to Paris? I thought the whole point was Paris.

Not only are the destinations still up in the air, so are the dates. The only window of time open to us all—given Georgia's First Communion on May 24 (she's not coming to Paris, but obviously I want and need to be here for this big event), given Ardis's daughter's sixth-grade graduation (they both want to come) and given that Trina, Anna and Nadia must work in their respective restaurants over Grand Prix weekend, there is exactly one week available: May 26-June 2. Fabrice delivers all this news *pas-de-problem*, completely unruffled.

But when he comes over to talk to me a week later in the Lab, he looks stricken. There has been a misunderstanding. The prices that his travel agent has been quoting to him for the past five months—$1,400 for Paris, $1,800 for Rome—do not include airfare.

"Oh, my God," I say, turning off my mixer.

"*Mais oui*," he sighs. He's a big man, but today he looks smaller.

"We're talking another $700-$800 per person. Who's going to be able to afford that? Not these kids. I'm not sure I can come up with that," I say.

"I told my agent, 'You crush my dream,'" says Fabrice.

But how could this miscommunication have gone on for so long? How did he not know these were not all-inclusive prices? How did he not know any of this since he'd just organized a Paris pastry trip last semester? I wonder this later, after Fabrice has reassured me that somehow there will still be a trip to Paris, that he will make it happen. And later still, I think, no, the travel agent didn't crush his dream. He helped.

When I mention the situation to Trina and the others, assuming Fabrice has talked to them as well, I realize I'm the only person he's shared this critical piece of news with.

"You know," says Trina, standing by the ovens with her arm around Jen. "I'm not that upset about not going to Paris."

"Really?" I say. "I am."

"But we can go somewhere else, somewhere closer," says Trina. "I've always wanted to go to the Niagara area, visit the vineyards."

For a moment it sounds almost okay. And then it doesn't. Wine is not pastry. And Ontario is not France. It's nowhere close. It's hard to believe Fabrice can somehow still get us to Paris, but for now I want to believe he can and will.

In other news, Passe-Partout, the baby of über-baker James McGuire, has gone bankrupt. Both the multi-star Montreal restaurant and the *boulangerie* are gone within the week. Rumours have been circulating for days, fuelled by Trina's recent experience. Trina the Brave called McGuire to see if she could do her *stage* at Passe-Partout. When McGuire called back days later, he was gracious, but non-committal. I'm probably going to be declaring bankruptcy soon, he told her.

"It's a real loss for this city and for our industry," says Ardis. "Every patisserie that closes is a loss, especially one as fine as this." I feel a pang for the croissants I missed, those legendary Passe-Partout baguettes. (Given the snooty French ladies at the counter, I was an infrequent customer.)

And other disheartening news: There will be changes to the pastry curriculum next year. Industry representatives from bakeries like Au Première Moisson sit on the curriculum committees of vocational school boards like ours apparently. What do they want? More Viennoisserie, which means more croissants, more Danish. No more Bread module and no more Ingredients module. In other words, less theory and more production. More "on-the-job training" for giant bakery operations like Au Première Moisson and Au Pain Doré, which means, to my mind, less of an education.

"What would happen to a student like me, someone who wants to do something besides work in a patisserie?" I ask Ardis. "That's not what I came here for."

"Exactly," says Ardis.

"I'm writing a letter," I say.

"Write it," says Ardis.

Do we need more classes in Viennoisserie? After three weeks with Pierre we're awash in Danish and croissant dough.

As with puff, we make dough in one class, shape it the next. The day before the croissant and Danish exam, we're to practise on our last dough, kept safe and cold in the walk-in freezer. Tara wheels in the trolley loaded high with frozen dough slabs. I find one, two, three frozen palettes of dough with my initials on them. I don't remember making all this dough. My Danish is having babies in the walk-in. A pastry program with fifteen more hours of Danish? There won't be room in the freezer.

But shaping Danish, looping them into figure eights, filling them with raspberry preserves, has a sweet side for me. It takes me back, makes me think of Regina, my imperious Hungarian Jewish grandmother, someone I spent only a little time with. She was the Danish queen.

Reggie's Danish were palm-sized, yolky in colour and tender from outside to inside. The square ones were filled with sweetened cheese; the crescents with cinnamon and ground walnuts. Every Rosh Hashanah she made trays and trays of Danish, dozens on dozens, enough to fill barrels.

The year I lived in New York—the year of Juilliard and bingeing—she invited me to stay with her in the Bronx over the Jewish New Year. I'd only just arrived in the city from LA and was nervous. What would we do—this eighteen- and sixty-five-year-old? What would we talk about? I'd lived on the other coast for five years, was part of that other family, the non-observant one. What I knew about Reggie was that she was Orthodox, kept kosher and liked to drink a dozen cups of instant coffee with cream every day. "My

Nescafé." She was my grandmother and I hardly knew her, though she was generously giving me $100 a month while I studied dance at Juilliard.

I spent the High Holy Days of 1965 on a hide-a-bed in my grandmother's spare bedroom. Next to the bed was a barrel and next to that was another barrel. Both were filled to the brim with Danishes. In the middle of the night, I'd reach for one or three of each kind, square and crescent. I ate them during the day, too, though not in front of her.

When my grandmother came to take a few one afternoon to enjoy with her Nescafé, she couldn't believe what she found. I could hardly believe it myself, having reached happily, blindly into what seemed like a bottomless supply of Danishes for several days. The three-foot-high barrels, both of them, were now half empty.

Where did they go? What had happened to her beautiful cheese and nut Danishes? How could I have eaten so many? How was this possible?

I guess I ate them in my sleep, was all I could say. My grandmother didn't yell, though I could tell she was nearly as shocked by my behaviour as she'd been when my mother ran off with my Puerto Rican father twenty years earlier. Later, I overheard her talking on the phone with my aunt, telling her in a hushed, incredulous voice what I'd done. Maybe my grandmother realized I was just a homesick kid looking for comfort. Still, I don't think she ever forgot my act of gluttony.

And I never ate a Danish as delicious.

When I arrive at my scheduled time for the first day of the croissant and Danish exam, I discover there are no mixer bowls or hooks. No mixers at all. Every piece of equipment is being used, something that's not supposed to happen with our carefully choreographed, staggered exam times.

Then I spot Wendy and Diane and realize that once again Wendy has bent the rules and come in early. She didn't want her exam slot, which was in the afternoon. It was not convenient for her. (This is Wendy's doing, I'm convinced. Diane, who has no car, literally goes along for the ride.) I hear Wendy negotiating with Pierre to come in early again *tomorrow* when we will shape and bake. That means a sure pileup at the ovens.

I see red. I tell Ardis.

The next day everyone is where they should be. "Wendy's trying to figure out who complained," Ardis confides to me, trying not to smile. "I wouldn't tell her, just that it was someone who was scheduled for the morning."

"It couldn't be Denise," Wendy had said. "She'd never do something like that."

I feel a pang when I hear this. But it's a little pang. Go to pastry school and learn how to make the dreaded mokas, how not to choke when you feel most like choking, how to stand up for yourself. Or at least, complain to someone who will.

My *stage* is set. The cookbook lady and I talked on the phone last week and she's willing to take me on. Jen's going to work for a Cambodian French pastry chef in Lachine, Trina's off to Pâtisserie Nancy in Notre-Dame-de-Grâce, while Tara and Jing will be *stagiares* in Loblaw's cake decorating department. Suzy's hired on with a Jewish bakery in Snowdon and Lorrie's going to my old hangout in Montreal West, Pâtisserie de la Gare. Min's found a deli-bakery in Westmount.

For our last day together for three whole weeks we prepare a knockout potluck—casserole bowls and Tupperware containers line the counter where Pierre sits smiling in his baker's T-shirt. He's the right teacher for the day. Some of us never even put on our checks.

We drift into the Lab with vague directions for shaping the mountains of leftover Danish and croissant dough. Some, like Rena, get right down to it. Jen and I find our dough frozen solid in the middle, leave it to thaw in its plastic bedding and wander off to talk. We can't stop talking today, especially on Bum Butt Alley where we've been working with Michèle, Nadia, Wendy and Diane since February. (Claudette seems to have forgotten her promise to move us every month). It's the narrowest, most crowded space in the Lab; also the coziest.

"I am so nervous," says Michèle, who's doing her *stage* at Pierre's patisserie on the South Shore. Pierre took the whole class there on a tour a few days ago. It's an impressive, bustling place. My respect for him has increased, especially after bringing home a loaf of his bread, two joined golden globes, *les fesses* (buttocks). Beauch says it's the best bread he's ever eaten.

"What if my chef only speaks French to me?" worries Jen, whose French is limited. "Or what if he only speaks Cambodian?"

What if, what if? We're speculating all over the place. And since we're asking questions, what's happening with Paris? Did Fabrice find an affordable trip? We won't find out anything until we come back from our internships at the beginning of April, pretty late to be picking dates and booking flights.

We keep buzzing. Every now and then I look up to see Trina bent over her dough, rolling up cinnamon buns, sectioning dough for croissants, or Tara and Suzy zooming around as usual, and feel a nip of guilt. I really should be working. But then I drift back into the warmth and ease of the company around me. Later, when I go over to talk to Suzy to ease my conscience, she's only too eager to put down her dough cutter and chat, flash me one of her surprise smiles.

We've run and hustled and freaked out and we will do so again. But not today.

"Are you nervous about your *stage*?" I ask Min over lunch.

She considers the question for a moment in that reflective way of hers, perhaps rifling through a dictionary in her head. "No," she says, opening her hands, then her arms. "I want to learn everything."

I'm baking in my own kitchen, listening to my own music. It's a little bit like the old days, except it's not. Every morning I put on my chef's jacket. Not to parade around like *le chef* as Beauch kids me, but to remind myself of what I'm really in my kitchen to do. I'm not here to call friends or make appointments, though it's tempting after months of being out of the loop and so behind on life maintenance. I'm doing a ninety-hour *stage*. I'm still in school. I'm in my kitchen to test recipes.

My boss for these three weeks is a well-regarded, classically trained baker, teacher and cookbook writer. But the Friday night before *stage* was to begin, I received an email from her: "I'll be ready to start testing recipes after Passover." Passover? Passover is a week after *stage* will be *over*.

The dates had been on the school forms I'd taken her to sign several weeks back. We'd gone over the dates again on the phone. Trying not to overreact, I emailed back, reminding her of the dates, adding that I was open to testing recipes after my *stage*, but that my availability would go way down once I was back in school. I spent the next twenty-four hours racking my brain trying to come up with alternatives. How was I going to find another *stage* at this late date? Her email the next day contained a cheery note and nine recipes. It was a warning sign.

The first day, I feel jumpy as a cat, as if I've never baked at home before. I feel like I'm wasting time, standing in my white jacket next to my white mixer (a new KitchenAid professional model with a whopping 350 watts), no agenda on the board, no Claudette on my case. But by mid-morning I settle in, the light off the St. Lawrence River coming through my kitchen window, Bach playing in the background. I start to feel purposeful with my stack of recipes for muffins, pies, bread, lots of bread. I bake two muffin recipes, taking notes as I go.

By the afternoon, though, the pleasure dims slightly. I feel the need to get out of the house, to talk to people. I miss my pastry school friends more than I ever expected to. I throw on a coat and go, gratefully, out into the world. These first recipes require many ingredients I don't have in the house: frozen blueberries, malt powder, a certain brand of instant yeast.

Searching for unbleached white flour in the baking aisle at Loblaw's, I hear someone yell, "Denise!" And there's Jing waving excitedly from a staircase. I knew Jing was doing her *stage* here, had hoped I might see her. We run toward each other, her perfect black bob fanning out from her face. I can't get over how happy I am to see her.

"The woman I work with, she's very nice," Jing tells me. "She explain everything. I mask the cake very slowly, but I see her masking so fast," and Jing demonstrates a hand whipping madly around a cake pedestal. "So I try and go like that, too." She looks at me with her usual self-deprecating smile. "I need to go faster."

Her lunch break proved harder than the masking. "I'm very shy, very quiet," she confesses. "I can't talk like Tara. That girl can talk!" And we laugh, thinking of our gang, now scattered around the city.

The first few days I tackle muffins and cookies, relaxing into my new pace and enjoying the down-home recipes. No gelatin sheets to melt. No sugar syrup to monitor. This is the way I used to bake. *Adieu, les mokas!*

I decide to wait a few days to start on the bread recipes. My *stage* boss had promised to show me how she made bread on the Thursday morning of my first week. We'd be in her kitchen; I'd watch, ask questions, take notes. A good learning experience. An internship is for learning, Ardis said.

Wednesday my boss emails that Thursday isn't a good day, after all, could I come Friday? It's the first of several schedule shifts. In between these negotiations, she emails me a question: Are you an organized person? I step into the answer hastily, eager to impress, say something about looking unorganized because I often take on too much, but that I'm a very committed person, and always committed to getting things done. Blah, blah, blah.

Her answer makes me realize I should have written, No, I am not an organized person. I am working for someone who is probably not terribly organized herself, someone who might feel threatened by someone really organized.

I'm not *that* organized, I write back. I just try hard to be. Which is more true than my first answer. And, I hope, less intimidating. We'll move to safer ground when we talk bread. She's the expert, not me.

Friday morning, as I watch her navigate the kitchen she's outfitted with a restaurant stove, baker's racks, giant bins for flour and sugar, I see what an expert she truly is. In fifteen minutes she has four different kinds of bread dough on the go—bialys and challah in the bread machines, soda bread in the KitchenAid, and something wheaty in the plans.

"You are taking the most basic ingredients and making paradise," she tells me, and I realize that whatever else is going on here, this woman *loves* baking bread and that this is what I will take from these weeks.

"The whole point of bread making is to slow you down." She gently, gently flattens the bialys on the wood counter. "Be gentle to your dough," she says, looking up at me.

By the time I leave a few hours later—generous bags of bialys for Beauch and soda bread for Georgia in my backpack—I've written down a few other rules: be spartan with the amount of flour you roll into your bread dough when shaping it; use a single pan for baking on the top rack, double pans for the bottom, her oven credo.

And so in the second week I begin to seriously bake and test the bread recipes. I make wheat bread, rye bread, white bread. I realize that, thanks to pastry school, I've overcome my fear of bread. I can bake bread. I love baking bread. My family loves my baking bread. I send scrupulous email notes on everything I bake, noting things left out on the ingredients list, little inconsistencies, vague directions, items that are nearly impossible to find for the average home baker, as well as writing warmly about how things taste: mostly really, really good. (I would include one of the recipes here, but I've been strictly forbidden by my *stage* boss to share the recipes with anyone.) I back carefully into the questions I pose, because I already know, or think I know, the kind of person I'm working for. Plus she's the chef, right? All chefs are sensitive about their creations.

I'm in my element. I'm a writer, an editor and a baker and I'm getting to do all three things at once. Is everyone happy? Well, no.

A week into testing, I receive another email from my boss, telling me (not unkindly) that matters of taste, procedure, technique and ingredients are her mandate, not mine. So what does that leave me to do? To bake. And to shop, it turns out, endlessly, sometimes fruitlessly. I'm also paying for all the ingredients out of my own pocket. "You have to eat, right?" my boss said, when I asked at the beginning who would cover the cost of ingredients.

Sugar, flour, eggs, cornstarch, even butter—okay, I figured in the beginning, how expensive can it get? In three weeks I spend $300 on ingredients, plus another $40 for two odd-size baking pans. Beauch is not too happy. He likes the bread, but how many loaves can you eat in a week? How many muffins? He's begun to feed his co-workers at *The Gazette* with my test cases. Not only do I "have to eat." So apparently do the multitudes.

But it's only in the last week that I begin to buck. I'm standing in the aisle of the upscale Metro grocery in Westmount—definitely not my neighbourhood store—for the fourth time in two weeks, hunting the aisles for Steen's Cane Syrup and Tate & Lyle's corn syrup—whatever they are—coming up with nothing, wondering where I should go next. And I think: hold it! I am going home and I am making this pecan pie with Crown corn syrup and Mother's molasses and I am finished shopping.

I tell my boss, of course, about the adjustments I've made—pleading the case that if I've given up trying to find an ingredient, the average home baker (whom she's earlier characterized as having both limited skill level and attention span) will definitely not make the effort. And I'm using orange extract in those biscotti, I add. For days I have been searching stores for orange, tangerine and lime *oil*. When I find out later they cost $20 a bottle, I'm glad I never found them. (My mother has already air-expressed me a bag of unsalted macadamias from Los Angeles for those same biscotti after I could only find little cans of salted in Montreal.)

I remind my boss again that my *stage* is over in three days, that Monday I return to school. This week, my last, she emails me twenty-three new recipes to test. I make as many as time will allow, not even half. As usual, we are right in step.

With Ardis, who's spending these *stage* weeks checking in on us, I visit Jen and Trina at their respective patisseries.

The shop Jen's working at is called Pâtisserie Fine Savoureuse, which sits like a little French jewel on a street corner in working-class Lachine. The shop is empty, except for an elderly Asian woman who greets us sweetly. It's the chef's mother we find out when Chef Pen Paul Pichitr comes out of the kitchen, Jen trailing shyly behind.

"Hi," she says with a little wave.

There are a few stiff moments, until Ardis begins to enthuse about the cakes in the case. They *are* lovely: mango mousse with slivers of glazed mango fanned across the top, Easter cakes studded with tiny bunnies and eggs, chocolate cakes topped with abstract chocolate flowers like the ones we made (what seems like years ago) with Alfred. Pichitr is forty, Cambodian born, educated here. He apprenticed for five years, he tells us, with one of the top French pastry chefs in the Gatineau, also Cambodian. He opened this shop only last summer. "It's been difficult catching on in the neighbourhood," he admits to Ardis.

In the kitchen—white, quiet, empty except for us—I ask Jen how it's going, really. "It's like having your own private teacher every day," she says, smiling. We don't stay for long. No one seems to have much to say. On the way out I buy a millefeuille Jen made an hour before. It's just the way I like it, with only Chantilly between the layers.

The next day we visit Trina at Pâtisserie Nancy in NDG, another pastry shop I've avoided for years because of the condescension of the counter ladies. But upstairs it's a working man's space—long wood counters, a wall of sinks. It's bright, yet somehow dismal. Trina is wearing one of her cute little hats, no hairnet, and glasses instead of her usual contacts.

"You look pale," observes Ardis.

I'd go further: depressed.

Trina and I have already talked on the phone a couple of times so I know she's not especially happy here. But I haven't been able to figure out the reasons. She says the French-from-France chef, Claude, smiling across the room at us, is a "teddy bear," pleasant, helpful. He's been letting her do everything, something many of our classmates are complaining isn't happening on their *stages*: Easter chocolates, mousse cakes, the whole French works.

When the dishwasher failed to come in on Saturday, Trina volunteered to wash the dishes. The all-male staff wouldn't let her. The owner did them.

So what is the problem exactly? Because there is a problem. When I spoke to Trina on the phone she had the desperate tone in her voice I'd heard only once before, right before the Pastry Olympics when she came to me, crying, "I don't have the heart to make the chocolate mousse."

"I don't know if I can finish this *stage*," she told me.

Part of the problem is the hours: she starts at 4:00 a.m. (2:00 a.m. on Saturdays), the only one of us with such extreme *stage* hours. "I'm not a morning person, I guess."

That first Saturday she'd gone right from her night *garde-manger* job at Il Sole to Pâtisserie Nancy as had been arranged. No one was there. She waited for two hours in the freezing March wind until someone showed up.

Still, it's clearly more than the hours and lack of sleep. I could hear Trina herself trying to get at the why. Why did she dislike this so much?

"I miss cooking," she finally said. "I miss being in a kitchen with a lot of things happening. I find this..."

And there was the word I remember thinking in the Chocolate module one afternoon, dipping ganache square after ganache square after ganache square, scooping the little fork under its two-inch squareness, *chablonnage* side down, lowering it into the tempered chocolate, lifting it out, setting it down on the parchment next to the other fifty ganache squares.

"...mind-numbing," says Trina.

She looks miserable in this kitchen. And Trina looking miserable is not like some of our classmates looking miserable. Trina's a happy gal.

She clearly doesn't want Ardis and me to leave. We drift to a corner to continue talking about our classmates' *stages*, Paris, the other teachers. Every now and then I steal a guilty look at Claude, now filling huge Easter egg moulds with chocolate. He never stops. Does he resent us for keeping Trina from her work? They're not paying her, true. But Trina doesn't seem to want to let us go.

It's not that she's unimpressed by her chefs or that they're unimpressed with her. My hunch is they'd hire her in a flash. But something about a traditional patisserie with its endless production, éclair after éclair, brings her down.

Her last day at Pâtisserie Nancy was gruelling, Trina tells me when our three weeks are up. "By six that morning I'd made twenty chocolate Easter eggs for the chef. At 6:30 I made thirty more. At seven I was asked to make another forty. Then at 7:30 the chef came over and asked me to make twenty more. I couldn't help but feel resentful at that point."

She knows, of course, that it was a good *stage*, as *stages* go. "But on the last day, walking home, I nearly cried I was so happy it was over."

10

Meltdown

"Seven a.m., in the Lab, in uniform, ready to work." Fabrice has never been clearer about what he expects of us.

But here we are the day of the Sugar Bush, one day out of *stage*, on a Sunday morning, Palm Sunday yet, in the pouring rain, and we're the only ones here. (Well, most of us are here: I don't see Suzy and a few others.) The school is locked tight. Seven thirty: still no teachers, no maintenance crew. A few of us have cars, so we clamber in them to stay dry and tell war stories about our weeks in the real world.

At 8:40 a teacher in the cooking program shows up and lets us in. We fly into our uniforms: Breakfast is at nine and nothing's been prepared. There are potatoes to fry, sausage to cook, eggs to scramble, loaves of bread to slice, vats of *pouding chomeur* to mix and bake. Not to mention hundreds of crêpes to flip, one at a time.

And then a woman comes screeching into the Lab. It takes me a minute to recognize the Wagnerian profile and voice: Dora Floros, the former grad who's made good. She is to be our supervisor in the Lab, while Fabrice manages the kitchen and dining room. She accuses us of being late, unprepared and unprofessional.

Cindy tries to explain that no one was here to let us in at 7:00 a.m., that we've just come back from *stage*, but Dora cuts her off, tells her she's making excuses and don't we know that in this business *there are no excuses.*

Cindy—don't mess with Cindy—interrupts again, "We were on time!"

And now we're in for it. "Start moving!" Dora barks. "You, I don't care what your name is," she points to Michèle, "you're on crêpes. Get cracking! "You!" she points to Anna, "go find out what's happened to the bread. Now! Why are you walking so slowly?"

We eye each other and start moving. I don't know where I'm going, but I don't want this woman to catch me standing still. For the next hour we scamper, crack eggs, sizzle sausage, whip pudding and keep our mouths shut. At some point I find myself crouched by the giant Hobart, wiping crêpe batter from the base, and realize that I'm hiding.

We're cooking, but by 11:00 it becomes obvious that our Sugar Bush is more like a very small shrub. Last year when the pastry class staged their Sugar Bush, Beauch, Georgia and I stood in line for half an hour to get served; this year, despite flyers plastered all over the school and coaxing friends, neighbours and relatives, people only trickle in. We never get a crowd. There are mountains of crêpes and no one to eat them.

Fabrice has hired Native dancers from Kahnawake and a clown for the afternoon's entertainment. By this time the school dining room is only a quarter full. In the Lab, I even attempt a conversation with Dora, who's still doggedly making crêpes, asking her about James McGuire and the fate of Passe-Partout.

Last week, Ardis had a brain wave for me. With Chef Maguire closing his shop, perhaps he'd be interested in working on a cookbook with a writer/collaborator. "You should call him," she said. Now, fresh from my *stage*, I feel bold enough to think "Hey, I could do that."

Dora's almost friendly as she tells me about the last days at Passe-Partout. But then I go too far. "So what are you going to do now that Maguire is closing?" Dora clams up and cuts me off, as if she's just remembered the difference in our status.

I drift back to the dining room, where most of us are catching our breath before the massive cleanup. The Lab doesn't look quite as bad as it did after Pie Day, but it's close.

"I feel this big," Diane tells me as we watch the dancers, and holds up thumb and index finger, an inch of space between them. I've heard her say this before—about how she's done on an exam, how a certain cake turned out, about the Olympics—but now she's talking about *stage*.

She and Wendy did theirs at a West Island patisserie called Gourmet Privilège, the shop that took over when Alfred's bakery went bankrupt. They were expected to come in at 5:00 a.m. and do the scut work: buttering pans, cleaning pans, that kind of thing. Wendy was convinced the owners didn't want them there, and after a week called Diane to say she was quitting. "Do what you want," she told Diane.

So, as usual, Diane did what she thought Wendy wanted and left, too. Though having to get to work for 5:00 a.m. without a car, she didn't have much choice. Only now Diane isn't feeling too good about having quit. "I didn't love it, but I could have stayed there for two more weeks," she tells me. Now the two will have to add two more weeks to their second *stage*—making it six weeks instead of four.

I see an opening after all these months. Of all the people in our class, I tell her, Wendy is the one I have the most trouble with.

"Really?" Diane's eyes go wide.

"We're all hoping you don't go into business with her," I say. "We all think you'd do much better on your own."

And then I say something else I probably shouldn't: "You're better at pastry than she is anyway, you know."

Diane looks at me, disbelieving.

But the next day back in class, it's only hugs and kisses. "I love everyone!" Wendy declares, clearly relieved to be here. We all are.

Pierre's our teacher for the first day of the cookie module (*petits fours secs*, as opposed to *glacés*). We re-enter the blur of assembling equipment and running for ingredients, but it's a slow-motion blur today, full of goodwill stops along the way. This is what I have missed, the pleasure of our company. I'm so happy I can almost forgive a day of learning little. Not only does it seem oddly placed—*cookies*, after the baking complications we've faced down?—but Pierre, while friendly and encouraging, lacks any sort of pedagogical objectives. We brainlessly bake tuile after tuile—so many we *could* tile a roof—until we run out of milk.

Ardis finds me late in the day and pulls me aside. "Can I ask you something?" Her voice is low. "How did it go with Dora yesterday?"

I tell her the truth.

Okay, she nods. My experience corroborates others. Not only did Dora yell at us, she insulted Fabrice. There'd been talk of hiring Dora as a teacher in the school. Now? No way.

"Can I ask *you* something? Where's Suzy?" I ask Ardis. Suzy's the only one missing this first day back. She hadn't come to work the Sugar Bush either.

"She had a rough *stage*," says Ardis.

A few of us get on the office phone. No one answers, but we leave a message: "Come back, Suzy! Don't quit now! We miss you!"

We're back. Love, drama, tuiles, whole damn thing.

There's much to learn from each other's experience, Ardis believes, so we spend our second morning telling *stage* stories.

Tara iced eighty cakes a day at Loblaw's and went through fifty cases of kiwis in three weeks, she tells us. "My bosses let me do everything. 'Just do it!' they said."

"If I had to ice eighty cakes in a day that would be like stabbing myself in the foot with a knife," says Trina, clearly not over her *stage*.

Lorrie cranked nearly that hard at Pâtisserie de la Gare. "It was a great *stage*," she tells us. And humbling: "I'm so slow. An hour and a half would go by and I'd still be making the same thing. These chefs roll two *chocolatines* at a time, one in each hand!" She also admits her "French French French" boss was difficult. "The last day I was there he was having a tantrum, kicking walls, because his ganache wasn't setting up."

Still, she held her own and they've offered her $8.75 an hour to work part-time until school's over (seventy-five cents more than the industry standard). "You have to be enthusiastic and ask questions," she says. "That's what saved me. Otherwise I would have been unmoulding muffins all day."

Yujie spent her three weeks at a Première Moisson on the Plateau. "It was very good. I feel very happy," she says. "People very nice for me." Ardis confirms this: when she went to pay Yujie a *stage* visit, her co-workers were listening to a CD of Chinese music that Yujie had brought in. "They want to know something about my culture," she says, and I feel a pang for her and all my Chinese classmates. We've allowed them to cook for us and give us gifts, but never has one of us said, bring in your music, tell us about your life.

Yujie admits, "I make big mistakes, very bad mistakes. I make dents in the cake sometimes. I offer to buy the cakes I damage, but the chef he say, 'It doesn't matter, we all make mistakes.'" Yuji also stayed late to finish things. "I was happy to because it was chance to practise more. I have only three weeks for *stage*!"

Jing's chef at Loblaws wrote on the evaluation that she was the best student he'd ever had. Jing blushes and giggles when Ardis tells us this. Loblaws wants her back for *stage* II, and this time they want to pay her.

Avedon ended up going to Sweet Sisters, the cheesecake lady Alfred had thought might be good for me. "The first day I did génoise all day," she remembers. "The second day I was up to my elbows in carrot cake. I had a wonderful time. She taught me a lot."

Diane Ryan, the owner, was herself taught by Claudette, who still periodically does stints at Sweet Sisters for extra cash and to keep her hand in. "She told me Claudette is worth $300 a day!" says Avedon.

Okay, says Ardis, people who had a bad *stage*. "Rena, want to start?"

Rena opted for an internship in the pastry kitchen of the *très haute* Queen Elizabeth Hotel where she's been working as a fill-in cook for six months. But that didn't give her a leg up.

"There I was in la-la land, staring at a wall, peeling apples in a room all by myself for five hours. The boss had no idea what my skill level was. I was just a peeler. I was a nothing."

The last day of Rena's *stage* the entire pastry staff went to a *cabane à sucre*. Rena wasn't invited. "They went to the party. I went home. I was so disappointed." I think Rena talked to Ardis about the problems, but Ardis seemed to have not taken them seriously enough to step in. There's a surprising tension between these two as the year is progressing, surprising considering Rena's one of the most talented people in here.

We've already gotten bits and pieces of the disastrous week Wendy and Diane spent at Gourmet Privilège. Ardis admits she herself has always had a testy relationship with the owner. "All students are the same," he recently told her. "You have to completely retrain them."

Along with washing pans and emptying the garbage, the two were assigned a génoise inventory in the freezer. After counting 600 cakes, they, too, were frozen. On the few occasions where Wendy and Diane were given some real pastry work to do, they found that each chef had a different way of doing things. "Then we'd get into trouble," Wendy says. "Frankly, I was expecting a lot more."

There's a pause before Lorrie, never afraid to speak up, says: "I think some people have too high expectations of a *stage*. I think giving a *stagiare* menial tasks is a bit of a test."

Wendy doesn't say anything, so Lorrie keeps at it. "At my place they all did things differently from each other. And they'd tell me, 'No! No! *This* way!' You learn how each chef works."

Feng didn't even work with a chef at her *stage*. Choosing to do hers at Iangelo, a pastry factory near her home, she was just one of many line workers. "It's very physical," she tells us earnestly. "You carry big bags of flour over your shoulder. You lift trays holding eight cakes each." After observing how hard people worked there, she was disheartened to find out how little they make: $7.30 an hour to start; $9 an hour after fifteen years. If you have a diploma such as the one we will receive, you start at $8 an hour. There are no benefits. Still, it's better than China.

Alfred conveniently comes in at this point with news about opportunities in other, less populous, parts of Quebec. "Forget worrying about language," he tells us, writing all the regions of Quebec on the board. "The point is there are opportunities out there for pastry-chef entrepreneurs if you're willing to move out of the city." Such as an $8,000 tax credit.

"Eight thousand a year in Gaspé goes a long way," notes Trina. "Just don't go to Trois Rivières," she advises Rena, who seems the most interested in what Alfred has to say. "There's one English family there, and they moved!"

"Okay, Suzy," Ardis says when Alfred leaves. "Tell us about your *stage*."

Our phone call worked. Suzy's back, looking as relaxed as I've ever seen her. "It wasn't *so* bad," she says, clearly impressed by some of our stories. "Except my chef got upset when I told him the strawberries looked ten days old and that you just don't put rotten strawberries on a cake." For her, though, the hardest part was "not knowing what to do next."

Michèle nods. "I was always asking Pierre what else I could do." She tears up, remembering. "It was really disappointing." But she brightens as she tells us about the afternoon she kept Pierre's patisserie from burning to the ground. "All afternoon we kept smelling something burning, but no one could figure out where it was coming from." It was only late in the day that Michèle discovered a propane torch burning on a back shelf. And no, she wasn't the one who'd left it there. "Weird things kept happening all week," she says.

I've been wondering what I would tell my classmates about my *stage*. Some, I know, are envious that I got to do mine from home, that I had no boss man or boss lady breathing over my shoulder, yelling "*Non, non, non!*"

"Denise?" says Ardis, and I tell them about the endless shopping, my thwarted mandate, even my loneliness. And then I tell them about the money.

"Three hundred dollars?" croaks Madison. "You had to shell out $300?" It's bad enough that we didn't get paid for our labour, but to pay for it? My classmates are incensed.

"But I did learn two important things," I say, surprising myself with what it is I unexpectedly learned. "First, it's not easy to write a recipe well, one that's clear, complete and concise, one that makes sense, that neither assumes knowledge nor underestimates intelligence. It's hard just to get the numbers accurate."

But the other thing I'm only putting together now. My boss could not handle even constructive criticism. *The Gazette,* I know, will no longer hire her to write food stories because she doesn't take to being edited. Stay as wide open as you can, I tell my writing students the last day of class. Stay teachable.

I've been given my own lesson.

"Now Trina is a special case," says Ardis, looking sympathetically at Trina. "I've saved her for last."

"It was a fantastic *stage,*" begins Trina. "They were great guys. Okay, one of the chefs was a bit of an ass."

"What do we say when the chef's an ass?" Ardis asks us.

"*Oui, Chef! Oui, Chef!*" we chorus.

Trina tells us about the two kilos of orange zest she went through, the 140 chicks she made out of marzipan, the 120 whiskers she made for Easter bunnies. "They let me do everything. They were superb."

"But what Trina found out," Ardis tells us, "is that while she still likes pastry, she didn't like being in a pastry shop. Okay, let's all stick our tongues out at Trina!"

Seriously, she continues, it's all about finding what each of us wants. "And you know, listening to you, I feel like I'm changing my thinking somewhat. There's still the traditional pastry career. Working very hard, doing what you're told. The *oui, chef, oui, chef* track. The like-it or lump-it school. This element will be there for a long time."

But times are changing, she thinks. "There's another reality taking shape. You guys are helping me firm up a hunch that there's more room to move around now, to do your own thing."

This doesn't mean there are shortcuts. She reminds us that it still takes *ten thousand hours* to become a pro, an expert, a virtuoso.

"How many hours is our course?" someone asks.

Ardis smiles. "One thousand, three hundred and fifty hours."

"We're almost there," says Suzy.

Many of my classmates have told me the person they missed most during *stage* was Claudette. "I missed her organization," says Michèle.

"I even missed her personality," says Lorrie.

"I need that stress," says Trina.

I'm both looking forward to class with Claudette and dreading it. But if I have any illusions about who Claudette is, and how she and I are together, they're shattered as I come hurrying in the back door at 8:14 a.m.

"Oh, Denise, late as always, eh?" says Claudette, who, my luck would have it, is walking down the hall toward me.

So much for turning over my new punctuality leaf, plus impressing her with what a fabulous teacher I'd make for this program. Ardis spoke to me during *stage* about my teaching a module next year. I'm flattered, thrilled and surprised. After all, I've never had a professional pastry job and I'm hardly the star pupil here. "But you're an experienced teacher," said Ardis. "And you're a passionate baker. Plus you'll soon be a graduate of this program. It would be such fun to have you here!" She'll bring it up at the next departmental meeting.

In the classroom, Claudette is chirpy, glad to see us, too. While we were on *stage*, she, too, was doing a stint at Dagobert, the mammoth Montreal pastry operation on the South Shore with nineteen pastry chefs and forty employees.

"Two girls told me I was piping my butter cream rosettes in the wrong direction," she tells us.

We gasp. Who would question the way Claudette makes anything?

"To tell you the truth, I never worked so fast in all my career," she says. "I had to tell myself, 'Okay, Claudette, you're only on *stage*. Breathe!' One morning I piped 900 miniature puffs."

More disappointing, though, is that she doesn't feel she learned much. Still, she's returning to Dagobert. Washing dishes constantly while she was there, Claudette noticed that the company didn't use Quatromyacide. "I'm going back next month to teach the whole staff about hygiene," she says.

But today she's still teaching us. We've been hired by the school board, she tells us, to make 250 miniature pastries for a conference on non-traditional jobs for women.

As we rush to gather an endless list of ingredients, I realize something big and true. I really do love this.

"I'll get the eggs and the almonds," says Jen.

"I'll get the pastry flour and sugar," I say.

We scatter and gather, in this now-familiar dance of industry and creation. I remember how I used to feel in those first weeks entering the Lab's swinging doors, recipes and tool box in hand. How would I keep things straight?

Now the blur feels exciting. This morning, joyous.

And it comes to me again—absence is good for clarity—that I've only begun to understand the meaning of teamwork here: Nadia standing next to me at the sink, a towel over her shoulder. Tara, Suzy, Wendy offering extra coffee butter cream. "Here, take ours." Cindy bringing over tiny tart pans for me and Jen, even while she struggles late into the afternoon with a retake for an exam. Michèle asking several times a day, "You guys okay?"

There's limited time for big truths, though, when you've got Claudette and 250 *petits gateaux* to make. I haven't wielded a pastry bag in more than three weeks and here we are making ten different varieties of complex, one-bite cakes, recipes courtesy of Farinex. I feel rusty after days of muffins and crumbles, but Jen, Tara, Jing, even normally insecure Avedon, have turned into piping queens over these weeks. I'm in awe.

We make toonie-size *macarons*, a variation on meringues—so much in French pastry seems a variation on meringues—for one of the most exquisitely fine things I've tasted all year: two *macarons* like a half-opened oyster filled with *crème légère* and raspberries. Our miniatures (which really do go down in one bite), are beautiful to behold. As each team adds their pastries to the trays, we're incredulous.

They're also beautiful on the tongue, the flavours so intense: passion fruit and raspberry, vanilla bean and pistachio. The coffee pastries Jen and I are assigned are especially packed with flavour: we'd doubled the amount of coffee extract by accident. Flavour, I'm discovering this year, is really important to me when I bake. Maybe that's another reason I don't appreciate the dreaded mokas. No matter their colour, they have only one flavour: sweet.

Good work, Claudette says at the end of the day. It is good to be back with her, rolling pin at the back, spatula between the shoulder blades.

It's been a tougher week than usual because Beauch is in Thailand.

"Go on a trip of your own," I urged him last fall as our Paris dreams were taking shape. So he organized a week visiting friends in Bangkok and another week in the north of Thailand working as a volunteer for a small newspaper. He would go to Thailand and I would go to Paris. Fair is fair.

The first couple of days he was away we managed to stay in touch through email, but on the fourth day, he called. Beauch's voice sounded thin, more than long-distance thin.

"Are you okay?" I asked.

"I had a little accident," he told me. "Nothing for you to worry about."

Thanks to a borrowed bike helmet (he never wears one), Beauch only sustained three crushed thoracic vertebrae when he failed to take a turn at the bottom of a steep bridge while biking outside Bangkok. When our friend went back the next day to look at the accident site, the mud in the river bank still bore an impression of my husband's face. Luckily there'd been no river water where he'd landed. Another tourist was still in a coma from swallowing toxic water after falling in.

I didn't know these details until later. I only knew Beauch had had a bike accident and that he was doing "better." In the meantime, I was negotiating mokas and parenting solo. On the third day, Pas de Chat, our beloved cat, snuck out the front door. I was so preoccupied with everything else I didn't realize he wasn't in the house until the next morning.

I somehow got Georgia on the school bus, both of us hoarse from calling Pas de Chat's name and from crying.

"I'm a mess," I announced when I got to school late.

"We'll find him," said Trina.

I was on edge all day, not helped by Claudette.

"Shame on you, Denise!" she said in front of the class after I'd failed to put a carton of milk in the fridge during break.

"You okay?" Michèle asked.

"Nope," I said, trying not to blubber.

When school was over, Trina and I designed flyers with Pas de Chat's photo and stapled them to trees, taped them to lampposts. While I went back to the house to tend to Georgia, Trina walked up and down the riverbank, calling his name, stapling some more. It was now at least twenty-four hours since the cat had gone missing. Hopes were sinking.

Spotting my neighbour two doors down, I went to give him a flyer.

"Funny," he said. "I just heard mewing a minute ago from under my porch."

There under the woodpile was Pas de Chat. He'd heard my voice and begun to meow. Trina was rounding the corner just as I lifted the cat into my arms.

"I knew we'd find him," she said.

"We lost the cat," I told Beauch the next time we talked. "But Trina helped us find him." I left out the serious details, just as he had.

"Leave it to Trina," said Beauch. "How old is she again?"

But before the bike and the cat, something else happened. After months of rumbles and rumours, after Fabrice told his travel agent that meals must be included in the price, and her saying, no, they couldn't be, after our Sugar Bush bombed, the news is official: Paris? *Non*. The director of the school herself has finally scrapped our trip. It was getting too contentious and too expensive. So...no long walks along les Champs Elysées, no *pain au chocolat* from Le Notre. *Non* to it all.

The reaction has been muted. So many people have dropped out along the way, that only a few of us are really disappointed, though Rena's suddenly in a proper snit about it.

"How could it have fallen apart?" she asks angrily.

"Where has she been?" Lorrie whispers to me.

But even being here every day tracking this thing, I'm mystified. Qiang comes to me as he has several times recently. "Deni, what happened to trip? Can you please call my wife and explain what is going on please? She think I don't understand enough of the English."

Qiang, I tell him, my English is pretty good and I have no idea what happened.

Fabrice probably knows better than anyone, but he's too upset to be clear about the chain of events and the director's specific objections. He's depressed, a mess, a man whose dream has been crushed like nuts with a mallet.

The day we get the final news about Paris, Beauch is in a plane high above the Pacific heading for Thailand.

"It's all I can do not to call him and say, 'Get your ass back here!'" I confess to Lorrie, who's always up for a little Get Hubby.

I'm mad, but mostly sad. Paris has been the pastry payoff, the thing to aim for all these months, the prize to make this gargantuan effort worth it. And it would, I can't help feeling, have put meaning into that effort, connected us to this grand, frantic tradition of piping bags and *pâte brisée*. It was to be the apricot glaze on our year. I can go to Paris with Beauch next summer. But I won't be bunking with Jen and Trina, getting into the back kitchen of Joël Bellouet with Fabrice, staying up all night with les girls, dunking tuiles into café au lait. Now that we're not going, I realize how very much I wanted to go.

Plastic spoons hang from our mouths.

"You've got to try this one," says Jen, and sticks hers into the pistachio. I've already sampled the vanilla, the chocolate and the lemon sorbet. The pistachio packs a punch. We're not going to Paris with Fabrice, but we're going with him to Iceland: Module Fifteen, Frozen Desserts.

Fabrice, sounding surprisingly like Claudette, has already read us the riot act about the $8,000 Taylor ice cream maker our twelve teams will be sharing for the next few weeks. This hard-working piece of equipment must be scrupulously cleaned between uses. And we'll need to be patient and wait our turn using it. The Taylor can only make one litre at a time, working from light to dark, vanilla to chocolate.

He's also giving us more freedom than we're used to having in pastry school, challenging us to come up with our own recipes and flavour combinations.

"Lichee!" says Michèle.

"Mint chocolate chunk!" says Wendy, looking at Diane, who licks her lips.

"What about herbs like thyme or basil?" muses Lorrie.

I start thinking about all those macadamias sitting in my freezer from *stage*. What about butter macadamia instead of butter pecan? I already love the process of pouring in cream, egg yolks and sugar—crème anglaise, the base for most ice creams—and watching something solid, ice-infused, emerge.

Fabrice's Chocolate Ice Cream

Makes 1 quart (1 litre)

8 egg yolks
1 cup (250 mL) sugar
1 cup (250 mL) milk
1 1/4 cup (300 mL) bittersweet chocolate, chopped or in chips
2 cups (500 mL) 35% cream

Over a *bain-marie*, prepare a crème anglaise: Heat milk with 2 tablespoons (30 mL) of sugar. In a large bowl whisk yolks with remaining sugar until pale yellow. When milk is steaming, whisk it — in a slow steady stream — into the egg/sugar mixture. Return contents to the pot and cook over low heat, stirring constantly until the mixture coats the back of a spoon. Do not boil! (If mixture starts to overheat and curdle, immediately remove from heat and whisk vigorously.) Strain crème anglais over the chopped chocolate and stir until fully incorporated. Stir in cream. Refrigerate overnight. Pour into an ice cream maker. Follow the manufacturers' instructions for churning time. Pour into a litre container and freeze for at least two hours before serving.

All morning, as we work side by side, Nadia seems distracted, even upset. She is called out by Ardis. She comes back crying. She is called out again.

"What's going on with Nadia?" I ask Jen.

"It's something to do with Madison," Jen whispers, and it's only then that I realize Madison is also gone from the Lab.

Ardis comes in and asks us to stop what we're doing. Madison, she tells us, has stolen Nadia's tool box. Such things, as we know, are not tolerated in this school, and Madison has been told to leave. Nadia stands sobbing at the counter.

The decision is so final, so public, too. And as it turns out—I only learn this later—the infraction is more complicated than a simple theft. Madison had not taken the tool box at all. She'd watched a friend from professional cooking take Nadia's tool box and put it in her locker.

"Tell us who took it," Ardis had ordered.

But Madison had refused. She couldn't be disloyal to a friend. So out she went.

Madison wasn't the most mature member of class. She fooled around a lot, especially with Stinky, who was her partner and who was (not very secretly) in love with Maddie and her frisky seventeen-year-old blondness. I won't necessarily miss Madison, but the punishment feels severe for the crime.

According to Stinky the next morning, however, Madison is doing okay. "She's relieved, really. She wasn't into pastry anymore."

The first day of the Module Eleven exam I feel relatively surefooted. The second day I'm trying not to fall face down. Just the list of to-dos for the *petits fours glacés* and the mokas is daunting. Measure, cut, de-crumb, mask, decorate.

The tensest moment always comes as I stand, 14-inch serrated knife in hand, facing the cake. I'm not the only one scared of a cake. The morning of the exam, Tara, who's at the station next to me, knife at the ready, feet spread wide as if she's about to do the broad jump, begins praying out loud. She makes the first cut, then the second. They're good. She yells for joy, brandishes her knife like a fencer.

"Whoa, watch it there!" cautions Claudette, coming by.

I have no such hurrah, getting it close to right early on, then trying to make it more right and getting it increasingly less right. Ten minutes into trying to get my top layer perfectly flat, then making sure the other two layers are exactly the same height as the top layer, Claudette comes over. "I'd leave it be if I were you. It's fine. Put it in the fridge."

I could kiss her.

But there's still Part Two, because Part One produces only a trimmed, filled, but mostly bald cake. Rulers in hand, we measure off 3x5-centimetre rectangles, cut through our markings, then line the baby cakes up like dominos on a rack. For the first time, I fail to get the fondant thin enough and it lies like a thick cotton blanket on the little slabs. Two more times at the stove gets the stuff flowing *and* my rack looking like a punk hair-do underneath, the pink fondant hanging in stalactites.

I pass, losing a few points for the too-thick fondant, a few more for my not-perfectly square mokas. Will I ever learn how to make them exactly, precisely the same size? Probably not. I don't plan on making the dreaded mokas again as long I live.

Claudette looks nearly as relieved as I do at the end of the second exam day. Beauch and Georgia have come to pick me up. It's my birthday. Not one of my best, I have to say. Not just because of the exam, but because not one of my classmates remembered my birthday. I didn't even get to wear the party hat.

Claudette crouches low, talking to Georgia. Then, looking up at me, she says, "I'm so glad this module is over."

"I thought you loved this!" I say, almost in protest.

Claudette shakes her head. "It's so long." It's true: according to my notes, we began this module on January 4th. Here it is the last day of April. Four long, tortured and tortuous months. "It's a hard module for students," she sighs. "They get very frustrated." The exams are tough on her, too. "Two days top to bottom of checking twenty-three students' *mises en place*, their measurements, their fondant. Someone's always calling me over. And you know," she adds, compounding my disbelief, "I don't even like mokas."

Would I want to teach this stuff, assuming I could? The teaching scenario isn't looking as promising as Ardis had hoped. After conferring with Fabrice, Alfred and Claudette, she came back with the news that they were in agreement on my coming in to teach some theory next year.

"But I wouldn't want her teaching something like cookies," Claudette had said.

"Of course not," I told Ardis. Though, I added somewhat nastily, any of us could be teaching cookies the way Pierre's teaching them.

Word of our discontent seems to have reached Pierre. After our last cookie class, he looks deflated. Even he thinks we're producing too much, that our recipes are too big. He gazes at me sadly. "They want me to be more..." and he draws a line straight out from his forehead. More directive, more clear? I want to ask, but don't, because I'm one of those who's complained. "They push me out of teaching. That's not me. I like relaxed," says Pierre.

We're relaxing over dessert for once, taking small bites, breathing between stabs of our forks. No mousse inhaled, no doughnuts gobbled. Trina and I are back at school, seated at a plated desserts soirée in Le Saucier organized by Fabrice for a chefs' association. Each is spectacular in its own way—a square of puff layered with spicy chocolate ice cream, the richest brownie resting in a pool of crème anglaise, a spray of starfruit on the side.

We're impressed. And that's good. Since the collapse of the Paris trip, Trina has been less than impressed with Fabrice. I feel too badly for him to be as critical, although, I too have doubts that the truth of the trip has been fully communicated to us. Plus there have been the usual grumbles about his teaching as we hazard our way through ice cream.

But tonight we see his professionalism, even his perfectionism. We see him as *le Chef*.

Who in our group do you think will go places? I ask Trina.

Who do *you* think? she asks.

"Well, you. That's a given," I say.

She looks down at the tablecloth, smiles. "What about you, Denise?"

"Come on," I say. "I'm just going to write a book. I hope."

"And food stories, and maybe teach," she adds.

Truth is, I've also begun to nurse a private, small ambition. Maybe I could work in a bakery a day or two a week. To keep my hand in.

"Okay, you," I say. "Michèle, I think. She's talented and works hard."

Trina nods. "Jen," she says. Yes, Jen.

And Rena, if...we both sigh. Rena bounces from mood to mood, plan to plan.

Lorrie, our darling, maddening Lorrie, who wants this so badly.

Diane, Min, Qiang. They, too, are on their way somewhere.

But the next day every one of us is on the A-list. The miniatures we made for the women's conference nearly stopped the show.

"Oh, my God, did you guys look good!" Claudette beams, waving a thank-you letter from the school board. The women loaded their plates so high with our desserts that they ran out halfway through. "Your pastries," read the letter, "were the best advertisement we've ever had for this program."

11

Advanced Mousse

The evening class's work has always looked different than ours. Even last summer before I'd begun at Pearson, I could see the difference. We'd taken my parents, visiting from Los Angeles, to Le Saucier for dinner, and Fabrice, teaching that night, recognized me as an incoming student. He coaxed us into the walk-in freezer, eager to show off the cakes made by his evening students. (Given Claudette's seniority and reluctance to work evening hours, day class generally gets her more than half the time; evening class gets Fabrice.)

"Look!" he said, holding up a birthday cake studded top to bottom with bright orange butter cream rosettes. The cakes were decorated, all right. Over-the-top decorated. And, I couldn't help noticing this even as a novice, a bit...sloppy?

Sometimes evening class produces beautiful work. All spring we've admired their cake-top designs, on display in the glass case in the classroom. Their designs are far more creative than the colouring-book ones we've copied with Claudette. Still, even those of us in day class who struggle with Claudette are deep-down grateful to her. Call her picky, overly strict, nearly anal in her attention to detail, it's all been in the service of teaching us the guiding commandment of French pastry: make it perfect.

I'll need to chant this like a mantra—grateful, grateful, grateful—as we undertake two last demanding modules with her:

modern *entremets* and advanced decoration. We're meeting Claudette where she lives.

The first days of modern *entremets* are a blur of mousse cakes. Elderberry and passion fruit. Triple chocolate and raspberry. Harlequin and Mandarin. Pear Charlotte and Prince Noir. By the second day, I can't remember what we made the day before. The *mises en place* are staggering, the cakes themselves many-layered, many-stepped extravaganzas. These are cakes to make you proud—I made *that?*—and crazy. For two days running, Jen and I mess up the white chocolate part of the triple chocolate mousse cake. It won't set up properly, which throws off the layers of milk and dark chocolate mousse meant to rest above and below. We've got a seepage problem. All we can hope is that triple chocolate mousse won't be on the exam.

"The exam could be on any of...let's see," Claudette leafs like a demon through our textbook, "any of the cakes from pages 4 to 17." She looks up. "Did I stress you out enough? Good. I'm happy. My day is done." She adds that she can make sixty-five mousse cakes in a day. "And I'm slow. Okay, medium."

Despite eight months in this fast oven, I'm still slow. Sixty-five cakes? On the third day of advanced mousse I realize Claudette will only keep raising the temperature and the tempo. There are moments when I feel a frisson of something that makes me wonder about Claudette and what drives her. A streak of sadism? She's a terrific teacher, but cruel at moments. And she certainly doesn't go out of her way to win our hearts.

"Who's on ladyfingers?" The question bounces from team to team.

"I thought you guys were making them," Trina says to Wendy.

"I thought you were," says Wendy.

An hour later it filters down that we're *all* making ladyfingers for ice cream cakes. Fabrice couldn't be clear if his life depended on it. Back in October, his vagueness was unnerving; in December, somewhat amusing. By May, it's just exhausting.

I sat next to him in Le Saucier earlier in the week, a surprise lunch with Trina, Wendy, Tamara and Nadia, because the dining room had too few customers for professional cooking students taking their à la carte exam. Fabrice seemed down, not in the mood to talk about Paris, and not much else either.

He did tell me a little about his older brother, Patrice, a pastry chef who died of a heart attack at 41. At the time, Fabrice owned a patisserie in St-Jean-sur-Richelieu, a city about an hour southeast of Montreal. But when Patrice died, Fabrice sold it to one of his employees. He didn't have the heart to continue.

"My dream," he told me, "was to go in business with my brother."

You crush my dream. Maybe Fabrice is more of a sad man than a happy man, despite the jokes and "I kick your fucking ass." Maybe he's something of a tragic figure. Maybe there's a novel here.

It's not Fabrice's fault, though, that the day of our ice cream exam is an unseasonable 30 degrees Celsius and muggy, the hottest day so far this spring. Our exam is an ice cream cake with ladyfingers on the bottom, chocolate parfait in the middle, banana-orange ice cream on the top and sides. The entire cake is circled with halved wafer cones dipped in chocolate. It's cute when it works.

I flub my crème anglaise—there's a first time for everything, but too bad it's during an exam—so that flecks of chocolate dapple my chocolate parfait. Can I just call it chocolate chip? I ask Fabrice. But it gets worse when we have to put all the parts together in the heat. The ice cream melts as soon as it hits the air of the Lab.

Some of us try working in the air-conditioned classroom. "Put your cake in the blast freezer," Trina advises, hands moving deftly, delicately, as she attaches the cones to her cake. I keep my cake in the freezer for as long as I can, but all day wouldn't be long enough.

As I'm presenting my finished cake to Fabrice—"Show me something nice!" he told us at the start of the exam—two of the cones drop off. I stick them back. They fall off again. My cake is becoming a puddle. Fabrice nods and smiles. Another module down.

And another. I'm in the last group, the few of us spread out in the hollow-seeming Lab, for Pierre's cookie exam.

"They do good. The cookies they come out very nice," Pierre says before we even start, clearly wanting to encourage us by raving about our classmates who've already passed.

It shouldn't be a hard exam, given that we're only making *macarons* and tuiles. But suddenly, I can't remember a thing about *macarons*. Are these supposed to "fall" or not? Are these supposed to be shiny or not? And how long do you bake them for anyway? The famous last question we're always asking each other as we walk into the Lab before an exam, even whisper to each other as we slide things into the oven *during* an exam. Though by now we know the answer: they're done when they're done.

But it goes well, as Pierre fervently believes it will. My *macarons* perk up mid-bake, creating their little shelf so they look like proper *biscuits*. Not everyone's do this, I notice, peering into the rotating oven. I think I have finally learned to let my egg whites beat long enough.

I remember to double-pan the tuiles, though I fail to notice that the pans don't properly fit inside each other. The wet batter bakes slightly off kilter, producing disks with appendages that I surreptitiously cut off before sticking their hot little selves onto the curved metal surface of the tuile pan. Still, I end up with crisp, super-thin cookies. They look almost as good as the ones at Pâtisserie Nancy.

Afterward, Pierre tells me our performance makes him feel good, like we've gotten it, like he's done an okay job as a teacher. Studying for the exam the day before, I'd gone back to our text, mostly ignored for this module. It was surprisingly full of interesting theory on different kinds of French cookies, and I realized I've learned exactly one thing in this module, though I'd already been taught it by my *stage* boss: to prevent burning and insure better heat distribution, always double pan.

But today I don't feel like complaining about Pierre or anyone else. He's only a good man trying to do a good job. The locker room is empty when I come out of the exam. Strangely, sadly, achingly empty. We have only another month of classes. Then a month of *stage*.

There are signs that we're winding off like the last rosette in a butter cream border. We've had final-day parties now with Alfred and Fabrice, a barbecue potluck with Pierre a few days ago. Wendy's husband brought their family barbecue in his truck and we grilled burgers outside in the parking lot. I made mushy potato salad and Tamara made couscous and Min and Xiu Li brought dumplings. No one signed up for a dessert. "Someone make a mousse cake quick," said Lorrie.

On our last day with Fabrice he invents a new cake, one not found in our text, but definitely found in our experience: Team Cake. One team slices, two mask, three others pipe borders. Pretty cakes, generic cakes. We're cleaning out the freezer and the fridge, using up the last of the vanilla sponge and butter cream. Everything's got to be used and sold.

I've been waiting for this finale, *yearning* for it on the nastiest, toughest days, the days of killing fatigue and sky-high dishes. Now the yearning is deeper and more contradictory. I want it to end. I don't want it to end.

If Advanced Mousse is about speed, Advanced Decorating is about taking our time. All day we're sculptors, coloured marzipan between our fingers. We flatten, mould, tweak. We make little oranges, bananas, pineapples, pears. We stick a clove into the top of a pale yellow globe, dust it with a bit of green food colour, a dash of soft red. And there it is: a perfect, tiny apple.

We're having a blast, though no one seems to be having a better time than the speed queen herself. Claudette was all systems go on the *bûches de Noël*, the Christmas fruit cakes, getting the ribbon exactly so for génoise, even the dreaded mokas. But I can see that this is what she loves. Give Claudette a bit of marzipan and a sheet of rolled fondant, and she's over the moon.

She's warned us, though, about how tiring this module will be—"You stand and stand, bent over small, small work. You're not moving at all." She'll even accept our bringing in stools from the classroom. But after five hours the first day, we're still standing. We're no longer those girls of a few months ago, itchy to get home, whining about not wanting to make marzipan cats.

Later that day, Jen puts her head on my shoulder and looks up at me. "Have I told you how happy I am that you've been my partner all year?" she asks.

I'm so surprised and touched I can only squeak back that I'm so happy she's been *my* partner. "We've never had one fight!" I say, flashing to some tense, earlier moments she seems to have forgotten.

The girl is growing up. She even washes half the dishes since her *stage*. We've been working with Michèle and Nadia a lot lately, those unwieldy teams of four where inevitably one person runs the show. I've watched Jen seethe over Michèle's bossiness and it's made me appreciate the space we give each other. "You two are so calm and quiet over in your little corner," Tara said recently.

"Hey, let's stage a pretend fight before the year is over," I suggest, and Jen gets a naughty-girl gleam in her eye.

We will have our hands in the oven all day and we will be sweating like pigs, says Claudette. "I don't know where nougatine comes from. Egypt, I think." (That night I check in my *Larousse Gastronomique* about the origin of nougatine. There's no mention of any country but France—a village named Nevers where a famous nougatine cake was created in 1860. It's a French reference book and this is French pastry. Nothing existed before or since.)

But by the end of the day, we'll think nougatine came by way of hell. Although the ingredients are few—sugar, water, glucose, sesame seeds—the instructions are many and the pitfalls unlimited. Nougatine, Claudette admits, is very old-fashioned, hôtelerie stuff. "But it's classy, too."

It's not like we haven't worked with cooked sugar before. But this time we're taking that hot stuff and shaping it into an artful object, a basket for our marzipan fruits. The only way to do this, says Claudette, is to work fast (the F-word for me) because sugar goes from liquid to solid in seconds.

We get our sugar bubbling on the stove, oil our chef's knives, cutting boards, baking pans and rolling pins with canola. Nothing must stick and nothing must slow us down. We pour sesame seeds into the napalm in our pots and wait for the right shade of gold. As with crème caramel, too light's no good, too dark's no good.

And then in a moment it's the right colour, a luscious light caramel. We take our pots and run to our work stations where we pour the nougatine onto the oiled cutting boards. Off with the oven mitts, on with the rubber gloves. Roll, roll, roll. You've got to get this sticky, seedy stuff thin. Even with rubber gloves, it's burning hot. It's also, unfortunately, cooling off by the second, which means we must spatula the hot mass back onto the baking tray and into the oven for a few minutes to get it malleable again. We cut eight-inch disks with *entremet* rings, banging the metal rings into the hardening sugar with heavy plastic mallets. This is hot, fast and loud.

"Denise, you're so tough!" yells Nadia over the din. I'm banging as hard as she is, maybe harder. Yeah, I am tough.

The disks get a quick sculpt over the bottom of a soup bowl. It looks like a large sesame snap, those thin, crunchy wafers you can buy for cheap in any dépanneur. The basket handles are trickier, involving cutting a one-by-twelve-inch strip with perfectly straight edges. I haven't used my giant chef's knife much this year, but this is a job for that steely monster. The first handle cracks; so does the second, and by now my nougatine, which has been waiting in the oven as I rolled, cut and chucked, has gone from golden to brown. It's back to the beginning, which means back to the stove with a whole new pot of sugar and seeds.

By three I am sweating like a pig, a frustrated pig. Sensing trouble, Claudette comes over and tries to force one of my handles into a curve. It breaks. She takes a bite out of it. "Oh, well," she says, which pretty much sums up working with nougatine. Eventually one of my handles holds, bends without snapping and gets attached.

Between those million trips to the oven, we've whipped up batches of royal icing and cut and folded half a dozen paper *cornets*. Thick, white and sweet, royal icing is really just an extremely stiff

French meringue. Even though we've made royal icing several times before, this shouldn't make us cocky, Claudette warns.

"This is where people lose marks on the exam. At the end of the year, they've forgotten how to make a French meringue. They end up with something white in their mixer bowls, but it's not a meringue."

We decorate the edges of our basket with our tinted icing—delicate twisty vines and miniscule five-dot flowers, then fill them to the brims with our marzipan fruit. Everyone's basket is a treasure. Even when Claudette tells me I should never have used a straight line as a border, I am thoroughly pleased.

Ottawa has become Paris. And only nine of us—for varying reasons—are going: Jen, Lorrie, Wendy, Diane, Trina, Min, Michèle, Nadia and me. Some people, like Anna, Rena and Qiang, have to work. Tamara was going to go until Wendy made a remark about those who'd helped at the fundraising events and those who hadn't, and Tamara said, "Who needs this? I'm not going where I'm not wanted."

Except for Min, none of the Chinese women are going either, all pleading babysitting problems, though I sense there are other reasons. Maybe they feel as Tamara does. Suzy, who has never said she was going on a trip anywhere with any of us, definitely feels this way.

"Nobody likes me," she told me this week.

"I like you," I said. Suzy's delivered some of the funniest lines all year. She can be helpful, even generous. There's a basic good heart under that edge.

Suzy hasn't made herself popular with Ardis, though. While the nine of us are touring the Cordon Bleu in our capital city, it's school as usual for the rest of the class.

"Why?" Suzy keeps asking Ardis. "Why, when they're not coming in?"

"Because it's school regulations," Ardis keeps answering. "They are going to Ottawa for educational purposes."

"So why do we have to come in?" Suzy asks again.

For once, Rena and Anna are on Suzy's side. (Anna and Suzy had a fight the week before, with someone calling the other a bitch.)

Rena and Anna are also angry at having to come in while we're away, but after protesting against the injustice, they let it be.

"I don't see why we have to come in when the rest of the class is having a good time in Ottawa," Suzy says again today.

"I'm getting very frustrated," says Ardis, and for the first time I see her walk away from a student.

Whether we're headed for magical Paris or boring Ottawa, someone is going to get their panties in a twist. And there's a new wrinkle in those panties: Fabrice is no longer the tour director. Claudette is.

She's hoarse from shouting at us for three days.

"But you made a great job yesterday!" she says. "I push you hard and you make it. It was wonderful. Some people said to me that pushing that hard, they didn't learn much. But that's part of the life."

I don't actually remember what we made yesterday, though I've got two more white bakery boxes in my fridge. Raspberry mousse, I think. And mint mousse maybe. There is so much thinking that goes into this on-beyond-mousse module, so much inner planning, and so much hard-scrabble work, that the finished cakes are almost beside the point.

And *my* doing this, *my* making virtuosic cake after cake has also become beside the point. In the beginning, even until recently I have to admit, I was conscious of the novelty of this year, and the novelty of me, fifty-seven-year-old writer-me who never intended on being a pastry chef, doing this. Watch me ace a butter cream border. Watch me nail the dreaded mokas. A kind of how-did-I-land-here self-conscious astonishment. Has pastry school finally stopped being another world I'm just visiting for eleven months? Am I now immersed in what Claudette calls "the life?" Has this in fact become my life? Maybe I've lost myself. Maybe this is not a bad thing.

Deep into the afternoon, I somehow get the glaze on my *Opéra* right. Not too thin, not too thick. I don't fiddle with it like I usually do. A few glides with my offset spatula and I put it down decisively on the counter. Claudette walks by and gives me the thumbs up. She yells out, "You want to see a perfect glazing? Go see Denise's cake." My classmates come over and congratulate me. Claudette comes over and shakes my hand. "She *never* shakes anyone's hand," Tamara says later.

12

Out of the Oven

We're running out of days. What's left is full of relief, sadness, and stress. We've invented a new speed on the Hobarts, gone from high to warp, or as a co-worker once described a hyper boss: "He has two speeds—fast and purée." Make mine raspberry.

There are papers to write, *stages* to arrange, graduation photos to take, exams to pass and modules to finish. Advanced decoration alone will involve the design, construction and final flourishing of a three-tier wedding cake. There's even a new module we'll do from start to finish: Plated Desserts.

To teach plating—a restaurant skill that's part presentation, all bravura—Ardis has brought in Danny Gagnon, a former student, now pastry chef at the Queen Elizabeth Hotel. We met Danny back in September when he came in to share the story of his ten-year career. Danny's worked in pastry factories, at Château Lake Louise in Alberta, at the Palais des Congrès. He's worked twenty-three-hour shifts. If it's brutal and involves a pastry bag, Danny's done it.

He's a little guy, which takes getting used to after barrel-chested Fabrice and towering Pierre. "Where's Danny?" I ask Jen on our first morning with him. And then I realize he's standing right in front of me. My eyes were scanning higher. Danny is quick and sharp. When I walked in at 8:25, he said, "Denise, you're late," obviously warned about our small, end-of-year rebellions. (Okay, I've been rebelling all year about our start time. Okay, all my life. "Easy breezy," Lorrie calls me.)

"Plated desserts means *desserts à la carte, desserts à la minute,*" Danny says first thing.

"It means stress," says Wendy. And for once, I completely agree with her, especially when Danny tells us this module will involve making desserts in real time and serving them to real customers. In two weeks, we'll invite friends and family here to Le Saucier for a special plated desserts afternoon. Half of us will wait tables for the first sitting, while the other half bakes. Second sitting, we'll switch places. Oh, and this will be our exam.

We'll have three items on our menu: a *vacherin* (meringue layers with ice cream), a warm chocolate soufflé, and a molten chocolate cake, each resting on a plate in various coulis and adorned with baubles like spun-sugar nests and tuiles. We're talking beautiful.

We tackle the chocolate soufflés first, working from photocopied recipes Danny gives every team. But something's wrong, we realize after a few dips of our plastic spoons. The soufflés don't taste chocolatey, they taste eggy—even Danny thinks so—and they spill unattractively over the edges of the ramekins. We make another batch adding more chocolate this time, but it still doesn't cut it. Warm! Chocolate! Soufflé! It's got to taste as good as it sounds. Anna and Rena keep cranking them out, adding and subtracting, getting scientific, but even their results are less than stellar.

We've never had outcomes so all over the board. *We* have made mistakes this year; the recipes haven't. It makes me appreciate the unfailingly well-tested recipes in our text. And it makes me nervous. We don't have time for this.

Danny suggests we try warm lemon soufflés instead. Within minutes we're zesting and juicing lemons, whisking in sugar and yolks, making quickie, two-egg white French meringues. These are better—at least they rise more uniformly, but they still taste mostly of egg. Tweak, tweak, tweak. By the end of the morning, we still haven't arrived at a definitive *recette*. The garbage cans are full of failure. "So many soufflés to bake and throw away!" James Beard once said about the life of a food writer.

During a lull, Michèle confides that Claudette can't believe we've put a soufflé on our plated desserts menu. "I'd never risk that for service. They're too hard to do well, too iffy, too stressful," she told Michèle.

We try the second item on the menu: a heavy-with-butter-and-chocolate molten cake. We measure exactly, dust the custard cups neatly with cocoa and keep a strict eye on the oven. But when Jen and I cut into the finished cake, the centre spills up and over the edge of the plate. The thing tastes like chocolate all right: raw, runny, unbaked chocolate.

Thank God for the *vacherin*: three crisp French meringue discs layered with caramel ice cream, vanilla ice cream and rosettes of Chantilly. Keeping it from all melting together will be a challenge, but at least this *tastes* good.

Granted, we're as untethered as the recipes today. We talk, joke, play pranks. Michèle gives Jen a piggyback ride around the Lab. We must be a handful for a new teacher. But Danny's had worse days in a kitchen. He takes it like a chef, not hovering like Pierre, but setting us to work when he sees us drifting. One chatty team makes spun sugar nests—lacy webs of carmelized sugar "woven" by waving a wooden spoon back and forth, something Ardis taught us back in Ingredients—while another is assigned miniature spiral tuiles. Placing these on actual china plates reminds me again that someone real will eat this.

"I didn't even have a wedding cake when I got married." Claudette does an imitation of her husband's who-needs-that attitude. "So we went to a restaurant where he ordered an ugly Black Forest cake made with Nutrafil." We burn with shame for her. Of all the people to not have had a proper wedding cake! Even I had beautiful wedding cakes: a ganache-filled génoise from a real French patisserie for my first wedding in 1970; triple-chocolate mousse cakes for my second, to Beauch, twenty-three years later.

It's the first day of wedding cakes and time for show and tell (all). Claudette's brought in a four-tiered wedding cake she made a few years back. It's fake, she reassures us. No microbes growing: the rolled fondant has been stretched over Styrofoam forms, not génoise. It's still spectacular—a vision in white *pastillage* with a hundred filigree sails spiralling round the edge. It's all detail, white on white, delicacy on delicacy. She assembles and reassembles the tiers, showing us how it's put together. When she nearly drops the top tier, we shriek.

"Some days I have butter hands," she says, unperturbed. "My husband says it's a disgrace."

I have never seen Claudette so…happy. Even stories about her husband don't get her down this morning. "I love wedding cakes," she tells us, and watching her face, we believe her. "When you make wedding cakes with Claudette, you feel like you're being taken into her confidence. It's very sweet, very intimate," a former evening student told me back in November.

Claudette begins our trip down the aisle with some general, hard-earned advice: plan every inch of your wedding cake in advance, aim for continuity in the elements and keep it simple. And something specific, but key: never wrap fondant around a frozen cake. As it defrosts, humidity will build up under the fondant. You'll get bubbles, but not the kind you want at a wedding.

Claudette pulls off a hunk of marshmallow-white fondant, places it on the demo table, drops in a few shots of red food colouring, and begins rolling so that the white becomes shades of pink, the darker streaks fanning out in waves. She keeps rolling until the fondant is spread thin and large, then using a pizza cutter, makes several cuts deep into the circle. She lifts the segments gingerly, draping it over the top of a Styrofoam disk, adding one section at a time. They form gentle folds that cascade into a pool of marbleized pink, grace itself.

"You want me to finish?" Claudette stops to look up at us. Is she kidding? We're in thrall. "You guys are hard on me," she says and cheerfully goes back to work.

It would be nice to think we'll be asked to make wedding cakes on our second *stage*, but after the first *stage*, we're more realistic. We're also more methodical in our search, more clear about what we're looking for.

I have a crazy idea for mine: three *stages* in three different places over four weeks. I want to learn as much as I can from as many chefs as I can. I want the exposure, the experience. I also want to save myself possible humiliation. How much trouble can I get into if I'm only in a place for a week, a week and a half?

I even pitched the idea to *The Gazette's* veteran food editor in the hopes of writing three stories for the paper's Food section: a behind-the-scenes experience with some of Montreal's top pastry chefs. Her answer, when it came, was what I've come to expect after fifteen years of freelancing for my city's only English newspaper: "As usual, you are a woman of great energy, Denise..." After this flight of condescension, the food editor went on to say she thought stories about Montreal "pastry cooks" would interest few readers. And that she'd been told by "people who know" that our city's pastry chefs were nothing to get all *bruléed* about anyway.

"What is she talking about?" huffed Ardis when I showed her the email.

I decided to pitch the stories to another editor and to do my *stages* the way I wanted to do them, stories or no stories. But first I had to visit the chefs and the shops.

We'd met Rita Djerrahian when she was a guest lecturer in one of Claudette's decorating sessions earlier in the month. Rita didn't have Claudette's speed or organization, but she was clearly an artist with sugar, and has been running La Gâterie, a successful cake-decorating business, school and store on Montreal's West Island for a decade. Plus Rita seemed *flié* enough to make a fun, not-too-demanding boss for a week. Plus Trina wanted to do a partial *stage* with Rita, too. We'd drive out together to La Gâterie every day. That in itself would be a treat.

So ten days with Rita, then on to *stage* Number Two at Le Fournil, an artisanal bakery in Westmount; then finishing up the month in Lachine with Pen Paul Pichitr, owner of Pâtisserie Fine Saveureuse where Jen did her first *stage*. This seems a fitting way to end the year. With Jen's beloved "Cheffie," as she calls him, I'll experience *le vrai chose français*.

I make the appropriate calls, setting up the three appointments for a day Trina and I are both free. "I'll come with you for all of them," she's promised, having already arranged her remaining *stage* weeks in the pastry kitchen at Brontë, a très chic downtown restaurant. No way is she ever going to work in a patisserie again.

La Gâterie is a speck of a shop, packed with models of cakes, photos of cakes, supplies for cakes. What are cake supplies for sale and what are decorations being readied for a cake in progress? It's hard to tell. But already I love the smell of the place. Like marshmallow fluff and cotton candy. I've never realized that sugar—all those tubs of rolled fondant stacked against the walls—has a smell: soft, sweet, *pink*. It reminds me of my bedroom when I was six.

Rita, who's Armenian, but was born and raised in wealth and comfort in Ethiopia before the Communists took over, is a bundle of nerves and words. She pounces on us at the door, eager to tell us about everything at once: her clients, her classes, her competitors. She's aggrieved about her lack of visible success—no stories yet in *The Gazette* (no surprise)—and how hard she has to work.

"Do you know how exhausting it is to have, for example, a mother come in to order a cake with a Strawberry Shortcake design? Only, the woman insists that it be the *updated* image of Strawberry Shortcake," Rita sighs. It means she has to go online to find the two versions, note the minimal, but apparently crucial, differences between the original and the update, and produce a beautiful and accurate cake. All for fifty dollars.

We shake our heads appreciatively. The phone rings for the third time in ten minutes and when Rita ducks behind a dividing screen to answer it, Trina whispers, "I'd love to spend a week in here just organizing things."

Rita's dense West Island shop is worlds away from Pen Paul Pichitr's patisserie in Lachine. There is the obvious neighbourhood difference: newer suburbia versus older working-class. But Pen Paul is as quiet as Rita is talkative, and the white, uncluttered space of his kitchen feels like an ashram after La Gâterie.

Pen Paul is a gentleman in a tall chef's hat. He has kind eyes. Yes, he would be happy to have me do a *stage* there. Yes, he likes Jen very much. He wishes he had the money to hire her, but as we know he is just starting out. Trina and I buy a slice of his pizza and a little maple-mousse cake and go sit on the edge of the Lachine Canal. The mousse is deeply maple. We've done nothing with maple all year, I realize.

"It's too expensive," says Trina. "I think you're going to have a good time there."

Le Fournil is as funky as upper-crust Westmount gets—a cozy, railroad-narrow bakery that smells as it should, of warm bread. The chef I introduce myself to doesn't look like the voice on the phone. Natalia Adams is young, round and not overly warm. Maybe she was expecting someone younger. Much younger. But the *entente* gets signed. I'll start right after Canada Day.

Trina and I buy a brownie on the way out. It's gooey and cakey all at once, everything a good brownie should be. We stand on the corner eating and talking about the contrast between the three shops, about the irony of Pâtisserie Fine Savoureuse in Lachine and Le Fournil in Westmount. Maybe it's about what we yearn for... machinists in Lachine longing for the Parisian sophistication of *une mousse au chocolat*; monied Westmount matrons wanting something down-home like sticky buns.

We've been waiting for him since our very first day: Edward Kraczyk, the tyrannical chef from the Queen Elizabeth Hotel, the man Ardis called "the real, European thing." But Edward won't be coming after all. Hernia operation, I think. I'm disappointed. I like extreme characters, at least to write about. But I'm relieved, too. Someone like that could tip us over the edge right now.

Instead we get Jürg Bangerter for a day's demonstration of sugar work. He arrives, without apology, a half-hour late for Ardis's class, a blond, unsmiling man of fifty with a Swiss-German accent.

Jürg sets up wordlessly, plugging in his heat lamp, readying his glucose. He seems almost angry about being here. He begins to melt sugar for a sculpted rose.

"A rose," he says, looking up at us and nearly smiling, "is a very sexy, erotic flower. Everything is round on it."

Erotic? We have been spooning and licking, moulding and rolling all this long year, feeling the texture of butter cream on the tongue, the way *pâte sucrée* yields under the fingers, but erotic is not a word I have consciously thought of once. Erotic. We titter. Where is this guy from? Candyland?

He twists and pulls the pink-tinged sugar, shapes, snips, pulls some more and in ten minutes holds up a hot-pink rose, transparent as glass. It is erotic.

Don't bother making the leaves by hand, he tells us. Save your efforts for the petals, since real rose leaves are not that attractive. "They're the only thing I don't like in nature."

Now that he's begun to talk, he doesn't stop: advice, gossip, war stories, bits of too-personal information. "Oh, French chefs and their chauvinism," he says, pulling molten orange sugar that will become the ruffled collar for a clown. "In Switzerland, women have always been welcome in professional kitchens. But the French have a disadvantage, you know." He looks at us significantly. "They're *very* disorganized."

He's worked all over: in Morocco setting up a hotel school ("more or less a disaster"), as a chef in Jasper, Alberta ("a party"). He taught in upstate New York at the famed Culinary Institute of America.

And every year he would compete in the big annual pastry show in New York City. "I think competition is good when you're young," he says, and I see on his face that he wishes this weren't so. "You see the best and the worst at these shows. There's so much jealousy among pastry chefs, such great rivalry."

He passes around his portfolio, evidence on every page that he, too, is the real European thing.

"And after all that, he ended up in Dorval," Ardis says, laughing. Bangerter's of Switzerland, a cute little shop with a bright orange sign on the lakeshore, specializes in handmade chocolates and Swiss cakes. Summers he makes ice cream.

"Of course, ice cream is more like a hobby," says Jürg. "It takes so long to make a litre of the stuff."

He's Swiss, pragmatic, and not afraid to talk money.

"How much do you think you can charge per person for a wedding cake?" he challenges us.

"Ten dollars?" says Wendy.

"More like $3.50," says Jürg and Wendy's face drops.

Meanwhile, Jürg's sugar clown has turned into a real person. He stands on one leg in his striped balloon pants, hands open, mouth grinning, as if to say, "Are you laughing yet?"

After a month of unanswered phone calls, emails and faxes to Le Cordon Bleu it looked like even the Ottawa trip might get cancelled. This week they deigned to answer. Yes, for $900 we may attend a pastry demo at their school. But now that only seven of us are going—with Claudette as den mother—what about everybody else who worked so hard for Pie Day and Valentine's Day and the Sugar Bush? "Everyone will get something," both Fabrice and Alfred assure us.

The Ottawa-bound gang holds an official meeting in Le Saucier. We're pretty much the same people who sit on the grad committee, which has been meeting for the past month. I don't know how I landed in either group, especially since it means mega-doses of politics and big personalities.

Now that we know we're really going, the big question emerges: Who is going to sleep in what room? Earlier I'd promised Tamara I wouldn't let her share a room alone with Claudette. ("I'm afraid I'll fart in my sleep or something," said Tamara.) But with Tamara not going, it's Min and me who'll be sharing quarters with Claudette. The others will be in a two-bedroom executive suite with a whirlpool bath. The fun suite. Wendy's arranged it all. I bristle, but just a little, because, after all, we are getting to go *somewhere*.

Rena's not going to Ottawa, but she's the chair of the grad committee, made up of students from cooking, pastry and butchery.

She's at her business-school best as she officiates over balloon colours and how we should list names on the program. My official job will be to give a short speech about our teachers. Rena's asked me to look over her speech, too. We haven't picked a class valedictorian, but she's giving the sort-of valedictory speech.

"I really was hoping we would pick a valedictorian," she said to me yesterday. She was going in, I was coming out of the walk-in. "I would have picked you, Denise."

It's good I wasn't holding cartons of eggs in my arms. They would have landed and scrambled on the floor. "*Me*? But I would have picked *you*! You have so much talent. I'm such a slowpoke, such a slow learner!" I was sputtering, thinking, is she nuts? And then, a darker thought: Is she making fun of me?

"No," said Rena, and looked me straight in the eye. "If there's anyone in this class who deserves to be class valedictorian, it's you, Denise." I kept protesting, but she kept insisting. And finally I just hugged her because otherwise I was going to cry.

Rena is a woman of surprises. Along with having a diploma in cooking, a half-completed university degree in commerce, she also has a diploma in hairdressing. "I need a haircut," I told her a few weeks ago. My last haircut—short because of the hairnet—was an expensive butcher job. "I'll do it," said Rena. "Ten dollars, okay?" We picked a day she'd come over after school.

"I need my bangs trimmed," says Tamara when I mention it. Ardis, overhearing us, chimes in, "I need a haircut, too." Trina decides maybe she does, too, and so at 5:00 p.m. on a day that feels almost like summer, four of us sit on my deck waiting to be shorn.

Ardis has beautiful long red hair, hair to envy. "Just a trim, right?" I ask as she sits down on the stool.

"No, all of it," she says.

Masses of hair hit the deck, blow off into the garden. I'm nervous for both of them. Ardis and Rena have had an uneasy relationship this year with Rena's up-and-down bouts. And now Rena is cutting her hair.

Neither looks especially nervous, though. And in the way of women, the five of us begin to talk. What's going on with Pierre and his plan to keep teaching. What's happening with the people who don't get to go to Ottawa. And why Claudette is coming with us when she's had next to nothing to do with any of our fundraising events.

It's been the most difficult year she can remember, admits Ardis. "And it's not just been among the students," she says, keeping her head down as Rena snips. "All the conflicts between the teachers have come out in the open, too."

And since we're not bothering to protect people, Trina says something about her struggles with Lorrie. It's gotten really quiet at their table in these last weeks.

Meanwhile, Rena bends intently with comb and scissors and Ardis's hair falls and falls. In the end, Rena makes Ardis into a new person—a sexy lady with copper curls and flashy green eyes. Ardis has lost years, yet somehow gained in maturity. We can't take our eyes off of her. Trimmed and shaped, we don't look half bad ourselves.

"I think I'm in a bad mood today," says Claudette. It doesn't show on her face. But then Claudette looks crisp and pulled together every day.

Why today? It's our last time with wedding cakes, the make-it or break-it push. Besides, we've grown accustomed to a kinder, gentler Claudette in these final days.

Not that I'm feeling especially gentle myself. This morning Claudette marched us up to the library (Pearson's version of a library: a big, ugly, bare room with a scattering of books on the shelves) for a twelve-page written exam on sugar work: What are the various properties of *pastillage*, royal icing, rolled fondant? Label all the botanical parts of a flower. The material is word for word from our text. But studying at the kitchen table at 6:00 a.m. this morning, my half-shut eyes had stayed on the page for exactly thirty seconds. She'd never include this stuff on an exam. She did.

I'd been up even earlier, since five, cutting and forming the last of the little flowers for our wedding cake. Last week Jen and I realized the only way we were going to finish the myriad flowers for our three-tiered heart-shaped cake was to bring the gum paste home and roll,

roll, roll. Jen had the periwinkle and white; I had the two shades of pink. The best hours to work, I'd found, were between 5:00 and 6:00 a.m. when the sun was just up, its light muted. I rolled the pink gum paste thin, very thin, then cut it with the smallest flower cutter, placing the flowers to dry and curl in the giant sponge Claudette had lent us. It was surprisingly relaxing, like meditating at dawn.

When we'd first read the directions—we were modelling our cake on one from a British wedding cake magazine—we'd laughed where it said, "This cake takes approximately 400 flowers." Four hundred flowers? We'd be lucky to make half that. So our cake would look more...Zen. In the end, without intending to, without realizing it, we cut more than 500, each of us going into a gum paste trance in the early morning quiet of our kitchens.

But now this is it, the final-day fussing, and there's nothing Zen about it. Some, like Tara and Suzy, are adding the last sugar daisies to their drape. Others, like Cindy—still struggling to get her Styrofoam cakes covered with fondant—are far from finalizing anything. Jen and I have at least masked our cakes, though that had nearly prompted our first tiff. The day before, I blew the first roll-out for the bottom layer—the fondant drying and cracking practically as it hit the air—and started to roll again.

"You can't roll it twice," said Jen. But I didn't listen, rolled again, failed to make it large enough again. I rolled again, Jen silently watching beside me. This time I rolled it big enough and thin enough. I lifted, smoothed, tucked, nearly hyperventilating.

So cake covered, flowers cut. Now we just have to attach everything, plus stencil the repeated heart pattern in royal icing along all the sides of all three cakes. It's a task we've both been dreading. I'm assuming Jen will do it, with her steadier hands and defter, luckier touch. We've cut our own stencil, poking out teeny-weeny holes in which to dab the pale yellow powder that we'll pipe over later. Jen tries twice, cursing all the way. The stencil leaves a yellow smudge, nothing resembling a heart.

"Make your holes bigger," says Claudette, coming by. We get bigger yellow smudges.

We've been so excited all week, encouraged and hopeful. Now we have this yellow blight. It's faint if I look at it objectively. But who's objective? The yellow screams at us. Jen grabs her piping bag and places royal icing dots over the smudge: a perfect, pointillist heart. We'll only do the top layer, we decide, as she finally puts down the bag to rest her arm.

Behind us, Wendy is finishing her pretty, pink, girly cake and Jing and Xiu Li are affixing large, deep-red sugar dahlias to the top of theirs. One counter over, Min and Qiang add more royal icing ornaments to their regally draped white-silver-gold masterpiece. Their cake has an almost pre-Columbian feel, though I think they were aiming for a Victorian look. Either way, it's a stunner.

I glance behind me at the deadly quiet back table. Lorrie and Trina are not doing a cake together. Trina's is dressed in unadorned white fondant save for six blue-purple gum paste lilies she's laboured over all week at home. Lorrie, Trina tells me when she comes over for a break, admiringly touched one of Trina's lilies earlier today and broke it, upsetting Trina not a little.

Lorrie's cake? I don't really have words to describe it. "What is she trying to prove?" Trina asks in private. Drapes, flowers and whatnots festoon the three layers of Lorrie's cake. There isn't a blank space. Every time I've gone over to check on my friends, Lorrie has been deeply bent over her cake, breathing heavily and muttering, "This isn't working." At lunch, she's even worse, not talking, sitting hunched over both my place and hers at our counter, dipping fries into a dozen ripped-open packets of ketchup.

But now it's after lunch, and those wedding bells aren't chiming, they're clanging. Placing our multi-coloured blossoms on the three cakes, we discover the obvious: we've made about triple what we need. Thankfully, we still need flowers for the little bouquet that will sit on top. Claudette shows us how to stagger the blossoms and graduate them by size until we have a miniature bouquet worthy of a cake-size bride.

By three, everyone is done. (Except for Cindy, still trying to figure out where to put the crimson roses on her hot-pink cake. It's nowhere on the French-pastel spectrum, but it's pretty anyway.)

Claudette goes from station to station. Already she's told Tara and Suzy that the back of their cake is too bare, that they need to make another drape.

"But it's perfect the way it is!" I told Tara, when I saw her cutting more fondant.

"I know," Tara sighed.

So now their cake wears a bustle at the back. It not only doesn't add, it detracts.

Still, the cakes around me are simply beautiful, worthy of the most elegant nuptials.

Ardis said so herself when she came in earlier to see our progress. "I told Claudette that each year the wedding cakes get better, more professional looking," she told me. "And I told Claudette that this must have a lot to do with her. "No," Claudette replied. "The students get better every year."

At the back table, Claudette tells Trina she needs something else besides the blue lilies on her cake. Trina quietly declines. Claudette says the same thing to Tamara and Avedon, who have made, to my mind, the most exquisite cake in the room: three oval layers, dusted at the base with gradations of gold and covered with single rose petals of sun-washed yellow. The sugar petals look as if they've blown off their stems and scattered themselves, randomly, languidly, over the layers. Their cake is all movement, all grace.

Claudette tells them they need something else on top beside the handful of petals.

"What else could you add that wouldn't gook it up?" I ask Tamara as Claudette continues through the room.

"I don't know," says Tamara, not making a move to do anything. "I have no idea."

When Claudette finally arrives at our table—leaving not one rave in her wake—the first thing she sees is the yellow smudge. But this doesn't bother her as much as the fact that our flowers have no centres. We'd tried doing this to a few, piping in pinhead-dots with royal icing. No, we decided. The dots made the cake look cute, not elegant. We wanted a more abstract effect.

We explain this to Claudette.

"Put them in," says Claudette. "Otherwise I don't consider this cake done and I can't give you a mark."

Jen tries to explain again. Her voice, louder than I've ever heard it, shakes just a little. "We tried it and it didn't look good."

"You need the centres," says Claudette and walks away.

Jen and I look at each other as she silently fills a *cornet* with royal icing. I do the same. And as we move from flower to flower like angry bees, our entire cake goes into a decline. One little dot makes all the difference.

As I walk around the room at the end of the day, taking photos of Qiang and Min's gold and silver treasure, Trina's understated blue elegance, Michèle and Nadia's triumph of will and orchids, Tamara's falling petals, Tara's and Suzy's now over-bustled daisy cake, I move from anger to dismay. What does Claudette not see? How has she missed the obvious? We've come so far, and we've come so far because of *her*.

"She's still the chef," Beauch says to me later that night, when I tell him about the day, how this wasn't a matter of proper technique like rolling our gum paste too thick. This was a matter of the eye. "*Oui, Chef! Oui, Chef!* Remember?" Beauch says. "She still knows way more than any of you." I remember the insistence in Jen's high little voice, Trina's benign refusal. Yes, of course Claudette knows more. And yes, we need to be done now and on our way.

But not before another plate of drama. Though it's a lot less exciting than Paris, Ottawa has become nearly as contentious and almost as doomed. The story is that Alfred and Fabrice wanted to take the people not going to Ottawa out to supper in Chinatown. This came out only when Wendy discovered we had $1,000 less in the Future Chefs account.

"That's one hundred dollars per person! For Chinatown!" fumed Wendy, who was as usual right in the thick of things.

"He lied right to my face!" said Trina, about Fabrice's explanation for the loss of the money (which got reinstated within the hour).

I worked like an investigative reporter all afternoon to piece it together, but then gave up in exhaustion. Who *knows* what happened?

We need to continue to trust and respect our teachers. We need to hold it together for just one more week. For the second time today, it comes to me: we need to be done.

For our last class with Claudette we make the last recipe in our book: *Pédrégal à l'orange*, a cake with so many mousseable parts I've lost count. I'm worrying, too, about my own part of this construction: the chocolate *succès* spirals I squished my way through a month ago, one of the many layers in this architectural wonder. But it has to work and it has to look good: I've already pre-sold my *Pédrégal* to the reporters and editors in *The Gazette* newsroom for their election-night buffet.

We also have to make twelve varieties of bite-size beauties for tomorrow's grad, plus organize a last-day party for Claudette. It doesn't feel like just one thing too many today, but twenty.

Still, when Claudette takes out that packet of Farinex recipes and begins rattling off assignments for the miniature pastries, we don't fold. We've made these before, for the job conference for women, two and a half very long months ago.

Fortunately, Jen and I don't get assigned anything with coffee this time, instead landing *croustillant praliné et pistache*, a compressed disk of *macarons* and pistachio crisps layered with butter cream, pastry cream, pistachio cream, a *palet* of pistachio and praline cream. "I give to you this time, Denise," says Claudette, "because you're always curious to learn." Seven parts in all, but today, alongside the *Pédrégal*, they feel almost like a snap. We actually enjoy ourselves, laughing when it comes time to mix the pistachio paste into the butter cream. It's the colour of baby diarrhea.

But hanging like a threat over this labour-crazy day is lunch. This is, after all, our very last day of class with Claudette. It is, after all, an occasion. We've had potlucks for our last class days with Alfred, Fabrice, Ardis, even Pierre. But who in here has the time or energy to cook and bake this week? Who has the energy to organize yet another event?

And besides, I keep insisting, this is Claudette. This isn't Ardis, an adventurous and generous eater who will appreciate glutinous rice balls or bean paste dumplings. Claudette won't touch the stuff. Lorrie and Trina, however, are convinced Claudette will be insulted that we haven't cooked for her as we have for the other teachers. But Tara, like me, is positive Claudette would much prefer takeout from Dani's, our favourite Greek restaurant in LaSalle. By dint of general exhaustion, and our just going ahead and doing it, Tara and I prevail. But even the simpler plan has its complications, including keeping Claudette from buying her lunch in the cafeteria, trying to finish at least part of the *Pédrégal* before setting off for Dani's at noon, and making it all look like nothing's afoot.

Returning with drippy bags marked with twenty-five people's orders, Tara and I get a grumpy greeting. "If I don't eat soon, I'm going to be sick," declares Trina. The others have to be dragged away from their *Pédrégals* to eat at all. But the most disappointing reaction is Claudette's. She acts unimpressed by her double serving of chicken brochettes, unimpressed by the gift certificate we bought her from Rita's cake supply shop. Somewhere in the silence of our eating she says, "Well, don't take too long. We've still got a lot of work to do."

Tonight we graduate.

But first, another exam. Plate presentation is all done with smoke and mirrors, though, thankfully, Claudette has talked Ardis out of using the mirrors we were originally supposed to be tested on. (Nothing like trying to wipe a smear of mousse off a mirror.) Instead we've got large, black plastic trays and the miniature pastries we made the day before. Colour, line, contrast, shape, height, texture. These are the elements we're to keep in mind as we arrange our pastries in concentric circles, triangles, diagonal lines, and try not to mangle them in the process.

I'm nervous, but nothing like the nervous I used to get. We slip on our latex gloves and survey the trays of pastries: fifteen hundred *Opéras* and mini-tarts, *macarons* filled with *crème légère* and raspberries, and our *croustillant praliné et pistache*, proud little stacks of everything but the kitchen sink. Tonight we will serve these to the people in our lives who know what this year has meant, what it has given and what it has cost.

Now we just have to make the place look worthy of an occasion. The upstairs auditorium is like the rest of the school, a hulking, impersonal space; we set upon it like fairy godmothers. Cindi from professional cooking has brought in a helium tank, bags of white, black and gold balloons, string and paper clips. "It will look really nice," she promises of the balloon arch these bare-bone supplies will produce. I blow up balloons for a while, then help Nadia wrap Christmas icicle lights around the two fake ficus trees at the base of the stage. Up close it looks pretty pathetic, but standing at the back of the auditorium as the arch fills out balloon by balloon, rising with each addition, a little magic happens.

Then suddenly we're back to crisis mode. Wendy has somehow left Trina and two other students' names off the list of grad committee members on the program. Trina's pissed, Wendy apologetic—the first time I think I've seen her apologize for anything. I'm feeling guilty myself since I proofread the program. So much for my professional skills. There's only one thing to do: Wendy and I spend the next two hours in the classroom writing in the missing names.

I run Nadia to her house to pick up flower arrangements, then back to the auditorium where the arch is looking downright buoyant. At five I race home to shower and write my speech.

I was thrilled when my classmates asked me to write this public thank you to our teachers. I am the writer, after all. I even coached the two grads from cooking and butchery, who will be expressing their thanks to their teachers tonight—"keep it short, make it personal." But I have yet to write a word myself. At six I'm still drying my hair, writing furiously on index cards on the bathroom counter, and berating myself. I haven't learned a thing. I will be forever late for life and forever saying, yes, sure, I can do that.

There's so much to say and so many ways to say it. How to sum up these four complex, radically different, dearly beloved people? As I choke up trying to describe Alfred in fifty words or less, I realize I've avoided writing anything because it's been a way of staving off the inevitable. Graduating means goodbye.

Beauch and Georgia drop me off at school ten minutes late and speed off on a mystery errand. In the dining room, everyone's decked out under their clean white chef's jackets: heels, make-up, sparkly things that catch the light. Claudette's in a slinky black dress, her hair newly pouffed. She picks up Jing's little boy and presses her cheek to his.

A few of us had talked earlier about handing out hairnets to everyone and then, on cue, throwing them up in the air at the end of the ceremony, our version of mortarboards. But I remember this only when we're marching into the auditorium and then it's too late. We file into the front rows of the auditorium, past beaming parents, husbands, wives and children. We fold down our chairs, sit down…and suddenly I'm on the floor. My seat is broken; there's nothing to keep the seat perpendicular to the back. I get the chair and me back up, trying not to laugh because if I start I won't be able to stop. The only way I can sit at the same level as everyone else is to hold all my weight on the floor with my feet. Oh, my beloved school. It's broken but strangely beautiful tonight: the balloon archway, Nadia's Christmas icicles, our teachers sitting on stage, looking out at us, proud and happy, the best of stage sets.

Joe Mercuri, the celeb owner/chef of Brontë and a grad of Pearson's cooking program, was supposed to be our keynote speaker. But then his sous-chef got sick so he had to work in his place and then another chef was asked to speak, but he also got sick. So it's just us and that's fine. Rena goes to the lecturn and speaks about the life of a cook, about her father's doubts that a life in the kitchen was the right thing for her to pursue, about how he came to see that it was.

We file up on stage, class by class, shake Alfred's hand, and are handed fancy new aprons with the Pearson logo embroidered on front, keychains and pins, generous gifts from a school that can't afford to replace a chair.

And then I'm up there, index cards in hand. My speech isn't what I'd fantasized a month ago. It's not well-structured, not at all writerly, and probably larded with clichés. But I've kept it short and it is personal.

"A school is only as great as its teachers," I shakily begin, "and in Pastry we've been blessed with a stellar quartet. Ardis, Alfred, Claudette and Fabrice couldn't be more different in their teaching styles, but they're a united front when it comes to giving their all to their students. And they are united in their passion for pastry. Guys," and I turn to look back at them, "we wouldn't be here without you. Please accept this small gesture of thanks…from us to you," and I duck to pick up the bouquet of carnations I've hidden behind the podium. "Thank you for believing in us, for putting up with us, and for passing on so very much!"

Ardis stands and begins walking to the podium, an expectant smile on her face, though I haven't called her name. I was planning on starting with Alfred. Ardis keeps coming, keeps smiling. I must look surprised as I shuffle through my cards trying to find my notes about her, because Ardis suddenly looks embarrassed. Everyone laughs, even her.

"Ardis Root, your patience is legendary, as is your warmth. And your love and respect for chocolate has been contagious. You actually taught us how to temper chocolate.

"Alfred de Luca, you taught us as much about life and never, *ever* giving up as you did about timing charts for bread and how to roll puff pastry.

"Fabrice Frelat, you told us early on, 'Never lose your smile, girls!' Of course, we did, but your generous, allowing attitude eased the way so many days.

"And Claudette Groulx, hardly last and hardly least—you've given us an idea of perfection, something to aim at, something to strive for. That's a priceless gift."

One by one, they come up to get their single carnations. When Claudette, the last, crosses in front of the podium she gives me a look that is hard to describe. It isn't just a smile. All of her is shining out. She looks proud and humble and very beautiful.

"Let's go!" I say, raising my arm with the remaining carnations, and my friends, my team, cheers.

Ardis has spent weeks putting together a PowerPoint presentation from photos gathered along the journey: people working, people clowning, people learning and trying and hugging. Us in all our crazy glory. She's managed to find a photo of every single person graduating. There was only one choice for a soundtrack: *We Are the Champions*. As the photos come up and fade out, we hoot, we clap, we try not to cry.

Walking up the aisle later, Georgia thrusts a grocery-store bouquet, the mystery errand, in my hands and Beauch slips me a gift-wrapped DVD. (*Spider-Man*, what every new pastry grad needs after too many days making the dreaded mokas.)

We pose for photos: me with Min, me with Cindi from cooking. No one can stop smiling. In the dining room, we pose for group shots. Everyone wants to be photographed with Claudette.

But what's happened to our thousand and one pastries? Only a few trays have been put out. "Claudette asked me why so few of our pastries are on trays," Jen whispers to me, as we continue to throw our arms around each other for the cameras. "I told her we'd just done what Ardis told us to do. Claudette got really upset: 'Then why did Ardis tell me to make so many if she didn't need them, if she wasn't planning on putting them all out? Why is she doing this to me?'"

Georgia, lovely in her off-white dress with the silk flower on the shoulder, her First Communion dress, is among the few eating, popping pastry after pastry. I make sure to get my favourites, the *macarons* filled with *crème légère* and raspberries. "Try these," I urge Beauch. "They're the best things we ever made."

We're among the last to leave. "A lot of leftover pastries, eh?" I ask Claudette, who's gathering still-full trays.

She rolls her eyes. "Come into the Lab," she says. "I'll give you a box to take home."

The evening class is in the Lab making bread. They're all smiles and compliments, having watched the graduation from the back of the auditorium with Pierre. They stand at their work stations, eating our pastries and looking wistful. Oh, to be graduating.

Claudette packs us a box of cookies and another of pastries. And then she and her black party dress sweep out into the night.

Back home, I wash my chef's jacket for the three hundredth time and try not to think of the immediate future. Though we've technically graduated, there are still two more exams to pass: plated desserts tomorrow and advanced decorating on Monday. In between there's the overnight to Ottawa, a day at the Cordon Bleu, back by Voyageur bus just in time for the parish synod Beauch and I are coordinating Friday night and all day Saturday. Then Tuesday begins twelve-hour days at La Gâterie, followed by a week at Le Fournil and another at Pâtisserie Fine Saveureuse. Spider-Man thinks he's got it bad trying to save New York? If I stop, I'll crash or fall sleep standing right where I am, even if it might be in the walk-in. I am tired from head to foot, tired in my brain, tired in my lungs and legs. I'm conscious, too, that although I'm relieved and blissed out from the evening, I'm wistful, too. Oh, not to be graduating.

There's only bits of theory to study the next morning for the plated desserts exam. How to prepare for something so *à la minute*? As I pack for Ottawa—we're piling into cars right after we pile our customers' plates with *vacherins* and those still-pesky soufflés—I keep flashing back to scenes from the night before: Rena at the podium in her short, silky summer dress, the wiggly, giggly line of us taking photos, Claudette in her blonde and black glory, the look she gave me as she came up for her carnation.

The auditorium has returned to its natural state, nothing resembling glory. In fact, it's a shambles, none of us thinking to stay behind last night and tidy up. The balloon arch is a puddle of gold and black on the stage. Should we pop the balloons? we ask each other. We can't. Too symbolic. We move slowly, companionably, sweeping, unwinding the icicle lights. Something was accomplished last night. It's not just that we (unofficially) graduated. We pulled off a grand event. "Best grad ever," the director of the school told Ardis.

We drift downstairs, nearly forgetting what's coming next. But as I push through the swinging doors of the Lab, the barometric pressure shifts. In one hour, people—customers—will begin arriving for dessert. This is not like boxing mousse cakes, putting them on a trolley and wheeling them into the walk-in where they'll sit until someone buys them. This is *service*, a word cooking students understand in a way pastry students don't. We will produce, serve and take the resulting heat, all in real time.

Danny has divided us into two teams. I'm serving at the first sitting, baking for the second. "I've never served a table," Tamara says as we unfurl and smooth maroon tablecloths over the restaurant's dozen tables. I have, though decades ago, and with no fond memories. I never could get the hang of stacking plates from wrist to forearm. Luckily, we're ferrying single dessert-size plates out to our customers today.

Michael, Le Saucier's maitre d', arrives. He's my age, a retired engineer who's a graduate of both cooking and pastry. He wants us to get things exactly right at the front of the house and bosses us around as we scurry with napkins and cutlery. Still, I'm grateful for clear direction, something I won't be getting from the Lab or the kitchen, which we've taken over for today. Both are in an uproar.

Pretty much like my brain, which struggles to retain all the steps for all the desserts. Unmould, plate, nuke for the molten cake. *Vacherin*: four or five miniature scoops of ice cream, then pipe with Chantilly rosettes. But what number pastry tip? And the lemon soufflé, which we've been making and throwing away for two weeks now…juice and zest one lemon, or is it one and a half? Bake for eight minutes. Or is it nine?

What really has me more worried, though, is the part in our instructions that says "decorate the plate." I know this is what this entire module is about, but we've actually had very little do-it experience, Danny referring us to illustrations in our text: "Pipe small dots about one-inch apart, forming a ring between the dessert and the edge of the plate. Drag a small wooden skewer through the centre of the circles in one continuous motion to create a string of hearts." Oookay. We've made crème anglaise, chocolate sauce, berry coulis, but I've never poured a coulis onto a plate. We've spun sugar nests and rolled wafers into cigarettes, but I've never negotiated the proper angle to lay one on a *vacherin*.

The first customers to arrive are Linda and Gil, old friends. They're the only people I've invited, most of our friends having day jobs. Even Beauch can't come today. My friends come bearing gifts: a bouquet of roses and a copy of *The Soul of a Chef*, Michael Ruhlman's second book. These are friends who "get" it, though I can see that Linda doesn't quite get the *vacherin*, which I've recommended. It's so hard it bucks both fork and knife, slides like a puck across her plate. "How do you eat this?" she whispers, trying not to embarrass me.

More people come, more than the few who've made reservations. Orders are taken and desserts sent out, spectacular desserts. An oval lagoon of crème anglaise surrounds a molten chocolate cake. Sugar baubles sit angelically on a soufflé. Once again, I'm knocked out by my sisters in pastry.

My friends leave, the pace slows. I find Trina washing dishes alone in the kitchen. She's annoyed that she's been stuck here because she's the only one who knows how to run the dishwasher. First, her name missing from the grad program, now this. She shows me how to work the dishwasher and we stack and steam plates, cups and glasses for the second sitting.

By the time we get back to the Lab, it's nearly two. Everyone's at their stations, supremely ready, *mises en place* ordered before them: zested lemon, squeezed juice, separated eggs, scoop of sugar. Our classmates weren't taking care of the dishes; they were taking care of themselves. I run for containers and ingredients, my body trying to match the situation, but it's dragging from the output of the last twenty-four hours. I reach for my (top-of-the-line Henckel's) zester. Not there. Reach for my paring knife. It's not there either. I fight off a scream because there's no one to blame but myself and my Sure! Of course! Borrow it! generosity with my tools.

"Denise!" Danny's barking my name for the first order. I've got to get my head out of my toolbox and make something. At first I think it's lucky to be starting with the *vacherin*. Nothing to bake at least. Michèle's next to me, our scoopers going in and out alternately of the caramel and vanilla ice creams. "Shit!" we say at the same time, because the little balls melt as soon as they hit the meringue, their contours disappearing. We speed through the second layer, knowing it will only get worse. I move to the condiment table, grab a squeeze bottle of crème anglaise, make a little moat around the *vacherin*, plop a spun sugar nest on top. I show Danny my plate. "Okay," he says, neither of us overly impressed.

By the time, I get to item two, the lemon soufflé, I'm practically hyperventilating, and by the time item three, the molten cake, gets unmoulded into my decidedly freeform coulis puddle, I can barely speak. Lorrie tells me later a few people were worried about me—I'd turned a shade between shrimp and lobster.

And of all the days to have asked Ariel, my daughter who's interested in food photography, to come in to take photos! Through the afternoon she walks among us in one of my chef's jackets and a hairnet, trying to document the chaos but not be of it. I take a photo of her perched on a stool, eating my lemon soufflé, which, as it turned out, had no customer to claim it.

And then it's over: no more orders, no more customers. "Everyone passed," says Danny. Whatever went awry, he knows it was our first day of service and our last day of school. But it's only as we're cleaning up in the blessed blank after that it really hits. This is the last time we will all be together in the Lab. I'm standing at the sink when the tears come. Nadia's huddled over our table bawling her eyes out. "Don't look at me," Jen warns.

"I love you, Qiang!" sniffs Michèle and grabs him as he walks by.

"I love you, too, Michèle!" says Qiang, the only one among us who never lost his smile, though his is sad now.

We're a vale of tears, a deep, wide pool of coulis.

But Claudette is already here, dressed for travel, impatiently waiting to drive us to Ottawa. There isn't even time for a good cry. We clean up, change clothes, pile into the three waiting cars. This, like the rooms, has been prearranged. It's me, Min and Claudette in Claudette's car. Everyone else is in Lorrie's and Michèle's, the fun cars. Michèle has bought a jumbo size pair of women's underpants—

pink—with the words Pastry 2004 written in black marker and has skewered them onto her antenna. As we head onto the highway, it billows like a parachute.

On the two-hour drive to Ottawa, Claudette talks non-stop. This is what I find out: she's not happily married. Okay, she's miserably married. Her Czech husband had an affair on a trip back to the mother country last summer and wants to return this summer. "If he goes, I told him, he goes for good," Claudette says. He still denies the whole thing, although Claudette intercepted an email from the girl and Fabrice had a Czech friend translate it for her. Fabrice? So he and Claudette must have been close at some point. Min leans forward from the back seat, hanging, too, on every word. She's getting most of it.

What else we find out: nobody, not even Ardis, wanted to accompany us on this trip to Ottawa. Claudette didn't hijack the class outing. She was told by Ardis that she had to go with us. Also, the tension between Claudette and Fabrice hit new heights this spring. As we near the outskirts of Ottawa, she complains about his laziness, his sloppiness. But wasn't he also the friend who tried to help her pin evidence on her wandering mate?

By the time we drag our bags into the hotel lobby, I'm exhausted and depressed. Claudette's story is so desperately sad; I feel a new compassion for her.

She, however, appears energized. "Come on," she tells Min and me as we enter our freezing cold room. "We don't have much time. Min, you wash up first, then Denise will go, then I'll go. We've only got twenty minutes." My compassion shrinks by a foot. She never lets up. I hear shrieks of laughter from the fun suite next door.

We have reservations at a French restaurant in the Gatineau. It's nicely done traditional French fare and we make a big deal about ordering every dessert on the menu. It's not even that expensive, but I feel a pang for my absent classmates. They're not even getting a Chinese banquet for all those hours of fundraising. I think of screaming Dora, the apple peels and chicken gizzards underfoot, the fog of flour, hardened chocolate on every surface. We're being rewarded for those tough times. I hope they will be, too.

Back at the hotel it's a pajama party with everyone shooting videos on their digital cameras. Michèle wears the jumbo panties over her PJ pants, until Trina swipes them and puts them on her head. Min leans over Wendy, seated in a chair, exposing a good amount of cleavage. Min zooms in with her camera and shows Wendy the image. "Is that your bum or your breasts?" she asks. We all look at the screen; it's impossible to tell. Wendy laughs harder than anyone. In her quiet way Min has gotten her own back.

It's still freezing in our room when we turn in at midnight, and maybe it's this or the fear of snoring with Claudette present, or the Coke I drank at eleven, but I can't fall asleep. I toss as quietly as I can, trying not to disturb Min, who's sharing the bed with me. I stagger out of the lightest sleep at 6:00 a.m., our wake-up time, with a burning question: How *was* one to cut into those too-crisp *vacherins* yesterday? I have to know.

Luckily, the expert is standing right here in her PJS, though Claudette doesn't seem pleased to be asked a technical pastry question so early in the morning. Okay, she says, the meringues and ice cream should have been assembled ahead of time, then frozen. This would have softened up the meringues a bit, not to mention averting a whole lot of anxiety. "Thank you," I say. "I knew you'd know."

As we drive up the circular driveway to the Cordon Bleu it's really hard not to laugh. This yellow mansion with its "Toujours Provence" touches is about as far from the Pearson School of Culinary Arts in LaSalle, Quebec, as we could get. The only thing the two schools have in common is their purpose: teaching people to cook and bake. But getting there would be so different here. As we're taken on a hushed tour of the opulently restored mansion, through the student lounge with its cushy chairs, to the well-stocked library, into the teaching kitchens where each and every student has her own stovetop, oven and fridge, it comes to me where chefs get their attitude. One would feel like a member of the ruling class here, as in chefs rule! "A nine-month program here costs $40,000!" whispers Trina, who once considered coming here.

I think of our alma mater, poor, rundown old place. And then I think of the energy in that place, the pace of that place, how much we've learned, how much talent I've seen grow around me. And I'm grateful that I don't live in a world made to fit me, a world of sunny, South-of-France florals and tailor-made work stations with everything in easy reach. What a fall it would be from this to the real life of a working kitchen. I'm grateful that I've had to learn—as a writer, as a person and now as a pastry student—how to fit myself to the world.

We're ushered into a chic demonstration theatre. Warm, saturated-with-butter croissants and *chocolatines* wait for us in baskets, good coffee, too. Privilege has its perks. Laurent Pagé, a sweet-faced young Frenchman, comes in to introduce himself. He's a part-time teacher and full-time pastry chef in the school's restaurant, he tells us, and will be our chef for the day. And yes, he made these croissants just for us early this morning.

He's stiff, a bit condescending even. But an hour into his ambitious program (two ultra-complex mousse cakes, plus a *pièce monté* of pulled sugar), Chef Laurent must realize from our questions that he's not "baking for the ladies" today, that we've made a génoise or two, that we're nearly as keen (if not nearly as skilled) as he is, and that Claudette has been a pastry chef—in Montreal's top hotels yet—for more years than he is old. Then someone mentions LaSalle.

"Ville LaSalle?" he asks. "You're from Ville La Salle?" When he first came to Montreal to work as a pastry chef at the Casino, he lived on Boulevard de la Vérendrye. Good memories, it looks like. He smiles at us, we smile back.

It's wonderful to watch him. First of all, he's awfully cute (Trina seems especially smitten), with a Tobey Maguire smile and blue eyes. He pronounces "sugar" like a southern gentleman: shugah, and sift like shif. Charming. But more compelling is the way he moves. Laurent is in possession of a coltish, but controlled, energy I've seen in other French-from-France chefs: utterly alert, smooth, purposeful and seeming to enjoy every efficient move. It's the bearing, too: upright, bouncy on the balls of the feet. I could watch him all day.

He's been bouncing and baking more than half his life, it turns out. Began his training in the south of France at fifteen (he's now thirty-five), but always with the dream of coming to Canada someday. I notice the little red maple leaf embroidered on the collar of his jacket. "Europe," he says and shrugs.

Laurent begins with the basics: the various *joconde* layers, the various mousses with their *bains-marie* of melting chocolate and softening gelatin leaves, thirty-five percent cream whipped to just-right peaks. When he works with white chocolate for one cake, he looks up at us. "Be careful with the white chocolate glaze. It loves to set!" Jen and I look at each other. We know.

Through the morning's demos, I keep thinking: He's doing what we do! Yes, he's smoother, defter, more confident. He does things we haven't yet dared to do, like smoothing the top edge of his mousse cakes with the palm of his hand. But the method, that once dirty word, is the same. The method is in his head as it is in ours.

After assembling and decorating the *entremets*—encircled with thin ribbons of chocolate, like birthday presents—he hands out slices on china plates. One is a *dacquoise* with red fruits and white chocolate cream, the other a *biscuit Viennois au chocolat*. The flavours are separate and intense, the texture like edible silk.

But it isn't until the sugar demo that we see what Laurent is really made of. He begins with the heat lamps, with the *shugah* and glucose and microwave, plus the little pots of food colouring. We've seen Jürg at work and photos of the work of Swiss sugar master Erik Potter. But we really haven't seen anything until now. Laurent heats and pulls and sculpts the flaming hot sugar into birds and tropical flowers, then begins to attach them to foot-long cylinders of lime-green sugar. It looks treacherously fragile, but Laurent's expression never changes from its alert, all-is-equal state. He pulls and glues, bends and adds.

When the structure, an astonishing engineering feat, begins to droop—"Uh-oh," gasps Michèle and points—Laurent catches the sinking cylinder. Another section threatens to collapse, and this time Claudette, who's been holding back all day, letting him be the teacher, goes behind the demo table and holds up the part so he can bolster another failing joint. He kids with her in French, still adding decorations, reinforcing the weak connections. He does not panic, he does not choke. He looks engaged and pleased at every moment, even when the entire *pièce monté* looks likely to topple. And when he finally decides: *c'est fini*, he looks up at us and really smiles. The wildly curvaceous sculpture with its flaming-hot colours probably isn't what he'd originally planned. But something beautiful stands there, something that did not exist an hour ago.

We barely make it to the bus terminal; Claudette guns the car, Trina wrestles with the map, Min, Jen and I bite our nails in the back seat. If we miss this bus, we have to stay in Ottawa another night. (I'm due at our church in two hours to coordinate a weekend-long conference.) Claudette turns too soon and we end up in a one-way bind, a long block away. Trina jumps out of the car and runs toward the terminal, Min, Jen and me trailing behind.

When we make it into the station, there's Trina standing in line, tickets in hand.

"Oh, Trina," we sigh. Sweating, gasping for breath, Trina is still the most solid of us all. She's not just the strongest physically (she's the only one in class who never missed a day of school), we have all leaned on her in so many ways. She makes sure we're settled before darting back to Claudette, parked who knows where by now. We find three seats at the very back of the bus, Min between me and Jen, and too tired to talk, we fall asleep.

Only a handful of us are taking the advanced decorating exam the Monday after Ottawa. Everyone else, through a weird bit of scheduling, took it nearly ten days ago. The rest of the Ottawa gang basically went from our trip into *stage*, except for Wendy, who slid right into summer vacation. Pleading the need to spend the summer with her kids (who among us with kids doesn't need that after this year?) she petitioned to postpone her second *stage* until the fall. I know I won't envy her come September, especially since Wendy also has to make up for the two weeks of *stage* she skipped out on in March. By then I'll be free of school and *stage* and mousse cakes, but it bothers me now, especially thinking of the next frantic month. I've realized again this year that I really don't like Special Cases. (No Special Cases! I used to warn my journalism students at the beginning of every semester.)

Weird scheduling, weird exam. Instead of testing us on how beautifully we can sculpt a rose out of fondant or make calla lilies from gum paste, Claudette has us making nougatine baskets. There's no meditative rolling and shaping of soft, pliable dough today. We're firing up the ovens, oiling our cutting boards, taking out mallets for a burn and bang fest.

I start out instantly on the wrong foot by forgetting to rinse my pot with salt and vinegar. Claudette docks points for missing this step, so it's back to remeasuring the glucose. With my hands already shaking, it's a sticky, icky operation. And a first: I can't get the consistency of my glucose and sugar quite right. Rena and Tara are already sculpting their baskets—ultra-thin and multi-pleated—and I'm still at the stove guessing if the sugar's right.

I'm off-balance through the hundred next steps: can't get the nougatine rolled thin enough. It's thick like a flapjack and about as bendable as a frisbee. I start over again with a new batch, but number two is, if this is possible, even more of a dud. And the handles! When I put my weight into my super-size Henckels, the nougatine shatters everywhere.

See how much you still can't do? See what you haven't perfected? See what a crapshoot this still is? It's not supposed to end like this.

I'm banging and rolling and pulling my hair out when Michèle comes in with books for Min and me. She and Trina bought them for us in the Cordon Bleu gift shop after we left on Friday. *Dessert Techniques* is the most beautiful professional pastry book I've ever seen, glossy and packed with how-to photographs. Min and I are speechless. Where did the money come from? I ask Michèle, and she tells me we were each entitled to a book costing up to $50.

I turn back to see Rena and Anna watching this. What about *their* books? Fabrice and Alfred have told me that instead of getting books from the Cordon Bleu, which is what they originally wanted, they're being given something else. "It's all being taken care of," Alfred keeps saying.

Something doesn't feel right. I've had a night at a hotel in Ottawa, eaten in a fine French restaurant, watched a master pastry chef, even had my bus trip home paid for. And now this? I guiltily put the book in its silver Cordon Bleu bag under my table.

And then it's back to burning sugar and lost time. I end up having to decorate my first clumsy basket, hoping to redeem it with a delicate floral design in royal icing. But I'm too indecisive with my dots and vines and have to do them over three times. Trina brings her basket by. It's gorgeous, with blue posies and a pale-green filigree vine.

"Claudette must have clapped," I say, trying not to feel jealous.

"She told me it was *too* thin," says Trina, incredulous.

When I finally take my basket to Claudette, this small container for four hours of frustration, she looks at it for a minute. "Your borders are uneven," she says. She turns it around. "Not bad. You pass."

And that's it. I clean up slowly, pack up my tools. I go to thank Claudette—for everything really. For her vision of perfection, which has been both beacon and impossible dream. I change in the now-empty locker room and pile all my stuff—big toolbox, little toolbox—into the van. This morning I'd parked in the back parking lot, off limits to students, thinking what the hell, it's the last day. There's a note under the wiper from the director of the school. "If you ever park your car here again, it will be towed. This is a warning."

I am chastened in all ways: this cold note, my flubby little basket. I drive the few blocks home, stunned that the end has been so muffled. No sparklers, no trumpets. And stunned that this is, in fact, the end.

13

Into the Fire

Of course it isn't the end. There's *stage*. Or rather, *stage* times three. I'm wondering now about this brilliant idea of doing three placements in four weeks, the brainchild of someone with more pep, drive and chutzpah than I've got now.

It's only 7:45 a.m., but Rita Djerrahian has beaten Trina and me by an hour. "The heat's on, girls," she tells us, shepherding us into La Gâterie. "Welcome to wedding season."

She looks at us appraisingly—"You need coffee"—and sets to work grinding beans. "It's Armenian coffee. Strong, but you'll like it." We were only here a month ago setting up our *stage*, but I'd nearly forgotten how (I search for a non-judgmental word) stocked? crammed? dense? Rita's shop is. A few steps beyond the showroom of show-stopper cakes is the fifteen-by-thirty-foot work space that functions as commercial kitchen, cake-supply store, classroom, and congregating point for friends, family and customers. Cake pans of every persuasion hang from the ceiling. Plastic tubs of rolled fondant stand nearly person-high. I can smell the fondant's compressed sweetness, even through the coffee and Rita's Opium perfume.

Coffee poured, Rita clears two small places on a cluttered table and shows us how to roll, shape and sculpt stephanotis buds and flax blossoms out of gum paste. "Yes, like that," she says. Rita used to paint

Fabergé eggs in her native Ethiopia and her business card aptly reads "Sugar Artistry."

She fills us in on the week. Three wedding cakes are to be made for Saturday. The first, a three-tiered white cake, is for a couple from Nigeria. They don't have a big budget, so Rita's promised something pretty, but not too elaborate. The second is for a French-Canadian couple. The groom is a pianist; a crown of sugar treble clefs will stand atop their three layers of chocolate ganache cake. Last, for a couple from Hong Kong: three ovals of white cake to be adorned with sugar calla lilies. Rita shows us the magazine photocopy the bride brought in on her first visit six months ago. The cake looks complicated, with lilies coming out the top layer and stems showing through a narrow column of Plexiglas between the first and second layers. It will involve building a special stand.

The day flies as we fashion fields of flowers and calla stems, a symphony's worth of treble clefs. We stop for more Armenian coffee and a slice of leftover chocolate cake in the afternoon. I'm enjoying myself, sitting on my bum by the hour making flower after flower. And I find myself liking Rita more and more: she's funny, dramatic, and full of gossip about her competitors (who sometimes masquerade as her friends) in the West Island Cake Club. She's grateful and happy to have us here. She says so every few minutes.

While we sit, Rita bakes cakes and answers the constantly ringing phone. The Nigerian groom brings in family members to show off his cake and pay the rest of his balance. There are tense calls from the Hong Kong couple's wedding planner. Apparently they don't want to pay Rita's downtown parking when she delivers the cake Saturday, nor do they seem to know where the hall's parking lot is.

"How much longer are you staying?" Trina asks when we finally leave just before 6:30. "Oh, another five hours," says Rita.

More flowers Wednesday. And coffee and bagels and Armenian music on the CD player. "You go crazy otherwise," says Rita, who over the years has come up with strategies for keeping her sanity. There is a psychology of directing people, she tells us. "When Martha

Stewart comes up with some new look, everyone wants that. When it's impractical, I feel like killing them and her." Rita throws back her head to laugh. "So you take couples' photos, but you add your input. I want to make something that also gives me pleasure. I want there to be love in there."

By 2:30, it's cake time. We shave off the tops of all the layers to make them equal in height. I try hard to keep my hand steady as I guide the serrated knife. Try to keep my mind steady, too. Who's getting the chocolate cake and what kind of butter cream is going inside? While Trina and I fill and cover the cakes, Rita hurries off to the front to consult with a couple on their fall wedding.

"I did not receive the cheque yet and you didn't call me back about the parking facility." Rita's on the phone Friday morning with the Chinese wedding planner. She's calm but firm. "The cheque," she repeats. The balance should have arrived two weeks ago. "You want me to sit there Saturday and leave the cake unattended? I need to think about my car. I need to think about my cake."

When she finally gets off the phone—never having raised her voice—Rita looks more tired than she has all week. She rolls out a giant circle of fondant on a thick piece of plastic; then lifts it ever so carefully up and over the bottom layer of the Nigerian couple's cake—peeling off the plastic when it's in the just-right position, because once that baby's down, there's no moving it. She cuts the excess and strokes the fondant smooth over the top and sides. She's tried to keep the costs down on this cake by limiting the flowers, but it's a beauty even so.

Rita's husband, Levon, comes by to cut the Plexiglas platform for the calla lily cake. He's cheery, charming, a man who looks like he's been asked to do this kind of thing many, many times before. She raises doubts, questions. He reassures, he delivers. "Now I can breathe," she says, when he leaves. Between a visit from her sister and more calls from the Chinese wedding planner (now asking about the refrigeration requirements of the cake) she's redoing the treble crown for the musical cake. "We had so many discussions over it, I forgot what our final decision was," she says, unsticking the little royal icing roses Trina and I had attached earlier.

The nuptial hour is upon us. Overnight the cakes have been transformed. Rita has draped the lily cake with pale avocado-green drapes; the music cake with regal white ones. "I worked until two in the morning, then came back at six," Rita says. "I'm so tired I don't know if I'm speaking English or Armenian." Trina and I fit the lily stems onto the Plexiglas stand, add a final flourish of gold dust on the white drapes, pearl on the green.

At one, Rita dons a clean chef's jacket, packs up her cake repair kit—a jar of royal icing, white cotton gloves, extra flowers, Exacto knife, ribbon, floral tape—and we're off for the Dorval church where the Nigerian couple will exchange vows in an hour. My job is to sit in the back of the van—we've taken out the middle row of seats—and make sure the cake doesn't go anywhere. It makes me think of the time I was helping my mother with a big party, transporting a five-pound wheel of brie baked in puff pastry on the back seat of my car. When I arrived, I realized the pastry had sprung a leak. Five pounds of melted brie sat on my velour upholstery. (The car was known forever after as the brie-mobile.) I almost tell Rita this story, but don't. The mood has shifted; things are getting serious. I hold onto the rack tighter.

The church basement is alive with African music as we arrange the cake on the waiting table. Rita looks at the cake for a moment. It needs a little extra something, she thinks, so we add tiny pink flowers at the base. And then it's back to the shop to finish off the other two cakes. No one's joking now and no one thinks to turn the radio on. We dust the lilies—yellow inside, green at the base; Rita twists them into sinuous bouquets. Then we load cakes two and three onto bread racks and ease them into the van.

The sky is clouding up as we cross the bridge to Île Ste-Hélène. As we go around a curve, another cloud rises: the sweet (now nearly sickly) smell of fondant. We park, carefully lift the bread racks and hope for nothing underfoot. The banquet room in Hélène de Champlain is decorated like a music conservatory, the tables with name cards reading Vivaldi, Chopin, Mozart. Rita's three-tiered creation, treble clefs bobbing, is in perfect harmony.

But a few blocks from Centre Mont-Royal and our final delivery, it begins to rain. Where *are* we going to park? It's never been settled. Rita gives it her best guess and somehow we end up in an underground loading zone, find a cart to load the lily cakes on, find the right banquet room.

But it's only when Rita—white gloves donned, pastry bag in hand—steps back and looks at her cake in that still-empty room, that I'm reminded what this is about, what it's for. It's been easy to forget about marriage, happiness, commitment in the madness of this week. Love! Rita steps back, then steps in and removes one of the lily bouquets. She's right. In this case, less is more beautiful. There's love in the gesture. I remember this later when we're sitting in a Tim Horton's where we've gone to celebrate *The Gazette* agreeing to run my story on La Gâterie, a coup for us both. I've gone to another editor who thinks it could make a good summer story, this being wedding season. The editor also said something about food fights, which makes me wonder what he's expecting. But for now, Rita's ecstatic. All our cakes have been made and delivered and we sit there with coffee and pecan Danish, laughing with relief.

We've worked so many hours with Rita that I actually have a couple of days off between *stages*. I go back to the school to drop off the tax rebate form for my first *stage* with the cookbook writer, thinking it must be the last day for evening class before they take off for *their* second *stage*. But when I push through the back door, the store and the storeroom are dark. Passing Le Saucier, I see the back of Michael, the maître d', as he unfurls a burgundy tablecloth. Of course: the last day of service for the year.

I turn the corner, expecting to see the lights of the classroom on, Fabrice or Alfred cruising down the hall. But the lights in the classroom are out, the door locked, the stools upturned on the counters. The main doors of the Lab are locked, too. I peer into the darkness, making out the Hobarts, the stoves, the work stations, Lucy, the rotating oven. And I am hit by the terrible stillness of it. Michèle and Nadia aren't bent over the front counter, sculpting sugar lilies. Tara isn't dashing by, a tray of tuiles carried high. The Lab is like a ballroom with no dancers.

Back in my van, I turn on the radio for comfort. A big, fat Strauss waltz is playing. And I have to smile at the perfect timing of it. The empty ballroom, the remembered blur of movement.

A few days later when I'm rolling pie crust at Le Fournil in Westmount I find myself missing those funny fondant days with Rita. Le Fournil is a frenetic place, literally a sweatshop, with rich customers out front buying their $15 pies and $4 brownies, while we workers toil in the back next to the bread ovens in thirty-four-degree heat and seventy-percent humidity.

I'm lonely, too, working alongside Le Fournil's pastry chef, a young woman who barely speaks to me the first day. On day two she decides to talk and we have a lively conversation about books. She's an avid reader, especially appreciates good food writing. I come in on day three thinking we've broken the ice, but it's frozen over again. She opens and closes all week. By the last day it's so hot and I'm so tired, I don't even attempt talk.

But after this week I know something important: Pie is my favourite thing in the pastry universe. I love mixing the dough, I love rolling the dough, I love fitting the dough into the pan. There's something that's different about pie dough; the shortening/butter in there makes it yielding and compliant. I roll and it listens. Okay, I'll bend this way. Okay, I'll make myself as thin as you like.

I also learn that I can (mostly) follow directions and be a pastry employee. Natalia hands me a recipe written on a piece of paper towel and says, "Make this." Blondies, brownies, lemon-blueberry tarts, peanut butter cookies. I'm happy to be baking some old favourites. Do I miss *Pédrégals* and *Opèras*? Can't say I do.

I'm on my own a lot here, Natalia assuming that if she tells me something once, that's it. I do appreciate that she's willing to show me her way of doing things. After she dumps all my eggs into my butter/sugar mixture for blondies and I laughingly tell her that Claudette, our teacher, always wants us to add the eggs bit by bit (Natalia doesn't even smile at this), I realize I'm just going to have to say, "*Oui, Chef.*"

Something else becomes apparent this week. I could never, ever, not on your life, do this for a living. The heat, the repetition, the physical nature of this beast. I find myself, like Trina in her first *stage*, counting the days. I count the hours within days, the minutes within those hours. I begin to resent the fact that I have to do this at all. Haven't I already proven everything I needed to prove to myself? To my teachers? Enough already. I'm a writer, I want to cry. And in that endless last day I see that I loved *learning* to do this. I just don't want to keep doing it and doing it and doing it.

The last day proves to be the toughest of all with huge orders and oppressive heat. Even Natalia, who's been doing this job for four years, nearly passes out from dehydration. We're panting, side by side, our bandanas soaked.

Before I limp home, I visit Trina at her second *stage*. She's at Brontë for the next few weeks, the celebrated, major cool restaurant where she's working with pastry chef Mark Tan, another grad of our program. I met Mark the year before starting pastry school, spent two days trailing him in Claudette's class. He's from Taiwan, spent five years as a line cook in a top restaurant there and has paid his dues with Canadian chefs like Rob Feeney in Vancouver. But you'd never know about Mark's fancy past from talking to him or even watching him in a kitchen. He's kind, calm, controlled. When I find him and Trina in Brontë's pastry kitchen at five, they're prepping for service, but there's nothing urgent in the air. They're talking about the properties of buttermilk versus cream. Mark's trying out a new ice cream, has been experimenting on and off all afternoon. Trina looks her happiest self.

I'm glad to see Mark again, to talk to him now after this year's education. He's optimistic about the profession. "Things are changing," he says. "The older chefs, the older ways, are making way for something new. There's room now." And as I watch Mark, an Asian man, and Trina, a woman, take ramekins of basil ice cream from the freezer—Lorri was right in step when she came up with this for the ice cream module—I feel as if I'm getting a sneak preview of this future. The ancient, revered hierarchy that excluded anyone not French, male and white, the old traditions (basil ice cream!) are finally, finally giving way.

Pen Paul Pichitr looks like he might belong to that tradition with his tall toque and his display case filled with mousse cakes. But after a few days, I see he's part of both worlds.

It's pleasant this first morning to drive my new commute: fifteen minutes along the lakeshore against traffic. Min and I will be here together in our last *stage* week. All those extra hours at Rita's the first week amounted to nearly a fourth week, a great relief. I'm also relieved to have company again, especially because I know from Jen that Cheffie doesn't talk much. Of course I'm nervous, too. New chef, new expectations, new ways to mess up. Plus it's back to palmiers, éclairs, and mousseline this week. Back to perfection.

Min and I take turns changing in Pâtisserie Fine Savoureuse's windowless bathroom. The chef seems pleased to see us when we emerge, introduces us to his mother, a tiny lady who smiles a lot and helps out in front. I think she speaks French, though I'm having a hard time understanding her so we mostly bob at each other.

As Min and I watch Pen Paul fill éclairs and bake palmiers, he tells us about himself. He's much more forthcoming than Jen led me to believe, or maybe he's just responding to my writer's barrage of questions. The only negative thing he wrote on Jen's evaluation was that she didn't ask enough questions.

He's Cambodian, he tells us, having immigrated to Montreal with his family in 1980. During his first year of CEGEP, Quebec's junior college system, his father died. "I took over his *fruiterie* in Ville St. Laurent. But after a couple of years I realized I didn't really like the fruit store. It didn't seem like a real business to me."

Attracted to the "happy occasions" nature of the pastry biz, Pen Paul looked into the ITHQ's program for night students. "But you needed six months of pastry experience to even get in." Frustrated, he called his friend Rasmey You, proprietor of Pâtisserie Fine Fidélice, a pastry success story in the Gatineau. Chef You promised to teach him everything he knew.

"I was there for five years," says Pen Paul, running his serrated cake knife under water. "I started with croissants and after two years I graduated to mousse cakes." In the process, he discovered that he not only loved making pastry, but that he was good at it. "I could also work very quickly, which is important."

He seems to sense that speed is not my thing and since it *is* so important and since Min is better and quicker than me and since I seem content to sit on a stool and ask him questions, that's how we spend much of the first couple of days.

I'm happy to sit and watch, because I'm too tired to do much else. Those hot days at Le Fournil have finally done me in. I've even noticed my checks are tighter. I must be eating more to fuel myself. At any rate, I have no energy to impress. I barely have the energy to butter a pan. I wake up Wednesday morning and realize I'm having trouble breathing. Beauch talks me into going into the emergency room, where I'm given a puffer. I'm not asthmatic, but here I am with a puffer. "Exhaustion, maybe?" shrugs the ER doctor. Maybe I've just breathed in too much flour.

I call Cheffie to explain, praying he doesn't say I'll have to make this day up next week, because all my hopes and plans are pinned on this Friday being the once and for all. But he doesn't say anything about the lost day. "See you tomorrow," he says.

When I return, it's clear Min has moved up a peg. *She* is dipping the éclairs, *she* is making the butter cream. I offer to help, but Pen Paul seems happiest to have me play nurse to his doctor, handing him spatulas when he asks for them. He's also happy to keep telling us about himself and his shop.

"When I told a friend last year that I was opening a patisserie, the friend laughed and said, 'Oh, you'll be working twenty-four hours a day!'" He admits that the friend has been pretty much right. Seventeen months after opening, he has yet to take more than a day a week off to spend with his wife and infant son. Sometimes not even that. "In a patisserie, there's always something to do. At one of my first jobs, my chef used to ask at the end of the day, 'Are you done?' I'd always joke and say, 'I'm not finished, but I'll stop.' In this business, you don't count your hours."

Plus it's been a hard sell for Pâtisserie Fine Savoureuse in a neighbourhood that's more used to Tim Horton's. Plus he had some bad history to erase. Choosing Lachine for its low rent and wide-open market, Pen Paul was puzzled by the question every customer seemed to ask in his first month of business: *Are your cakes fresh?* Fresh? Of course, they were fresh.

He eventually learned that Pâtisserie Fine Savoureuse was following on the heels of a failed bakery at the same location. Stale cakes had been their undoing; stale cakes made them go bankrupt in seven months. Pen Paul countered the freshness question by telling customers, "Take the cake and don't pay me now. If you're satisfied, come back and pay. If you're not satisfied, you won't come back anyway."

Of course, they came back. Who could resist pastries made with 100 percent butter and with such respect for tradition? The previous Christmas, Pen Paul gave away more than a dozen *bûches de Noël* to neighbouring businesses. What this gesture generated in goodwill and referrals was worth the cost of the butter, he says.

"If you think about saving money all the time, you're in the wrong business." He's masking what will be the bottom layer of a *fraisier* wedding cake. I enjoy watching the dance of his spatula against the butter cream. "If you're using shortening instead of butter to save money..." he breaks off, laughing at the thought. "I'd rather save my reputation than save a cake for too many days."

Yet Pen Paul is thrifty like all the chefs I've met this year, with tricks at the ready. He makes fake display cakes for his case, while keeping the real mousse cakes in the freezer. He uses day-old baguettes for garlic bread. He fills and finishes only half a dozen éclairs and millefeuilles each day. All this keeps waste down, profits steady.

Some things he won't stoop to, however. Watching strips of génoise fall from his knife as he trims the layers for the *fraisier*, I ask what he's going to do with all the cake crumbs. "I don't know yet," he says. "Most bakers use them for brownies, adding them in with the flour. I don't make brownies. Brownies are not my baking style. You have to stay true to your style."

Part of his style, unfortunately, is mokas. At least Pen Paul's are not fussy little squares that have to be symmetrically, agonizingly trimmed. His are made in round mousse moulds. Still there are a hundred ways to go wrong. At some point, as he's talking about his growing client base, he turns to us: "So don't smash my little cakes, okay?" I didn't expect him to be such a joker, so fun to be around.

Pen Paul does mokas, but he doesn't want to only do the tried and true. "You have to try new things. This year I did a mango mousse cake with chocolate. New flavours are so important."

On our last day, Pen Paul sends Min and me to the open-air market down the street. "Get the freshest strawberries you can find," he tells us. The thirty-degree heat makes our walking slow. We're both exhausted, though Min says she's had a good week.

"I learn a lot," she says. She doesn't know what she'll do next, where she'll look for work. Like Jen, she'd love to be in the employ of Pen Paul, but like Jen she knows he doesn't have enough business yet to hire anyone on a steady basis. And steady is what Min needs now. There's always Loblaw's, where Jing and Tara are doing their second *stages*. But Min had hoped for higher things. She'd like to be making *fraisier*, not strawberry shortcake.

In our last few hours we watch Pen Paul quickly, expertly assemble and decorate the five wedding *fraisiers*. But after eleven months of *fraisiers*, it's as if I've finally given myself permission to be impatient. My eyes can't stay off the clock. I hope Cheffie doesn't think this has anything to do with him or that this is anything like boredom, but suddenly I feel that if I don't get out of this white room and out of my white jacket and get home and back to my life NOW, I don't know what I might do. I might jump out of my skin. I might jump into that cake.

All that keeps me grounded is watching the chef's progress. He folds the strawberries we had sliced into the mousseline, fills the layers in a few spatula strokes, rolls, cuts and places the crucial marzipan top layer. Times five. He performs microsurgery on the remaining whole strawberries, turning them into fans, then pipes rosettes of Chantilly, beds the strawberries into them. The cakes—studded with fruit now—are out of a fairy tale. All these months later it still seems more like magic than mechanics, that someone can take eggs and sugar and flour and make *this*.

Then it is five and even *stage* is over. Min and I hug goodbye—we'll see each other next week at our official farewell potluck back at school. We thank Pen Paul for taking us in and sharing so much. He'll be here for another four hours at least. It's his brother's birthday and he still has to make the cake for the party tonight.

"What are you making?" I ask. "Not another *fraisier*?"

"I'll see," he says. "Something the family will like."

"Did you make your own wedding cake, Chef?" I ask.

"Everyone expected a big elaborate cake," he says, grinning. "But no, nothing, no wedding cake at my wedding." Min and I tell him the story of Claudette and her awful Black Forest wedding cake. Why don't pastry chefs have wonderful wedding cakes? Maybe it feels redundant, or expected, or maybe it's just too hard an act to match. Maybe they're just tired.

Pen Paul picks up his pastry bag to add a few more Chantilly rosettes. He looks more happy than tired. Earlier today when I pressed him for what he loves about his profession, he told me he likes making people happy.

Pastry does that, doesn't it? Even after all these months of anxious baking, crafting cakes and cookies that had to "count" in a way they never needed to when I was blissfully untrained, there is a happiness at the other end. I think of Cynthia, Georgia's sitter, trotting home with her bakery boxes many afternoons, Beauch's face when I presented him with my first baguettes, Alfred's eyes when he tucked into perfect crème caramel. Even Claudette looked happier after a slice of my chocolate cheesecake. Which of course, made *me* ridiculously happy. It's so simple, really, so uncomplicated. Bake, eat, love.

What was I expecting? I walk in my usual five minutes late, gift bags in tow. I've cleaned out one dollar store of every cake tester in stock. "Denise!" the cry goes up. But it's a quiet cry from fewer people. Trina, Lorrie, and Jen aren't here. Michèle comes up and gives me a great, long hug.

"How did it go at IGA?" I ask. After the disappointment at Pierre's patisserie for her first *stage*, Michèle decided to try a grocery store pastry department.

"Fine, good," she says, smiling.

Lots of others aren't here: Suzy, Avedon, Rena, Yujie, even Min. Trina and Lorrie, back to being friends, arrive and a louder cry goes up. They've brought Timbits, which is good because hardly anyone thought to bring food this morning. I somehow forgot the cream cheese to go with Tara's bagels.

We stand around, awkward with each other in a way we haven't been since last September. I don't know where to sit. Qiang is on my stool. In five weeks we've forgotten where we fit.

Alfred and Ardis show up and it begins to feel like school again. Alfred opens the manila folder filled with our *stage* evaluations. He begins reading them out loud, not just random compliments, entire, no-holds-barred evaluations, our names announced at the beginning of each.

"What is he doing?" I ask Lorrie. "This is supposed to be confidential."

"I know," she says, wincing.

He just keeps going: the good, the blushingly bad, the indifferent. Most of us have already seen our evaluations. Would someone please stop this man? I've been reminded in recent months, especially the months when we were no longer his students, that Alfred can be less than perfect. He can be officious. Sometimes he's indiscreet.

For my part, I have a tendency to idealize. I remember how surprised I was a couple of months ago when I came into the pastry office with Georgia, and Alfred playfully placed his extra-tall pleated chef's hat on her head. It wasn't made of starched, crinolated linen, after all, I realized, when I gave it back to him. It was made of paper.

To our credit, we stop listening to the evaluations. They're repetitious. And besides, it's all over now. Alfred keeps reading and we go back to what's always been interesting: each other.

But then people start to leave. Cindy, Shirley, Stinky, Michèle and Anna have to get back to work.

"We love you, Denise!" Jing says and hugs me.

"Bye, Deni!" says Qiang. We exchange emails and promises to stay in touch. Ardis and Alfred bow out, promising the same, and then it's just me, Trina and Tamara standing at the Lab door, looking in one last time. The lights are on, but no one's there. Yujie dashes by, too late for the gathering, her *stage* report for Ardis in hand.

"Yes, I go back to China," she says to our questions. "But I come back." She's nodding happily.

A wind-up pool party at Nadia's has been in the works for weeks, though I've nearly boycotted it on the grounds of discrimination. All or none, I've been saying, over the protests of Wendy mainly, who wants just the in-crowd to be invited. In the end, it doesn't really matter: Wendy and Diane are drying themselves off to leave as we arrive. It's friendly, but muted. They promise to keep in touch and let us know what comes of their café/bakery plans.

Tamara, Lorrie, Trina, Nadia and I talk pastry under the umbrella. I tell them about Cheffie's *fraisier*, about his version of mousseline. We compare mousseline and *crème légère*, everyone pitching in an opinion, a preference, a different ratio of heavy cream to pastry cream to butter.

"Everyone else starts going to sleep when I talk about this stuff," I say. "You guys are the only people I can talk to anymore."

"I know," they all agree, and we start in again, on butter cream this time. Swiss versus Italian versus fondant, butter cream holding us together before we go our separate ways. Jen and Tamara are already enrolled in professional cooking for September; Nadia will be attending Pius X because her parents want her to learn Italian cuisine. Trina is scouting jobs as a restaurant pastry chef, while Lorrie is hoping to work with Rita. Me? *The Gazette* business section has told me they're interested in a profile of Chef Pichitr and I'm cooking up a series of holiday baking stories. I've got to get writing.

Then it really is time to go. I hug Lorrie at her car, then drop Tamara and Trina off at Trina's apartment. When the door closes behind them, I drive off fast, not wanting to look back. I miss them already. I'd give anything in this moment to be baking in the Lab with my friends. Really, anything.

fin

Acknowledgements

I am indebted to the Pearson School of Culinary Arts for many things: a first-rate education, support for this book, and permission to adapt and use the included recipes. Thanks beyond measure to my teachers: Ardis Root, Claudette Groulx, Alfred DeLuca, and Fabrice Frelat. Each gave us everything they had. Pastry chef Trina Rehel tested all the recipes, leaving me three pounds heavier and eternally grateful. My daughter, Ariel Tarr, took the cover photos and ate my lemon soufflé when no one else wanted to. Karen Haughian, my editor, whipped the book into its final shape. My husband, Ray Beauchemin, performed his usual magic on the manuscript (times three) and supported me in every way through my pastry year, even when he couldn't bear the sight of another one of "those apricot-glaze things." Thank you especially and forever to my team: Jen, Lorrie, Avedon, Madison, Min, Diane, Lane, Michèle, Andrea, Yujie, Susy, Anna, Wendy, Tamara, Shirley, Nadia, Tara, Rena, Qiang, Trina, Jing, Cindi, Xiu Li, and Feng. Let's go...